Freedom *from* Failure

Forge Books by Jaqueline Lapa Sussman

Freedom from Failure
Images of Desire

*F*reedom *from* *F*ailure

How to Discover the Secret
Images That Can Bring Success
In Love, Parenting, Career, and
Physical Well-Being

Based on Ahsen's Image Psychology

JAQUELINE LAPA SUSSMAN

A Tom Doherty Associates Book
New York

The imaging exercises in this book were developed by Dr. Ahsen and are the result of his work and research which spans most of the last half of the twentieth century. The images were edited from their original versions for linguistic reasons, to meet the needs of the present audience. The final instructions were developed in consultation with Dr. Ahsen and meet with his approval in present form. This also acknowledges that Dr. Ahsen holds the copyright for the instructions and that he has extended his kind permission to reproduce them here.

FREEDOM FROM FAILURE

This book is printed on acid-free paper.

A Forge Book
Published by Tom Doherty Associates, LLC
175 Fifth Avenue
New York, NY 10010

www.tor.com

Forge® is a registered trademark of Tom Doherty Associates, LLC.

ISBN 0-312-86910-X

First Edition: February 2003

Printed in the United States of America

0 9 8 7 6 5 4 3 2 1

I dedicate this book to
Richard, Zachary, and Lila,
who are deep in my heart.

Contents

Acknowledgements

I am most grateful to Dr. Akhter Ahsen for his inspiration, support, and wisdom during the writing of this book. His friendship and guidance in this project have been invaluable. Akhter Ahsen is a fount of information. It is with deep gratitude for all he has taught me that this book is possible.

To my family
I want to thank my husband, Richard, and my children, Zachary and Lila, for their ongoing support of my work, their love and devotion. They are my true cheerleaders.

To the people at Forge
Much thanks to Linda Quinton. It was her belief in seeing what Eidetic Imagery can do for the general public that led to the publishing of this book. I am very grateful to her for making this book possible.

I am indebted to my editor, Bob Gleason, for all the time and thought he gave to this second book on Eidetic Imagery. His expertise and knowledge have proven invaluable, as was the case with the first book.

Thanks are also due to Jennifer Marcus and Jodi Rosoff in publicity. Their constant availability and personal warmth have made it a pleasure to work with them.

I also owe thanks to Brian Callaghan for his thorough editorial assistance.

Special thanks to those who helped shape the book
To Carol McCleary, my agent, for being the primary person whose vision, enthusiasm, and perseverance made this work a reality.

To Hilda Podrug, who has been most generous in transcribing hours of taped case materials.

And to Bob Griswold for his diligent feedback and editorial assistance, and Judy Einzig for helping to simplify a difficult concept.

I want to thank all the people who have generously contributed their life stories, problems, images, and transformational experiences contained in the pages of this book.

Introduction

This book offers you a miraculous journey. It gives you the steps to go within and discover answers to life's major questions from a fount of wisdom that is completely accurate, totally personal, already within you, and waiting to be tapped. *Freedom from Failure* provides "prescriptions" to help you discover your own powers, abilities, and unique personal solutions that emerge from within and are appropriate for you. The answers you seek for the questions you ask are in keeping with the person you are.

Through *Freedom from Failure* you will discover amazing powers you never knew you had and abilities you never dreamed were yours. You will find the solutions to your life's problems plus the energies that you need to succeed emotionally and physically, at work, while at play, and in your relationships. Those who have experienced this work said that it was like finding pockets of gold in the psyche.

Best of all, it is easy to discover the solutions you seek in *Freedom from Failure*. The solutions are far more effective than anyone outside can give you because the illuminations all come from your own personal, lifelong storehouse of images.

We have become a culture dependent on opinions of experts and silver-bullet cures for all that ails us. We have forgotten the wisdom of the ages. If *"all the answers are within,"* how do we go within? How do we discover our greatness that is within us? And, how do we discover solutions that we will know are right for us? This book shows you how to answer your questions and how to chart out the inner journey. *Freedom from Failure* tells you exactly how to find the "Gifts of the Gods" within you.

I hope you enjoy reading this book and experiencing the inner bounty that awaits you. When you discover stories and images in the book that are especially relevant to you, make sure to follow through and "do" the image yourself. The instructions are made purposefully simple and you don't need a professional to "take you" through an image.

On a separate note, Chapters 11 to 17 deal with sensuality. For a more in-depth knowledge about tapping into your sensual self, please refer to my first book, *Images of Desire*, in which I fully cover the topic.

As you read *Freedom from Failure* and work through images, please let me know of your results.

You may reach me by e-mail at: **jackielsus@aol.com**. Take a minute or two to click on my website, **www.jaquelinesussman.com** to stay up-to-date on eidetic imaging, new books and new imaging workshops around the world.

*F*reedom *from* *F*ailure

1

Discovering Our Gifts with Imaging

Eidetic imagery enabled me to pinpoint the sources of my character, its strengths and weaknesses, thereby helping me to identify specific capabilities. Imagery can be a useful tool for anyone interested in maximizing his or her business potential as well as personal development.

Hon. William Simon, former U.S. Secretary of the Treasury

Confucius tells us that a picture is worth a thousand words. That statement is a thousand times truer when we scrutinize ourselves and seek to discover the person we would like to be. With images, mental pictures of ourselves and those around us, we can peel away the layers of our life and personality and uncover negative aspects that keep us from succeeding, and positive ones that propel us toward our greatest fulfillment.

Over the past two decades I have worked with thousands of people who have used self-imaging to achieve their goals, people at the top of their profession in the worlds of the arts, science, major league sports, government, and business. Some of these people are household names, women who led social revolutions and men who have managed America. Corporations, whose products are in every home in America, have hired me to work with their creative and management staffs to improve productivity and profitability.

And I have worked with men and women who wanted desperately to find love and just couldn't make a relationship stick, people who are stressed by situations at work or going through emotional meltdown from problems with their spouse or children.

By using imagery, Jacqueline Sussman allows us to re-enter past experiences and understand unexamined emotions. She gives us a map for inner traveling.

Gloria Steinem, author, publisher, social revolutionary

No matter what our initial goal is, a man or woman seeking love and fulfillment, a top executive wanting more success, or a professional athlete sweating out the last ounce of inspiration, the process of self-discovery through images is the same.

All of this work is done in the field of eidetic (*i-det-ik*) imaging.

Eidetic images are visual memories that each of us keeps stored in our mind. They are the emotionally charged record of the events that shaped us into the person we are today. Accessing them gives us deep insights and perceptions, not just about other people and situations, our lovers and bosses, our career or other goals, but about *who we are* and *how we got to this point in life*. They also reveal the grandeur of our beings. Deep within each one of us is a reservoir of tremendous power and ability that lies dormant waiting to be found. Eidetic images reveal our greatest potentials.

The images are not products of our imagination or fantasy, but are the actual visual record of the events of our life. They are prime memories full of meaning and emotion. While a simple apple may be part of our visual memory bank, an image of a person we love—or hate—is an emotionally charged image that we can examine with eidetic techniques to draw fresh perspectives about the person, ourselves, and the situation. We can tap within and discover new strengths to deal with any problem life throws at us.

This book evokes on your unique personal images, the visual record of the events that shaped you from birth. At birth each of us was endowed with natural talents and abilities and from that day forward we have been shaped and molded by the people around us, by our parents, teachers, friends, and society in general. Unfortunately, few of us have managed to reach adulthood without layers of negative self-images being imposed during the process. Often the people around us were well meaning, but the images they projected for us are still fraught with anger, fear, or anxiety. We have to dispel the layers of negative images and replace them with the positive images of the potential that already exists within us.

What were we like—*what did the future hold for us*—before other people layered upon us their false images? We can know our full potential by looking within and discovering the images of our greatness, which are like jewels in the psyche waiting to be mined.

Eidetic imagery has worked with my team of designers in a traditional corporate environment. Through use of eidetic images, the team was able to work through

destructive behavior that was based on their perception versus reality. The images
reveal insights that words could not convey.

Ivy Ross, Senior Vice President of Worldwide
Barbie, Division of Mattel Toys

Most forms of self-assessment focus not on this all-important, all-powerful imagery that controls our actions, but on its insignificant symbol—words.

The importance of personal imagery is apparent. History, literature, and religion redound with examples of overpowering imagery. Genesis tells us that before God created the world there was darkness and chaos. Then there was light and imagery (which the Bible calls "form") and it was good . . .

In this modern age we likewise recognize the unique power of imagery. The illustrations in children's books and movies remain with us long after the words and storylines are forgotten. The famous pictures of Abraham Lincoln, Marilyn Monroe, John Kennedy, and electrifying images of war and terrorism haunt us after the words describing those subjects are forgotten.

Shakespeare understood the transcendence of imagery over words. Hamlet is driven to death not by words but images of his father.

"My father, I see before me my father."
"Where, noble Hamlet?" Horatio asks.
"In my mind's eye."

Hamlet is likewise tormented by vile images of his father's killer, whose face he contrasts with his father's "as Hyperion to a satyr."

Eidetics give us the insight to unleash our full power.
Rick Peterson, Oakland A's Pitching Coordinator

Unfortunately, even those of us who have had the nicest parents and most comfortable circumstances have to unearth and resuscitate the marvelous person *that is us*, the person we were at birth with all our natural potential intact, before layers of fear and self-doubt coated us or left us at war with our emotions. To be the best we can, we need to *rediscover* our radiant essence. All of us have inner voices, images that whisper negatively and sometimes even cruelly over our shoulders, whether we are up to bat in the World Series, shyly eyeing someone across a candlelight dinner, or standing up to a domineering boss. We submit to these negative nuances without consciously thinking about it; when that happens, world-class athletes hit 300-foot foul balls instead of 400-foot home runs, our natural inner warmth and sensuality are not communicated to the person across the table, and fears keep us from expressing our true feelings to a boss or spouse.

Sometimes the negative images seem subtle and simplistic:

"Jane, don't be silly, you can't do that," and "Paul, you have to be practical . . ."

When we have been subtly and inadvertently "programmed" to believe that success and happiness are out of our reach, we are not going to reach for the stars. To see ourselves clearly, we have to probe beneath this programming and discover our true radiant self. For most of us, rediscovering our unique selves will be as exciting as uncovering a treasure trove.

"This goes a step beyond Jung."

Elizabeth Kübler-Ross

Let's do a simple but important image that can give you insight into many situations in love and work. All you have to do is imagine someone swimming in a running stream. The person can be your lover, a coworker, someone you are having a problem with, someone you feel competitive with, or simply a person you want to know more about.

Relax for a moment. Then, keeping your eyes open or closed, whichever you prefer, see the person swimming in a running stream.

Watch how they swim. How are they swimming? Fast, slow, easily or with difficulty? Aggressively or just flowing with the current?

How do you feel as you see the image? What meaning or insight do you gain about them as you see the image?

This image allows you to gain insights into the person that are stored in your own mind. Every interaction with the person, all the subtleties that you would not recall if you were being giving the third degree by the police, coalesce and are drawn out when you see the person in your mind's eye performing the task. As you use other image tools set forth later in the book to probe the person, you can draw more and more insights about them or about your relationship with them.

These images are not fantasies but imprints of true, factual life. For example, an even more dramatic example of how these images are real imprints concerns our parents. It doesn't matter how old you are—we carry with us from birth to the grave images of our parents. To do this image, "see" your parents standing before you in your mind's eye. Examine the image for a moment. See your parents standing in front of you. Do not worry if you see a clear image or just a sense of your parents. Who is on the right side—your mother or father?

Now, try to switch their position. Is there any tension or difficulty doing so? Whose side appears stronger, mother's or father's?

See yourself touching your mother's body. How does it feel? Is it cool, warm, or hot to the touch?

Now see yourself touching your father's body. How does it feel? Is it cool, warm, hot? Allow the sense impressions that you get while seeing the image to come forth. Just take your time.

Most people see the image of their *mother on the right side* and their father on the left. There is what is called an inversion of the images if this is not the case. Inversion will be explained later.

The fact that your parents had a certain body temperature (and the left-right positioning) in your images of them has significance in terms of not only your connection to them but to your own life energy. No matter how old we are, no matter how long we have been away from them, we tend to unconsciously emulate our parents—or react in the opposite. As we get into imaging and its results, we will discover that things as simple as the body temperature of our parents and their position in our image has influenced how we deal with the world—and why.

In doing these and dozens of other images you will gain enormous insights about yourself in terms of relationships, careers, and most other important aspects of life. For example, have you ever thought about why some people are sensual regardless of their features . . . and others aren't, no matter how physically attractive they seem to be? In imaging you'll discover that sensuality is an energetic mind-body connection not unlike the mind-body connection that business executives and star athletes use to achieve success in their fields.

Throughout this book you will probe into your storehouse of visual memories and, just as you peel an onion to reveal layer after layer, you will make discoveries about yourself and learn how you can turn limiting images, thoughts, feelings, beliefs, abilities, attitudes, and reactions into positive ones. You will have the opportunity to look at your unique "history," all of those personality-shaping aspects from childhood to relationships, from school to careers, from failures to success. It doesn't matter if you have risen to handling millions of dollars as an investment banker, just want to be *happy*, or if you simply want tools to overcome negative states of mind! The women and men who have used the imaging process to find the treasures within them range from successful people who want to be more successful to people who simply want to succeed at a loving relationship, to those desiring to discover peace at times of stress.

The results are usually immediate and are often startling. And the most incredible thing about imaging is that it is simple to do in the privacy of your home and the results will be self-evident—you will not need anyone to interpret the insights you gain.

All you really need is the desire to take a journey inward and know thyself . . . to discover the source of your strengths. Within each one of us, lying just below the surface is a treasure trove of energy, abilities, and power waiting to be released.

Eidetic imaging techniques are as old as the ancient Greeks and as new as the cutting edge of modern psychology. Just as many of the great movements of the past century's science of mind are identified with specific people (Freud, Adler, Jung, Skinner, and others), the pioneering work in imaging in the last half century has been performed by Dr. Akhter Ahsen. Today, as a result of Dr. Ahsen's seminal studies, the doctoral practitioners of imaging are associated with many of the great universities of the world (Harvard, Stanford, Yale, etc., not to mention great institutions in Britain, France, Italy, and around the world).

> *I have found that these eidetic images effectively and permanently free blocked energy that allows people to get on successfully with their lives.*
> Carol Jenkins, former Fox Five News Anchor

In a sense we will be taking the Hero's Journey, that path in life that each of us must take to understand ourselves, discover our innate strengths, and our place in the universe. Only this journey will be an inward one.

As you turn the pages, remember that this book is about *you and your journey* in life. Learn from the experiences of others, apply the techniques that have been so successful with others, but never forget that it's all about *you*. Looking inward can be thrilling, but is never lonely; even the best and most successful have had to search inwardly to discover their greatness.

This is your journey, but it is a well-trodden path, one in which the spirits of giants will be walking alongside of you.

As a key commissioner, I have to deal with severe challenges as a lobbyist for my agency. Eidetic images have bolstered my self confidence and made me feel invincible when I needed it the most.

Patricia Russo, Commissioner, Connecticut Permanent Commission
on the Status of Women

An exciting and ingenious way of getting at conflict areas.

Contemporary Psychology

A unique and important contribution to the scientific study of healing with imagery.

New Age Magazine

2

Journey of Discovery

I created you human beings because I desired to see you lead a joyous life.

Ofudesaki

There is a tale told in India about the strange stripes that appear on the moon just before the monsoon season. When the full moon comes, it sails across the gloomy night sky, a swollen amber ball with shadowy stripes. People call it the "tiger moon" and a story is told that the King of Tigers has leaped aboard the moon.

Because he has tasted the forbidden flesh of other creatures, the all-powerful Brahma punished the tiger, making him run alone, always the hunter and the hunted. However, Brahma is merciful and once a year, just before the monsoon rains fall, the King of Tigers is permitted to leap aboard the moon and ride around the world, looking for a place where he will find love and happiness. He is doomed to keep repeating his journey every year because his reputation precedes him . . . and no one wants a tiger for a neighbor.

The moral to the story for me is that the tiger is looking in the wrong place for love, happiness, and success. And too many of us are like the tiger, looking for a *place* to be happy—that place may be in someone else's arms, a different career, or even another town. But peace emanates from the *inner person*, it is not found in a place or thing. Cars and boats and houses may excite us, but can't bring us happiness. (Wasn't Princess Diana a classic example of how all the riches in the world couldn't buy happiness for a woman who wanted inner peace?)

UNCHARTED SEAS TO THE SELF

To discover, or more appropriately, to *re*-discover ourselves, we need to keep in mind that we are really *three* different people:

First, we are who *we* believe we are. This persona is comprised of what others, usually our parents, teachers, and friends have told us we were during our growing years.

Second, we are the public person we show to the world, a persona that we think looks good to other people. This persona is not our genuine self and is heavily affected by the expectations that our parents and society placed on us.

Third, we are the person we truly are, with our own natural blend of attributes, gifts, and unique spirit. The more true to ourselves we can be, the more we can express genuine joy in the world.

Unlike the frustrated King of Tigers, we are not going to strive to find a place where we will be happy and successful. We are already at that place—it is inside of us. Rather than jumping on the moon, we will turn ourselves inward on a voyage of adventure and self-discovery.

The most famous journey of self-discovery is of course the epic tale of the hero of ancient Greece, Odysseus (called Ulysses by the Romans). After contriving the Trojan horse that brought down Troy—and blinding Cyclops, Poseidon's son—Odysseus was condemned by the gods to a ten-year odyssey of discovery. Braving the Furies and countless struggles, he at last reaches home, a wiser, more compassionate man. The tale has come to symbolize the journey through life that each of us must take, the battles we must fight, the demons we must vanquish . . . and like Odysseus, the soul searching we must undertake as the road gets harder.

We don't elect to make this journey. Rather, it is a rite of passage for all men and women. At a certain age we are expected to leave the home (tribe) we came from, leave the security that we are attached to and that binds us, and go forward in the world. Through trials and tribulations we are to deal with those who wrong us, battle difficulties, face challenges, discover strengths, and come back home (our self) with wisdom.

While the monsters we face may have changed since Homer's time, the Hero's Journey is still a rite of passage that each of us must take, young or old, to achieve inner peace and fulfillment and to find the sources within us to be able to love, to overcome fear, and to achieve our goals. It's an exciting journey for all of us, and if we keep moving forward, taking one curious step after another, we will come to believe in ourselves and find the courage and strength that we need to transform limitations into achievements.

While few of us get launched from home and our own tribe with the physical and emotional gifts of Odysseus, all of us have gifts stored within us—powerful rejuvenating images—and we can use them to make ourselves the person we were meant to be.

Imaging is an *internal* process and the Hero's Journey is an *inner* passage to the self to awaken those gifts we were born with but which were buried beside the bumpy road from childhood to maturity.

When we feel better about ourselves, the world looks brighter. The way we see things after imaging *affects reality* because our perception of ourselves shifts. When our perception shifts, we naturally act more positively toward others. When we do that, they will automatically act better toward us. We may find, for example, that we are giving too much power in a relationship to another person—a lover, a boss. After imaging, we are not stuck in feeling disemboweled, our tires spinning like a car stuck in mud. Instead, we find new strengths with which to deal with the person or situation. In doing this, our perception shifts. Now they do not look so powerful anymore. We may see the fear or vulnerability in them that we never saw before.

Before we go into actual imaging examples and practice, I have outlined the major subject areas we will be covering.

Rediscovering Our Self:

All the answers to the quest lie *within us* to live fulfilled and empowered lives, expressing our many gifts in all that we do. No person and no material possessions can make us truly happy. True happiness comes from discovering the unique essence inside us. We didn't come into this world with a load of negative baggage, and we can peel back the layers of our negative history and allow the positive images of our genuine self to flow and imbue our lives with joy and radiance.

Love and Relationships:

We all experience falling in love, later on followed by stormy seas. Eidetic imaging can restore intimacy and bring joy into our relationships. At first there is the thrilling experience of falling in love. Then, our history takes over (the self-images we and our lovers have carried into adulthood from our upbringing), and suddenly passion becomes conflict. Positive imaging can bring us back to that idyllic state of love before our history clouded it. The techniques reveal many strategies to find love and then to keep it alive.

Sensuality:
Beauty and sensuality are not the same, but our society has put such an emphasis on superficial outer beauty and sexuality has been so commercialized that many men and women have been emotionally debilitated, no longer knowing how to connect intimately. Sensuality isn't a perfect body, but a warm, glowing radiance from within that has been lost for many, but can be reignited.

Parenting:
The frantic nature of our rapid, modern life and the challenges posed by adolescent sex and threats from drugs test our parenting skills. Most of the problems between parents and children relate to a lack of *intimacy* and *connection* between them. Seeing yourself through the child's eyes and other techniques can give a parent an entirely different perspective, and reveal solutions to the problems with their children.

Success and Careers:
There is a "high" feeling when a great salesman is selling a product or performing well in a business that is similar to the high states of energy used by athletes, dancers, and other performers. Discovering the "high," the passion in what you do, is the key to unleashing your greatest potential. Imaging your boss, coworkers, clients, and work situations gives you fresh insights on how to deal with the problems that keep you from successfully attaining your goals.

Creativity:
We are constantly challenged to be creative, whether it is on the job, in relationships, or creating a work of art or literature. Imaging takes us deep into our spirit to release a flow of original creative ideas that easily pour forth, one after another, like jewels from our psyche.

Sports and Physical Activities:
The mind-body connection is the key in physical pursuits whether it is recreational jogging, losing pounds on a stationary bike, or competing in sports. Through "High Imaging" we can awaken untapped energies within us and put ourselves in a peak performance state, sending neuro signals from our brain to our limbs, activating and enlivening our bodies and enhancing our ability to excel.

The Future Today:

Many of us feel empty, as if there is a void in our life; there is often an expectation that something in the future will fill the void—a promotion at work, a better romantic relationship, having a child. But the void is still there because as it is filled, what it desires changes and we are left feeling empty again. Imaging can bring forward that precise inner quality to fill our emptiness.

Genetic Roots:

We were not created in a test tube but are the product of thousands of years of human development. Within us are the genetic imprints that go back an eon. Regardless of our personal cultural heritage, whether our roots go back to the highlands of Scotland, the steppes of Russia, or the savannahs of Africa, we are formed and imbued by those roots and can gain knowledge about ourselves by accessing the positive powers of those roots through imaging.

Mystics, sages, and wise men throughout the ages have said that all the answers lie within. Yet most of us have been trained to look outside ourselves, to the outer world, for answers. We don't realize that there is a whole storehouse of incredible knowledge and wisdom within. Many of us think that we are empty inside. But the truth is that by looking inward we can discover so much! We can expand our awareness and find illumination. We can discover strengths that we did not know we had. We can discover practical and ingenious ways of dealing with difficult situations. We can heal ourselves. Eidetic imaging is the tool to bring all that is stored inside of us to the fore . . . like pockets of gold in the psyche, waiting to be mined.

BENEFITS OF EIDETIC IMAGING

1. It provides instant *insight* into the people around us, spouses and lovers, bosses and competitors, parents and children, and into problems and other situations we are involved in.
2. It reveals where we are stuck and brings *effective solutions* to deal with these people and situations.
3. It allows us to tap into unrealized *inner powers*, strengths, and abilities we were born with but that have laid dormant.
4. It enables us to *see clearly* where others are coming from in our

life because imaging permits one to view a situation from several points of view, including the viewpoint of others.

5. It takes us from *negative emotions to positive ones*, such as helplessness to power, fear to love, "judgmentalism" to compassion and understanding, . . . all from within our own inner wisdom.

6. It brings *healing energies* to the body, healing illnesses, psychosomatic disorders, and restores us to a natural state of well-being.

3

Beyond Paradise to *Self*

For him who has conquered his self by the self,
The self is a friend;
But for him whose self is not conquered,
The self remains hostile, like an enemy.

The Bhagavad Gita

There is a song from the 1980s I like. Written by Ken Kirsch and Ronald Miller, it's called "I've Never Been to Me" and it's about a woman of the world who wakes up one day and discovers that she's missed something by not discovering who she really is. Part of it goes like this:

I've been to paradise, but I've never been to me.

As in the song, *I've been to paradise and never been to me*. Not, at least, until I was introduced to eidetic imaging and the inner journey to discover my *genuine self*.

Through imaging we can learn to know and love ourselves and end warring with our own emotions. On the following pages we will learn how to use imaging to find the source of our greatest strengths, and weaknesses. We will start with an actual imaging example that will show you again how quick and easy it is to do imaging.

Even though the imaging session will be of another person, the techniques are exactly the same as you will be using in a great variety of different situations (love and relationship problems, career goals, enhancing physical activities such as jogging and sports, discovering your sensuality, and many more areas).

The narrator experienced life's struggles, finding love, losing it, finding it again, and is now a happy career woman with a husband and child. Her experiences in finding answers through imaging will guide us when we do our own sessions. Her name is Karen, but she could be any one of us, of either sex, because imaging tools apply equally to men and women.

Following the imaging example, instructions for self-imaging have been laid out. These initial imaging tools are only a few of the several dozen we will be using.

This is Karen's story. As you read it and see how she used images to solve life's problems, think about your own struggles.

KAREN'S STORY

"I have always been interested in being all I can be in the sense of living a fulfilling life. I have always desired to find inner peace, true love, and a career that was rewarding. However, like so many others, I was struggling with the challenges life set in front of me every day. In my twenties, I reached out and did some tentative explorations, attempting to look within by taking some classes and workshops. But in those days I hadn't discovered the vehicle that took me along the path to the inner self. In a sense, I still needed the challenges of daily life, the hurdles we all must overcome, in order to learn that I could take charge of my life. I learned that all the difficulties I had encountered were the teachers for my growth. They drove me to look within myself to ultimately find the answers I was seeking.

"Eidetic imaging was the vehicle I ultimately used to make that journey. And along the path I found facets of myself that had long been dormant and that needed to be awakened for me to succeed in the challenges of marriage, family, and career.

"Today I am a successful career woman with a husband and child, but when I first looked into myself it was like Columbus discovering America. I found a whole new and exciting world. I had been looking outside myself for too many of the things I needed to make me happy and secure. I thought the answers were found in a perfect lover, lots of money to be secure, job prestige, or the admiration of others.

"The first thing I dealt with was love. I was struggling. I am a diehard romantic. I believe in love, true love, eternal love; all kinds of love. I thought true fulfillment in my life would come when I found that 'perfect' relationship. How wrong I was! I was striving to be happy but looking in the wrong direction.

"Years after I had walked away from one marriage, I found myself in turmoil with my new husband. I thought I had been unable to find that 'perfect' guy. I was in despair, blaming myself. That began a journey of discovery about myself and about my new husband. Through the process of self-imaging I examined my relationship myself and with my husband and discovered truths about both of us that gave me the strength and capacity to learn how to be a loving person. I discovered a profound love for myself and for my husband that went beyond just marriage. I learned that the most basic and essential foundation for success of any nature—love, relationships, careers, sports, creativity, parenting, etc.—is a *sense of self*."

This is the platform from which we vault into life. How high we leap will be directly related to how solid that platform is. A little later we will discuss at length this sense of self and how imaging helps shape us into the person we genuinely are. In Karen's case, imaging not only provided new insights about the people around her and the situations she was facing, but let her tap into inner resources and strengths that she didn't know she had.

Karen continued. "If you are going to take a trip into my psyche with me and measure my soul, you should know a little bit about me. At the time of the crisis with my husband, Vic, I was thirty years old, college educated, and did design work for an advertising agency.

"I had one marriage behind me that lasted only three years. Somehow, after I managed to survive a divorce, start a career, and marry again, I found myself feeling driven to find an inner meaning for my life.

"When I met my second husband, Vic, we discovered that we were shining examples of the maxim that opposites attract. But the flip side is that *opposites also repel*. Our attraction came from an intellectual stimulation and sexual charge of two people between whom sparks flew every time we walked into the same room.

"I sensed that he had integrity and emotional courage, and an intelligence that I wanted to learn from. However, one of the most significant conflicts between us was how we handled our need for closeness. I tended to want more interaction between us, to talk, to bond more emotionally, and Vic tended to need more emotional space. The more I reached out for him, the more he slipped away, and the more he slipped away, the more I desired him. The next step would be anger and recrimination at the way he treated me and I would back off. Backing off would bring him closer to me, until I reached out again.

"If one is going to spend one's romantic existence arguing Zen and making love, the opposing cosmic forces of a strong-willed man and strong-willed woman coming into collision are pretty exciting. However, when you throw in the dirty laundry, house payments, and stress at work, coming home to cosmic collisions is not as appealing.

"Yet I loved Vic, I wanted to merge with him. I believed that merging was love. I thought that if I had him the way I wanted him, I'd be complete, body and soul. But arguments were ripping us apart. The love was there, but there was something inside each of us that too often turned us into wild cats with long claws. I was to learn that before there could be a union with him . . . *I had to find myself*.

"I wanted very much to save our relationship. Even with all of the yelling and recriminations that could erupt when we bumped head to head, I knew Vic and I were meant to be, that we had come together because of that mysterious process called Kismet and that there was something worthwhile about our relationship that made it important to save. There was something beyond us that kept us together; we couldn't separate, yet we couldn't live together in peace. But I was clear that this was the man I wanted to father my yet unborn children, the man I wanted to go to the future with. I wasn't going to walk away from the relationship without giving everything I had to make it work.

"I knew through my discoveries with imaging that the answers to the conflicts between Vic and me would be found within *me*. That did not mean that I was at fault, nor he, but if I looked within myself I was sure I could find the keys to unlock our relationship dilemma.

"I was told that because I had interacted with Vic, that all those impressions—his actions, reactions, moods, feeling states, body language—were recorded in my mind, just as they were for other people with whom I had interacted. The data is recorded in the form of *eidetic* images, a movielike history of our relationship that is stored in the form of visual images in our mind, Jaqueline Sussman told me. These bits of information about Vic and me, or about my parents, daughter, people at work, are stored in our brain, that living computer we carry around; stored rather like the 'bytes' of information stored on a computer disk."

Our brains are constantly processing information and when we see the image, the information we've stored comes together in a whole new way that we were not consciously aware of, bringing with it insight and revelations. By seeing these stored images, with all their nuances, known and unknown aspects which the images reveal, we are able to gain insight into the obstacles to our happiness.

I told Karen that to probe her personal storehouse of images, she needed to physically get into a quiet place where she would not be disturbed, and distracting sounds would be at a minimum. She chose the living room sofa at a time when she was home alone, but that was just a matter of personal preference, The bedroom, a chair, any place in which one feels comfortable and at peace will do. I told Karen that once she learned the simple techniques involved in imaging, she could do imaging virtually almost anywhere and at anytime.

Karen sat down and relaxed her mind for a minute and cleared it of all the fleeting thoughts that sometimes flash by. She preferred to close her eyes, but again, that is just a matter of personal preference. Many people prefer to keep them open. She verbalized in her own mind the problem she was facing. She had a need for more emotional reinforcement from her relationship with Vic, and Vic had a need for more space. She knew that she would have to examine Vic, and even go back further, back to the antecedents of her own shaping as a person.

4

Images of Love

The human face is really like one of those Oriental gods;
a whole group of faces juxtaposed on different planes;
it is impossible to see them all simultaneously.

Proust

Karen continued. "Clearing my mind again, I saw a mental picture of Vic. I looked at his image from a distance and then I moved in closer, taking a good look at him up close. I looked at his eyes—his eyes were clear, there was no guile in them; rather, what I saw was depth and warmth. He had a slight smile on his face, and I understood the smile was for me, that he really loved me.

"I am not seeing a mental picture of Vic as I would an apple. The image of Vic is an emotionally charged prime image, an *eidetic*, and it has *meaning* for me while the apple is a neutral object."

The image of Vic that Karen sees is a snapshot of him, but it is also a reflection of *his* emotions. Just as she can access Vic's emotions, she can clearly become aware of her own feelings about him. Seeing an image of a person, we get clarity, insight into how we feel about the person because the image invokes an emotional response from us. In a sense, an eidetic image of our lover, parent, or the person who bugs us at work, is composed not just of the physical attributes of the person, their body language, gestures, facial expressions and nuances, but is also a composite of their inner emotions.

How does Vic's emotional state get recorded in her memory? Every interaction she has ever had with Vic, from the way he argues to his sensuality, facial expressions, body postures, voice intonations, and other subtle cues, are stored in Karen's brain. When she sees the image of Vic, the sum total of her interactions with Vic and the emotional states he has revealed to her are found in the images stored in her mind. When she sees those images, her emotional feelings toward him become crystal clear. Even though the impressions may have been subtle or she was unaware of them, they become clear in the image. (There is no need to take notes following Karen's experiences; I will take you through your own imaging sessions.)

"Up to now it's still just a picture of Vic I am seeing," said Karen, "and I know I have to take another step. I have to closely examine the picture to get different levels of meaning and by *relaxing* and *concentrating* I am able to see different things in the image. It's like those puzzle pictures in magazines and the comic strip page that you stare at until objects suddenly take shape that at first glance didn't appear to be there. The image of Vic is like those pictures; by close examination I can get beyond the surface and his emotions will take shape."

I think of this process as getting into the eye of the hurricane. Everyday life is like weathering a storm with the wind blowing and the waves coming at us. This is especially true if the maelstrom is a problem with a relationship. Once we are in the eye of the storm we are suddenly able to see things clearly—even seeing the sharks around us. We are able to see all of the subtleties that usually escape us. By getting ourselves into a quiet place and imaging the person, we are able to examine the situation closely and gain insight that simply *thinking about* the problem doesn't bring, because imaging allows us to see the situation in depth and understand it from different perspectives.

Keeping the image in mind, Karen began to use one of the tools of imaging, a process called *walking-around* the subject. By moving around the image and looking at it from different angles, we get a three-dimensional view of the person. The image is like a hologram, through which you are able to view all six sides of the image resulting in more information emerging from it. Or, think of it as looking at a fine Chinese vase; pick it up and slowly turn it, allowing your eyes to absorb all of the fine detail that the artist put into the work. It is that sort of detailed examination that will bring to the surface the mental and emotional states that went into making Vic what he is today.

We will return to Karen in a moment, but at this point it is time for *you* to see *your* own image. You can see an image of a person about whom you want more information, someone you'd like to know better, lover, friend, a coworker causing problems, a parent, the choice is up to you.

The instructions for the Walk-Around Image are set out below, as well as in the Appendix of Images found at the back of the book.

You can keep your eyes open or closed while you are seeing the image.

You *do not* have to memorize the instructions. The image will be there as you go back and forth from reading an instruction and seeing the image.

SPECIFIC INSTRUCTIONS: WALK-AROUND

This technique is used to gain insight about a person. By imaging the person, you expand your consciousness about the person's motives, fears, and emotions.

WALK-AROUND IMAGE

1. Relax, close your eyes if you like, and see an image of a person that you want insight into. If the image is vague just keep looking. The information will come anyway in sense impressions or feelings.
2. Look at the person from the front. What do you see? Notice their body language, the emotions that you can read on their face, and anything that strikes you. Let the information about the other person simply come to you.
3. How do you feel as you see the image?
4. Now move to the right side of the person and look at the person from that side. As you look at them, be aware of how they look, their body posture, the emotions you sense on that side. What do you see about them? Let all of the impressions come forward. How do you feel now that you see them from this side? Pleasant? Unpleasant? Neutral?
5. Now move to the back of their head and observe them from that angle. What do you see? Again, just let the information come, whatever it is. How do you feel as you see them from the back? Pleasant? Unpleasant? Neutral?
6. Now go to the left side of them. What do you see? How do you feel?
7. Go back to the front. What do you see? How do you feel?
8. Do you have a different understanding of this person than when you started?

We now return to Karen. After reading more of how she used walk-around, you may want to go back and do other images.

"I saw an image of Vic from the front. I saw his clear blue eyes exude warmth and his face light up with a smile. Yes, this is the Vic I was turned-on to and desired. I then viewed the image of Vic from his left side. It was essentially the same as the frontal view, with that smile still curving his lips. Yet, I realized the smile was a little tight, as if it was forced a little and that disturbed me. I understood that it meant that he was not totally relaxed with me and I sensed he was holding back some feelings.

"I kept the process going and looked at Vic from the rear, imaging only his head and shoulders and I noticed a marked difference in his posture. His shoulders were a little hunched, cramped up toward his neck as if he was protecting his heart.

"I moved around to his right side and got a feeling of sadness from him. Then back to a frontal view and discovered that there had been a change in his demeanor. There was pain in his face, hurt, and something else. Studying it I realized that what I saw was his face turning away from me, his eyes not meeting mine, not from guilt, but in the sense that he was drawing back from me as if in *fear*. Fear is a strong word and I knew Vic didn't fear me, not in a conventional sense, but that the emotion I sensed was his fear of being close to me.

"Next I looked into his eyes, for what had been described to me as 'the story in the eyes.' I sensed fear again when I looked deeply into Vic's eyes. A thought came to me about his father, a man who spent much of his later life physically handicapped. Vic was raised in a devout Catholic family. As I viewed the image, I remembered that Vic had told me that family members tended to be reserved about showing emotions. Vic's father developed heart trouble after a crippling work accident when Vic was nine. He deteriorated physically over time and became very inward as a result of his illness. Naturally, his mother's energies were devoted to caring for her invalid husband. Vic tried his best to be 'good' and he did not cause his mother too much trouble. Vic's childhood home was dominated by his father's illness, with his vibrant mother engrossed in her efforts to care for his invalid father. Vic felt an emotional void in terms of his own needs as a child, and also feared commitment because, in his mind, commitment meant you were 'stuck' and couldn't get out, just like his mother was. I saw a struggle of two forces in Vic, his desire to get close emotionally, and at the same time, his need to maintain his freedom.

"The image shook me up because I realized that I was gaining insight into Vic's Achilles' heel. Strong-willed and strong-minded Vic was afraid! I realized that the source of his fear was commitment resulting from being raised in a stressful environment in which his parents were emotionally remote from him because of the dire needs of his father. His father's dependence made it important for Vic to maintain his own independence."

Why did Karen look into Vic's eyes during her walk-around? As she said, there's a story in a person's eyes, one that is revealed to us when we look into them in the image. Most of us have heard that poetic phrase "the eyes are the windows to the soul." The phrase means that our eyes reveal our emotions, our love and hate, our jealousies and pity, our hurts and our strengths.

The eyes are like a mirror and when we look into them we see a reflection of the emotional states *inside the person*. Why are these emotional states revealed to us by looking at another person's eyes? Because we are looking into a hologram of that person's emotions revealed by our interactions with the person and stored in our memory as visual clips. We have created a single image from all of the clips, an image that is the totality of the emotional states we have learned about the person from interacting with them.

SPECIFIC INSTRUCTIONS: STORY IN THE EYES

The "Story in the Eyes" Image is used with other techniques; for example, with "Walk-Around" or with "Co-Consciousness," a technique we will go into next.

The eyes are an organ of silent communication and convey a story about the person (lover, spouse, boss, parent, child, etc.) revealing another layer of emotion.

Once you have imaged the person, such as in "walking-around" them, and you want to know more about them, do the following.

STORY IN THE EYES IMAGE

1. See a person standing in front of you that you desire to know more about.
2. Look into the eyes of the person you are imaging.
3. Concentrate on their eyes.
4. Do their eyes give you any feeling or tell you any story?
5. Concentrate on the story or feeling in the person's eyes.

Karen will now gain more insight about Vic and their relationship by *seeing herself* through his eyes.

This image is called "Co-Consciousness." She will perform it the same way she does other images—by relaxing, seeing the image, studying it, and gaining insight from it.

Before she examines herself through Vic's eyes, take a moment and use the tool yourself. Again, choose any subject you like—a lover, spouse, boss at work, a child, anyone you want insight into how *they see you.*

SPECIFIC INSTRUCTIONS: CO-CONSCIOUSNESS

This technique is used to see yourself through the eyes of someone you are having a problem with or that you just want to know better. You can gain insight and understanding about yourself and how others feel about you.

CO-CONSCIOUSNESS IMAGE

1. Relax, close your eyes if you like, and see an image of yourself in a situation with the person.

2. Where are you? See yourself in the environment where you normally spend time with the person (home, school, workplace, etc.). What are you doing?

3. See the person. What are they doing? How do you feel as you see them? Let the information unfold. The information will come forward. Don't worry if the image is vague or vivid.

4. Now see that the person is seeing you.

5. Now see through their eyes...they are seeing you. (In the image you can literally do this. Simply look through their eyes.) Allow the image to unfold. Don't second-guess the information coming to you. Just look at yourself through their eyes. You may see a full, vivid image or just get a sense impression.

6. What do they see? How do *they* feel as they see you? How do *you* feel as you see this image?

7. Now go back to your eyes. See that you are seeing them. What do you see? How do you feel as you see the image?

You can keep doing this, going back and forth, seeing them through your eyes and then seeing you through their eyes. As you do, more and more information will unfold.

The images are holograms, which means that there are stored pieces of information connected in the mind to other stored pieces of information.

Keep reversing the process, looking at the other person and at yourself, until you come to an understanding that is valuable to you.

To perform this imaging exercise, Karen put herself in Vic's head, seeing through *his* eyes, so that it was she and not Vic being viewed. Can she gain insight into how Vic sees her, feels about her? Absolutely. Vic's facial expressions and body language in dealing with her have been recorded in *her* mind as lasting visual impressions. His reactions to her lovemaking, her anger and joy around him, her frustrations and triumphs, her *everything*, is recorded in *her own visual memory bank* because she saw him react in subtle or overt ways and stored the memories.

A person's emotions are like light reflecting off of a mirror, shining out to affect the other person and bouncing back to us in the form of what our own minds registered about their perceptions of us.

In a sense, *co-consciousness,* looking at ourselves through the eyes of another, is being brutally honest with ourselves. It's hard for any of us to be totally objective about ourselves. If nothing else, we are so busy battling the storms that we never have the time to see the forest from the trees. This exercise clears our heads of our prides and prejudices and forces us to make an assessment of ourselves at a deeper level, at a level in which we assess *how others see us.*

Now let's see how it worked with Karen.

"I saw myself through Vic's eyes and just as I did with his image, I took a closer look at it and then started examining it. What I saw first startled me: There was pain on my face, too, and I was reaching out my hand for him. I didn't have to go any further with the image. I knew that Vic saw me as a person who was reaching out for him and that my needs were overwhelming him. And I realized from my examination of his seeing me that the fears generated by my need to be closer to him arose from his family environment in which his handicapped father drew everyone close and stifled them. As a result, Vic desperately wanted space and freedom.

"I had my own needs to bond emotionally with him that came from *my* family environment. My background was the product of an entirely different childhood family environment than his, one of closeness and sharing. I was devastated when I lost my parents, and needed someone in my life to cuddle me emotionally as my parents had.

"The two opposing forces were in collision—my personality shaped as one who expected emotional bonding and constant closeness, and his as one who expected more emotional space and who was ready to run from the commitment of marriage and children even after he had entered into the bond.

"The imaging gave me great insight into our relationship. Before I gained those fresh perceptions, Vic and I had been in a continuous process of racing into each other's arms and then recoiling with angry words, only to bounce back to each other as if we were attached by rubber bands.

"If I was going to be happy and successful, flow through life with energy and passion, and have a great relationship, I had to know what my strengths and weaknesses were. For that I would literally have to go inward and through the process of discovering myself."

> *This life's dim windows of the soul*
> *Distorts the heavens from pole to pole*
> *And leads you to believe a lie*
> *When you see with, not through, the eye.*

William Blake

5

Imaging Experiences

Now that you have experienced your first imaging sessions, I want to take a moment to explain a little more about the techniques and the results you may expect.

As you have already discovered, imaging is very easy.

While it is possible to see an eidetic image at almost any place or at any time, the best results are achieved when you are relaxed and ready to see the image and study it. If you are distracted, you are likely to get shallow results.

There are really only two prerequisites:

1. You should have the *desire* to look inward.
2. You should be in a physical environment where you can *concentrate*. "Concentrating" doesn't mean you have to work at it, it merely means that you have cleared your mind of pressing matters so that you leave yourself open to focus on the image.

Do not worry about memorizing the instructions—once you see an image, it will still be there when you go back to it after reading the next instruction. If you like, you may read all of the instructions prior to beginning so that the technique will be familiar to you, but that is not necessary. The instructions are short and simple, and if you need to look at them again while you are imaging, you may do so as it should not affect the quality of the image.

Once you have yourself in a "good place" mentally and physically to see an eidetic image, you are ready to begin. Now that you are ready and have left yourself open, the image will come to you naturally and spontaneously.

Remember, an eidetic image is neither mere memory nor a figment of your imagination. An eidetic image is an image recalled from the storage of visions in your mental bank. It may be an image of the lover you met last month or the parent who died thirty years ago. The length of time in storage is not important.

Keep in mind that the eidetic image contains three individual parts: first, the image itself, which can be seen vague or vivid; second, the bodily/emotional (somatic) response that accompanies it; and third, the meaning revealed by the image.

Also note that the *emotional response* may be very subtle—or earth shattering. Sometimes people experience very profound emotional responses, they will laugh, cry, and feel great joy or intense anger. Other times it is much more subtle, hardly detectable, a slight tension in the gut or chest, a vague feeling of coolness or warmth, feeling ill at ease, or just a good feeling.

Meaning refers to the insight you gain from the image. It is an automatic function of the image and you do not have to dig for it. If the eidetic image is there, the meaning will also be there. Often times it is an *Ah-ha revelation*, sudden insight and understanding that shouts out to you, *"So that's what _____ is all about!"* Or, "so that's why I can't do this or that, so that's what he means, so that's why she's so distant."

At other times it does not strike like lightning or flash like a neon sign but is a generalized sense of knowledge in which you gain information about the situation or person you are imaging. The image may be vague or vivid.

The important thing is that you understand to leave yourself open to *see* the image, *feel* the image, and *gain insight* from it.

Begin the exercise by finding a quiet place where you can completely relax and can sit or lie comfortably. You may keep your eyes open or closed, whichever you prefer.

We'll use several dozen images as we progress through different facets of our lives. All of the images are repeated in the Appendix of Images, found at the back of the book.

6

Rediscovering Ourselves

What Karen learned from her imaging of Vic was not only that he had carried the effects of his "history" into their relationship from his upbringing, but that she had also brought in her own childhood emotions and desires. She had a need to be fulfilled through being close to him, to bond with him emotionally. Even though he loved Karen, he rejected her need because of his smothering relationship with his father.

To uncover the source of our own attitudes and emotional conditions that are keeping us from being fully happy, we have to take an inner journey and examine our own "history."

We were not born "blank sheets" that became filled in by our environment. At birth we entered this world with many wonderful, natural attributes. As I mentioned earlier, we don't come into the world full of fears or doubts afraid to speak up to a boss or a spouse—that lack of confidence is a product of interactions with our parents and other significant people during our primary growth years.

We will go deeper into the subject of the traits we were born with, those natural aspects of the radiant spirit within us called the "gifts of the gods," in a subsequent section. But first we are going to look within to discover who we are and how we came to be the person we are. We do this with tools called the *eidetic parents images* in which we see images of our childhood home life to discover how our personality was formed. As I indicated before, it doesn't matter if you are six or sixty; you are still carrying around inside you the effect of those early years.

Self-defeating traits, like fear and self-doubt, come from negative experiences usually ingrained into our psyche during those formative years when our personality was molded and shaped. If we are going to understand ourselves, and if we are going to get rid of those negative images and the energies they emit that keep us from succeeding at love, career, or other goals, we must find their sources and replace them with the natural radiance that is our birthright.

The parents' images find the sources for us. The images tell us a great deal about our parents that we don't recall. The way they acted toward us and how we responded to them reveals how we deal with the world at large. Cold parents often create cold children who grow up and carry the chill into the marriage bed, or children who are consumed by doubt and in need of love. Parents who failed to provide a voice of encouragement continue on the feeling that we are not good enough when we try to succeed on the job today. The same dynamics hold true for almost every aspect of our lives.

For the most part I am not referring to "bad" parents. For example, many parents are not bad; on the contrary, they are loving and caring people. But even with terrific parents who do their best, their own personal limitations, ignorance, and stressful life circumstances get passed on to the children.

What we are today is a reflection of many things, but few things have the power to shape our personality as those impressionable years from conception to young adulthood. Shaping doesn't always mean you turn out like your parents. You will inevitably pick up some of your parents' traits, but other aspects of your personality will be formed by a reaction *against* their dictates or lifestyle rather than a monkey-see, monkey-do imitation. Or, you may form traits through "projection," a process in which we, as children, make up things that are not true but seem true to us at the moment. For example, if a parent constantly came home late from work during a person's childhood, it's not uncommon for the child to conclude that the parent's inattention was due to a lack of caring. That may be true or it may simply be that the parent's long work hours arose from the need to support the family, rather than from a lack of affection for the child. (We will go into more depth on this with imaging tools in the parent-child relationship section.)

The image of our "home" is also significant. A home is not just a place in which we once lived as a child. Unlike just visualizing an apple, the image of our home contains nuances, feelings, and emotions that we carry within throughout our life. It is the warmth or chill of the atmosphere, as reflected in our emotions while we lived in the house, that reveal things about us. The aura of the home and the emotional history revealed to us by imaging it are reflections of the people who occupied it. Back in the sixties we would have said a place had "vibes."

Vibes are feelings and what are left in our minds about places we have been are not just images of the tables and chairs but our feelings about the space they occupied. These feelings, perhaps decades old, are still with us today and we constantly experience them in our lives without realizing their original source.

Those feelings, which are clues to how we were shaped emotionally, are what we are searching for when we image the home. They are like knee-jerk reactions or imprints in our brain, staying with us our whole life, as basic personality imprints, emotions that we relive over and over.

At this point I will take you through some of the image tools from the Eidetics Parents Images. Developed by Dr. Ahsen, I have used them thousands of times with great success.

The images concern our childhood family home environment.

Images of our home should create feelings of security and warmth in us. The house we were raised in (and for most of us there will be more than one "home") contains our principal family members, our parents and our siblings. As we concentrate on the people in the house, one by one, our feelings attached to them will surface and become clear. In unlayering our emotions about them, we will begin to learn about ourselves. Normally, the image of the house should evoke warm and stable emotions. When the warmth and connection is not there the feelings evoked by the image of the house, pleasant or unpleasant, are the very same ones we carry into adult life.

We will begin by imaging our parents and then see our childhood home environment.

PARENTS' LEFT/RIGHT POSITION

In this image you will be asked to see your parents or primary caregivers stand in front of you. The images of one's parents usually get stored in the brain in fixed, specific locations. See where your parents appear and if you can easily switch them.

When this is not the case, there is an *inversion* (described below).

Parents' Left/Right Position Image

1. Picture your parents standing directly in front of you.
2. As you look at them, who is standing on your left and who is standing on your right?
3. Now, try to switch their positions. Are you able to switch them?
4. Notice any difficulty you experience when you switch them.
5. Now, see your parents standing in front of you again.
6. Who is standing on the left and who is standing on the right now?
7. Switch your parents' position again.
8. Do you again experience a problem when you switch them?
9. Notice the two different feelings: spontaneous and forced.
10. Notice that you have no control over your parents' spontaneous images.

Let's go back to Karen's story. She said, "I wanted to see if I could discover why I was so needy for Vic. I relaxed and got myself comfortable in a place where I wouldn't be disturbed, sat back and closed my eyes" (again, one's eyes can be open or closed).

"I started by seeing an image of my parents standing before me. In the image, my father is on the left and my mother is on the right."

Mother on the right and father on the left is the optimal position to see our parents when we see them standing side-by-side. Our parents are normally fixed in this position in our mind because for most people the earliest images of mother are genetically encoded on the right side of their brain. Primal bonding occurs when babies are held and nursed (or bottle fed) by their mothers. When the baby is held on the left, or heart side of the mother, the baby hears the mother's heartbeat in its right ear, thus her image gets stored first on the right side of the baby's brain. Mothers hold their babies on both sides of their chest, but the genetic cues are implanted more strongly on the side where the baby hears the heartbeat. While the baby hears the heartbeat and sees mother on the right, it usually sees the father on the left approaching or viewing the nursing scene.

The net result is that father on the left, mother on the right, is how parents' images for most people get encoded in their brains. (Have you noticed that through the ages, most artists intuitively have known this? They usually depict scenes of mothers holding their babies on their left or heart side.)

The position of mother and father, as people image their parents standing in front of them, appears fixed in most people. The inability to switch them easily indicates that the images are strongly localized in the mind. If you saw the usual pattern, father left, mother right, it means your mother and father had strong specific roles in your life.

Although fixed, the images should be able to be switched with conscious force. When the force is removed, they should spontaneously go back to their original positions. If they cannot be switched at all, meaning that the positions are overly rigid, it indicates inflexibility in your parents' relationship to you.

If switching their positions has pronounced flexibility (they switch very easy), it can indicate a weak relationship with your parents, emotional isolation, or extreme fear in relating to them.

If the images are revolving and not fixed in any position, it indicates an unsteady relationship to them.

When mother's image appears on the left and father's on the right, the image is called an *inversion*. This indicates that the influence of one of your parents is dominating your mental space. When growing up, you may have experienced one parent as dominating and the other weaker or absent. This means the influence of the "weaker" parent is less available to you.

Next, Karen saw the *home* that she shared with her parents. (This is called the *"House Image."*) She had shared several homes with her parents, but the one that came to mind was the home of her teen years, the most dramatic years in her family life. The image she saw was of the living room of the house with her father in an overstuffed chair reading the newspaper. Her mother was in the kitchen cooking.

Karen said, "My father was a Vietnam veteran. He volunteered for the war out of a sense of duty, leaving my mother behind with two small children, my brother and me. His decision to fight for his country turned out to have tragic consequences for him and his family. Wounded and captured, he was a prisoner of war for over three years. When he returned, rather than the hero's welcome our veterans of wars had received in the past, he came back to a society confused about the war, with many people angry not only at the politicians who kept it going, but even at the soldiers who fought in it.

"While his physical wounds healed, he never recovered from his psychological wounds. He often experienced bouts of depression and drank when depressed, taking out his anguish on my mother and on us kids. At other times he was overly protective, telling us that the world was a dangerous place and he had to protect us from the dangers. We had to stick together to be safe.

"Growing up in a household filled with these strong emotions, I never really understood their source because it always came down to something vague called 'the war.'

"I moved in closer to examine the image of my father, looking at his face, experiencing a well of emotion when I did. I had loved my father very much and my last memories of him are when I was seventeen. My high school principal called me out of class and drove me home in her car. She wouldn't tell me why I was being taken home in the middle of the day, but I knew something terrible had happened. When we reached home I discovered that my father had been involved in a fatal accident. He had been drinking and, thankfully, no one else was hurt.

"My father was a decent man who had suffered great emotional trauma from his experience in Vietnam. Since that time he experienced episodic depression, alternating with states of joy, warmth, and humor. Finally, his emotions plummeted him into a state of pain and depression."

Karen described what she saw in the image. "There was a sadness to my father's face that twisted my heart. I reached out and touched his skin and felt his warmth and melted with love. There was a noble energy about him, he seemed strong-willed, but there also was a refinement about him, almost a princely elegance. I looked into his eyes and saw that he was soft and vulnerable, and that the cruelties of the world were too much for him to bear.

"Next I imaged my mother. She was cooking, putting love in the food that she was preparing. There also was sadness in her face and she held one hand over her left breast, the breast that had been attacked by cancer. Mother always believed that her cancer was due to the stress of first 'losing' my father to the war, and then dealing with his emotional pain after the war.

"Her skin was warm to my touch, too, warmer than my father's, almost hot against my hand. I looked into her eyes and saw wisdom— love—and strength, but as I probed deeper, I sensed something else, a will and determination to move ahead in the face of any obstacle.

"I felt my mother was teaching me, that she wanted me to understand the difficulties she had lived through and to use her determination and strength to help myself and my own family. I saw her hand touch my shoulder and I instantly felt strength in my own being.

"Tears came when the images faded, but they were cleansing tears because in the images of my parents and our home life I had gained greater insight into my own needs.

"Although my parents had experienced serious problems, they stuck together and kept the family intact, probably because they were so dependent upon each other. Each in his own way felt that staying together meant strength and safety."

HOUSE IMAGE

Picture your parents in the house where you lived most of the time with them, the house that gives the feeling of a home. (If you lived in several houses, choose the one that most spontaneously comes to mind.)

HOME IMAGE

1. Picture your parents in the house. Where do you see them? What are they doing?
2. How do you feel as you see the house?
3. See your father. Where is he? What is he doing in the picture?
4. Do you experience pleasant or unpleasant feelings when you see him?
5. Relax and recall memories about the place where your father appears.
6. Now, see your mother. What is she doing?
7. Do you experience pleasant or unpleasant feelings when you see her?
8. Relax and recall memories about the place where your mother appears.
9. Where are your siblings? What are they doing? How do you feel as you see them?
10. Now see yourself in the picture. What are you doing?
11. Does the place give you the feeling of a home?

The home should create feelings of security and warmth in us. In the home setting appear the principal family figures: the parents and siblings. As you concentrate on these figures, the feelings attached to them will become clear and early childhood memories connected with them will surface.

Normally, the image of the house should evoke a warm and harmonious family relationship. Notice that the feelings you have in the house image are the same feelings you often experience in your life now, in your relationships.

7

Early History Images

In order to understand how her needs for warmth were clashing with Vic's need for space, Karen probed more images.

She closed her eyes and saw the "Warmth of Parents' Bodies" Image to learn more about herself.

Assessing the warmth of a parent's body in the image (cool, warm, hot) reveals the quality of bonding one had during their childhood period of dependency, the time when the parents look after the child's physical and psychological needs.

The feel of a parent's body and skin, its warmth and whether or not it accepts us, reveals the connection between us and our parents, and the depth of caring and nurturing we received.

When there has been warmth and nurturing from our parents, their bodies in the image will appear warm and impart a feeling of personal connectedness. Essentially, the images reveal whether our parents were able to express love in a tender and personal manner.

When we see this image and experience no sign of personal warmth, but rather cold, indifferent, or hostile parents, we know that there was a problem. The disconnection may come from the parents, who can't show affection, or suppress their feelings, or have other problems such as depression, illness, or anger and hostility. When parents' bodies appear cold, it usually means that they were not able to show us affection.

WARMTH OF PARENTS' BODIES

This image assesses the temperature of your parents' bodies, revealing the bonding and connection between you and them. The connection between our parents and us in turn reveals the connection we feel with the world at large.

WARMTH OF PARENTS' BODIES IMAGE

1. Picture your parents standing directly in front of you.
2. Which parent's body has more personal warmth?
3. How is the other parent's body in comparison?
4. Concentrate on your feelings concerning your father's body.
5. How do you feel as you see his body?
6. Relax and recall memories as you concentrate on your father's body.
7. Concentrate on your feelings concerning your mother's body.
8. How do you feel when you see her body?
9. Relax and recall memories as you concentrate on your mother's body.
10. Which parent's body do you wish to know more? Why?

"Going back and imaging my parents again," Karen said, "I see an image of both my mother and father. I draw a lot of richness and strength from them as I see their images. Being connected to them gives me a strong rooted feeling and a sense of strength that has been there for my whole life."

Many adults, who didn't have that kind of attachment, don't have that inner feeling of solidity. Good parenting really makes a child solid; it's like hatching an egg to give it the warmth it needs to hatch properly. Eggs and children need parental warmth. Lack of parenting leaves emotional holes in kids; empty holes that suck in garbage from TV and the streets. (We'll discuss this at greater length in the section on parenting.)

"From the images of my parents I feel a warm bond between them and me. My father's body is cool on the surface. As I probe deeper, there's warmth beneath. This brings back a positive memory of a time when my mother was on a trip and I was home alone with my dad. I must have been seven or eight and woke up with a bad dream. I was really scared and I ran into my father's bedroom and said, 'Daddy I'm scared!' He said, 'Get into bed with me,' and he put his arms around me and fell asleep embracing me. I remember his body was so hot, but it felt really good to be nestled inside his big warm body. I fell asleep. He was really there for me."

The skin is the next image. In our mind's eye we look at our parents' skin and concentrate on it. Does it seem to accept you, or reject you? Think about how you feel when you look at their skin. This image is important because the feeling of acceptance associated with the skin of a parent in the image conveys warmth and security. The care given by parents is reflected in the positive feelings that their skin generates when they come into contact with the body of the child. The contact results in the experience of acceptance and physical relief in the child. So normally the skin should appear warm and accepting, and it reveals whether the parents are accepting or rejecting towards the child.

"My father's skin accepts me but there's a feeling of pain inside, a little underneath his skin, a layer of coolness or a barrier. He can't let me in one hundred percent because there's pain. I know that the source of the pain is the memory of all of the people to whom he was bonded who died during the Vietnam War. I feel pain when I see this. It's not that he doesn't love me. It's just something from the past that is still there in him.

"My mother's body is warm to the touch and her skin is soft and she appears tender, I feel like I could sink into her. Her skin is warm and soft. It really takes me in. I feel very bonded to the warmth and love of my mother's nurturing skin, and it brings back memories of how she was there for me. If I had any problem I'd get in bed with her and cuddle like a child, talking out my problems. In fact, every Sunday morning my brother and I made brunch and brought it with the newspaper to my parents and we'd all jump into their king-size bed, read the papers, and cuddle. It was really great.

"My father enjoyed these times and accepted me, but there was a pain that wouldn't let him enjoy life fully. I took this personally as a child, thinking that he didn't love me at times. The images helped me to see that it was his past, not me, that created his inability to fully let me in."

PARENTS' ACCEPTANCE OF YOU IMAGE

Acceptance or rejection by parents is reflected in our sense of their bodies and skin. The care given to us by our parents as children is reflected in the positive or negative feelings that their skin generates when we come into contact with them. At the very least, our parents' skin should be warm and appear accepting.

PARENTS' ACCEPTANCE OF YOU IMAGE

The *Acceptance* image is:

1. Picture your parents standing in front of you.
2. Look at your parents' skin and concentrate on it for a while.
3. Does it seem to accept you or reject you?
4. How do you feel as you look at their skin?
5. Whose skin gives you the feeling of acceptance? To what degree?
6. Whose skin gives the feeling of rejection? To what degree?
7. Concentrate on your feelings concerning father's skin.
8. How do you feel as you experience father's skin?
9. Concentrate on your feelings concerning mother's skin.
10. How do you feel as you experience mother's skin?
11. Which parent usually touches you more?
12. Which parent do you usually touch more?

So far we have used the *Walk-Around* Image in which we see an image of a person we want to understand better and look at them from different angles, including seeing the *Story in Their Eyes*, and the *Co-Consciousness* tool in which we look at ourselves from their viewpoint, getting insight into how they feel about us.

In the present section, we dealt with rediscovering our connection with the world through assessing the *Left-Right Position* of our parents, the ambiance of the family *Home*, and the *Warmth* of their essence.

I am now going to introduce you to three further quick and easy images from the Eidetics Parents Images. They are the *Listening, Understanding*, and *Acceptance* tools.

Understanding what the child has to say, as opposed to just giving it "lip service," has a direct relationship to whether a parent is not just listening, but also understanding what the child is trying to communicate. Our parents' ability to pay attention to and understand what has been said to them by us creates *confidence* in us and serves as a bridge to reality when we deal with the rest of the world. If our parents did not listen to us, there will be a negative voice whispering in our minds when we want the rest of the world to listen.

PARENTS' UNDERSTANDING YOU IMAGE

The process of hearing and listening is connected to understanding. This is another way of assessing whether the atmosphere in which we were raised has undermined our confidence levels.

PARENTS' UNDERSTANDING YOU IMAGE

The *Understanding* image procedure is:

1. See yourself talking to both of your parents again.
2. Who seems to understand you better, mother or father?
3. Concentrate on how your father understands you in the image.
4. Do you feel understood?
5. Concentrate on how your mother understands you in the picture.
6. Do you feel understood?
7. See father. What kind of ideas would you like to exchange with him?
8. See mother. What kind of ideas would you like to exchange with her?
9. Which parent exchanges ideas with you more?
10. Which parent do you feel should exchange ideas with you more?

Karen continued exploring the image.

"I see my parents before me and I talk to them in the image.

"When I talk to my father, I get a mixed feeling. The way he hears me is that he takes what I say in chunks and he gets it. Then, there are parts that he does not get. I feel somewhat understood by him. What I sense is a small block within him; at times his mind wanders and he seems preoccupied so I don't think he hears me fully. I feel frustrated.

"For my mother to hear me, I have to really explain things to her. At first she questions what I say, but as I continue to explain myself to her, she understands. I realize my ability to stay with my point of view and explain things came from my interactions with my mother."

PARENTS' LISTENING IMAGE

Whether we believe that our parents really listened to us will affect our level of confidence about communicating with the rest of the world.

PARENTS' LISTENING IMAGE

The *Listening* imaging is done as follows:

1. Picture yourself talking to both your parents.
2. Who seems to hear you better?
3. How does the other parent hear you in comparison?
4. Concentrate on how your father hears you in the image.
5. When he hears you, do you feel secure or insecure?
6. Concentrate on how your mother hears you in the image.
7. When she hears you, do you feel secure or insecure?
8. Concentrate on the parent whose hearing creates security for you.
9. Concentrate on the parent whose hearing creates insecurity for you.
10. Which parent do you approach more for listening to you?

Karen observed, "When I saw my father, I know that he takes what I say in bits, but not fully. My mother hears me differently from my father. At first she questions what I'm saying, but as I continue speaking she gets excited by my ideas and cheers me on. I see that with my mother, I have learned to be clear and precise about what I'm communicating. However, my father leaves me feeling frustrated about not being heard."

The Gifts of the Gods

The glorious gifts of the gods
are not to be cast aside.

Homer

Now that we have started an inner journey, you need to know what you can expect to gain from the quest. We have talked about negative energies that keep us from happiness and success (fear, lack of confidence, self-loathing, rage etc.) and positive ones (confidence, excitement, energy, resourcefulness, etc.) that all of us were born with but are no longer bright and shiny in many of us. We are going to take a closer look at these "gifts" that each of us has but that life has dulled. To find those gifts, we will need to *rediscover* the person we really are.

Joseph Campbell, the well-known mythologist, showed us that the Hero's Journey was a universal theme throughout the world and in ancient civilizations. In the introduction written by Phil Cousineau to the book *The Hero's Journey, Joseph Campbell on his Life and Work*, Cousineau relates a discussion he had with Campbell. Cousineau had been on a motorcycle trip when he spotted something in a graveyard that struck him as being at the heart of the Hero's Journey.

> It was a crumbling tombstone in Boothill Cemetery in Tombstone, Arizona, the grave marker of an old gunslinger.
>
> The epitaph read: "Be what you is, cuz if you be what you ain't, then you ain't what you is."
>
> I can hear Joe's hearty bodhisattva laugh now and the clink of our glasses over the soothing sounds of the late-night jazz piano in the old redwood-paneled bar.
>
> "That's it!" he cried with that eternal look of wonder in his eyes. "That's what it's all about: the mystery of the journey."

To me, the *mystery of the journey* is discovering who we are, and one way to discover the real *us* is to unload the detrimental "history" that makes us what we "ain't."

In using imaging tools to look at others and myself I learned that many of us are not using our own full potential, that we have many qualities inside of us that were not being utilized. Even worse, we are not aware of them.

As children, we have enormous natural powers within us. Some of us lose touch with them because our parents tell us that we can't do or say certain things, or be who we are. Even champions in business, entertainment, sports, and other fields who succeed are always trying to find more of this natural potential and energy from within. They too have been told they can't do or be whom they truly are, but they have overcome these limiting messages and tapped into an inner reservoir of great ability.

You may remember that as a child you loved to speak out—and tell the truth. Remember the story of the Emperor's New Clothes? Like the child who spoke the truth about the emperor's clothes, people try to stifle what they don't want to hear or what they fear to hear. When we speak the truth as children, we are often told we aren't supposed to say those things. We aren't supposed to say someone has bad breath or his or her nose was very long. We learned to lie, be polite, and not to be ourselves. There are countless ways in which we as children still our honesty, vibrancy and enthusiasm because adults around us are threatened by it.

We quickly adopt our parents' attitudes in both dramatic and very subtle ways, often with no idea of how we got there. Assume, for example, you have a problem defending yourself. Through imaging, you may find you lost the ability to "battle" in childhood. Perhaps your brother was always hitting you and your natural impulse was to hit back to defend yourself, but you always got yelled at for it. Soon you learned that defending yourself was bad. When you grow up your ability to defend yourself is stunted.

Some of us have been suppressed to the point that we have lost contact with some of the most valuable qualities that we have inside, qualities such as curiosity, spunk, courage, and the ability to initiate. Some of us can't see beyond the box of rules and expectations we were put in. Children in a classroom, who may have novel ideas that don't fit into the curriculum or standard of thinking, may find themselves being pressured into the box, their creativity thwarted in the process.

At every turn, Odysseus faced this sort of problem as he struggled to accomplish his goals and break out of the string of boxes in which he found himself. Fortunately, he was quick and strong, brave and resourceful. He never lost hope and always looked to new paths.

His odyssey is also a spiritual, philosophical, and psychological pilgrimage. He survives the Cyclops, the deadly song of the Sirens, and even the seductive lure of forbidden love, not through brute strength, but through intelligence, cunning, and courage. He reached into himself time and time again and found he possessed within him all he needed to forge ahead.

Like Odysseus, we are not born a "blank sheet" to be filled in by life. Rather, each of us possesses traits at birth that can be called "gifts of the gods," natural abilities, and talents with which we were born. It is to these "gifts," natural abilities, powers, and talents within, into which we tap when we do self-imaging.

> *If you are very valiant, it is a god,*
> *I think, who gave you this gift.*

Homer

TAPPING INTO OUR GIFTS

Eidetics allows us to tap into and bring forth our own majesty and grandeur. The ancient Greeks called the glorious radiant spirit within "*eidos*." Imaging permits us to find the eidos, the very unique bounty and giftedness that is within each one of us.

Insight—the vivid powerful apprehension of these gifts and images—is indispensable to anyone wishing to experience joy, love, creativity, and especially success in business. The movie director needs this to create a work of art, the lonely man needs this to find companionship, and the ambitious woman needs this to gain total confidence to feel invincible with the competition.

In one of Dr. Ahsen's seminal works on eidetic imaging, he identified twelve qualities of the self which "insightful imaging" will allow you to access. Each of us is born with these energies, but some may have been lost to us during life's hard passages. Through imaging we can reclaim and revitalize all our energies.

THE TWELVE QUALITIES OF THE SELF

When all twelve energies are available to us, we feel whole and know that we can tackle the world with full power and confidence. Notice which ones are readily available to you and which ones you may have more difficulty accessing.

1. Happiness:
   We are all born to be happy. No one is born to be miserable. Feelings of pleasure, contentment, and joy are our natural birthright.

2. Alertness:
   Awareness and a keen perception of the world around us is our natural state. We are designed to be attuned to the environment around us.

3. Active:
   Vibrant energy as we perform in life is an inherent quality of the self. We need the vitality to fully participate in all we do.

4. Eagerness:
   The positive, hopeful desire to interact with life is a natural energy. Those who are eager emanate an infectious engaging spirit to others.

5. Excitement:
   It is the electric force that vitalizes and inspires us to participate in life. Those who still possess it fully are able to inspire others to action.

6. Interactive:
   To freely interact with people, objects, or ideas, is how our inspiration and genius freely flow from one idea to the next.

7. Hopefulness:
   Knowing we will succeed, expecting that good things will come our way, believing that things will turn out all right is the ability to trust life. This optimism draws good things to us.

8. Initiative:

Having the resourcefulness to start new things (projects, activities, ideas) and see them come into fruition is a natural ability of the self.

9. Exploration:

Venturing confidently into life, going to new territories (jobs, friendships) with a sense of openess and curiosity, keeping our horizons open is a natural potential we are born with.

10. Battling:

The ability to overcome obstacles and remove the things that impede us is a force found in our innate spirit.

11. Openness:

The capacity to be available to all life offers in an unobstructed manner. Those who are open have many life opportunities to draw from.

12. Resourcefulness:

The ability to tap into a bounty of resources stored within us to meet any challenges that life throws at us.

When all twelve of these qualities are fully accessible in us, we are in a natural state of joy and well-being. This is our birthright. Anything less is not being all that we are meant to be. When all twelve aspects are readily available inside of us we are whole and complete and can meet the challenges of life with full confidence.

We have to understand that we are not all born "equally." There are extremes of persona at both ends of the scale. Some people are born into tragic circumstances. Others are born into privilege. Some have loving parents, while others grow up in horrific situations. But within each one of us exist qualities that allow us to shine regardless of our outer circumstances. Success for most of us is something very personal within reach if we have the desire to draw from within and go for it. Our success already exists in our imagination. Take a moment and reflect, what is your image of success?

But the great Master said, "I see
No best in kind, but in degree;
I gave a various gift to each,
To charm, to strengthen, and to teach."

Longfellow

9

The Search for Love and Meaning

The salvation of man is through love and in love.

Victor Frankl,
Man's Search for Meaning

When I think about the tale of the King of Tigers, it reminds me of another tale from the "mysterious" East, a story of a place called Shambala. To Tibetans, who live on a three-mile-high plateau called the Roof of the World, an area twice the size of Texas and as cold as Edgar Allen Poe's "misty mid-regions of Weir," Shambala is a mystical green valley lost somewhere in a crack between the icy reaches of their Titanic mountains. It is a place of milk and honey where it is warm year-round and the trees are flush with food. Westerners have heard the Tibetan tales of Shambala and have launched futile searches to find the valley. Back in the 1920s James Hilton, the British writer, heard the tale and wrote his enchanting novel about Shangri-La.

These Western explorers searching for Shambala miss the same point the King of Tigers hasn't grasped about his own situation: Shambala isn't a physical place; one finds Shambala in the *heart* when inner peace and fulfillment are achieved.

There is nothing wrong with seeking love and job success or green pastures, but we will be doomed with failure and keep on repeating our quest, making our mistakes because we must first find ourselves *before* we are ready to take on the world or open our heart to others. You find your Shambala in the center of your own heart.

Finding ourselves, our true nature and abilities, is in a sense finding *love* in a place many of us have never accessed. Too often, we look for our fulfillment, our Shambala, in another person or place, expecting that someone else—a lover, a spouse, or child—will make us happy; or we look for it in our bank account or in our style of living. (Remember that bumper sticker that claimed "The one who dies with the most toys wins." The real winner is the person who *lives with the most love*.)

There are different types of love: romantic love, love of children, family, and friends, universal love for all people, and love of God. But true love of any nature has its roots in an emotional state that must exist before love can nurture: *love of self*.

Not a narcissistic self-love, but one of inner fullness and confidence, of being satisfied with one's self. When we are at peace with ourselves, we can expand that love to others and open ourselves up to the love of others. When we lack self-love, what we too often feel toward others is not the wisdom and compassion that is needed for a foundation of love, but emptiness, depression, or jealousy.

Some people try to hide their own insufficiencies by a veneer of misplaced confidence, portraying themselves as better, smarter, or whatever else they think it takes to gain the respect and admiration they crave. Others are so self-centered and are caught up with their own life so intensely that they don't understand that they are turning off the very people they want to turn on. They do not know how to give of themselves.

These people repel others rather than attract them. And if they are able to attract others because of special attributes—beauty, money, position or fame—they don't gain a true loving relationship but shallow companionship based upon external *things*.

We can't depend upon others to create our happiness for us. Relying on others are temporary "fixes" that give us an emotional high . . . only to crash later. Each of us needs a solid emotional foundation within rather than temporary fixes from others. Pinning our happiness on others is simply asking for trouble. Even if the other person reciprocates and provides the happiness we think we need, the person we kiss good-bye in the morning may not make it home that night.

We can't rely upon "things" . . . cars, grand houses, and boats are externals that also provide temporary fixes, but not permanent joy. As John Lennon and Paul McCartney professed back in the impetuous sixties, "money can't buy me love." (I also like Bob Dylan's musical comment that "money doesn't talk, it swears.")

We can't rely upon *entities* either, putting our faith and tendering our happiness to a group or organization external to ourselves. Too many people fill the void within them with devotion to a company, a government, or an organization because they have not accessed the fullness of their own heart.

True fulfillment is only found *within*. That's where it starts. Things outside us are only fulfilling if they are a product of the expression of our inner essence. Otherwise we just keep feeling empty—no matter what we buy or whom we are with. Marilyn Monroe is a classic example of emptiness. She had beauty, fame, money and talent—but didn't love herself and couldn't fill the emptiness with the men at her feet or the glamour that surrounded her. Finally, the pain of the void within her became so great that she took her own life. (Tibetans call death "passing beyond sorrow." I think that is a humane way to describe the pain of self-destruction that some people are driven to.)

We have that "emptiness" and fill the void with external things because we are victims of a storehouse of *negative self-images* gathered during those critical years in which we were being shaped by the conditions of our childhood. Negative images are the painful side of our spirit that was transfused into our psyche by the world around us. Too often our reaction to those events is to close down our hearts and live in fear or isolation. We lose our joy and optimism.

How we get rid of the negative images and replace them with positive ones is the focus of sections that follow. But first we must learn how to access the world within us and go to the very center of our beings and reopen our hearts so that all the positive energies within can flow outward, filling our own selves and those around us.

Evoking an eidetic image is also a *revelatory* experience, one that brings about sudden insight that expands our knowledge and understanding about others and ourselves, and "enlightenment" in the sense of an expansion of knowledge and understanding. It can bring deep layers of reality into consciousness and activate energies that have remained frozen.

Before we are able to truly open up ourselves to give and receive the love of others, to go for the gold in careers and life, we must first make that journey of self-discovery and rediscover the fullness within ourselves.

In the next section we will be discussing love and relationships. Before we go into that area, I am going to relate one of the most poignant and tragic tales of love that I have ever heard. It is not a story about a love affair, but of the *power of love*, a power so great that it can give us a reason for life itself.

A REASON FOR LIVING

Victor Frankl relates one of the most poignant and powerful personal experiences of the spiritual and psychological nature of man in his book *Man's Search for Meaning.* Because Frankl, a Vienna psychiatrist, was Jewish, he was imprisoned in the notorious Auschwitz concentration camp. In the camp all possessions were taken away from the prisoners and an effort was made to degrade them to the point where they lost all sense of their own worth and reason to live.

In spite of the brutal treatment the prisoners received, the prisoners' sense of spirituality increased and some were able to retreat *inwardly*, to a place where the beasts that imprisoned them couldn't come.

Frankl's personal salvation was an inner journey that reflected on his love for his wife. As he put it, "love is the highest goal to which man can aspire." Reading his description of his images of his wife, it struck me that the images had an eidetic quality to them.

> We stumbled on in the darkness, along the one road leading from the camp over big stones and through large puddles. The guards kept shouting at us and driving us with the butts of their rifles . . . as we stumbled on for miles, slipping on icy spots, supporting each other time and again, dragging one another of us onward. Nothing was said, but we knew: each of us was thinking of his wife; my mind clung to my wife's image, imagining it with an uncanny acuteness. I heard her answering me, saw her smile, her frank and encouraging look. Real or not, her look was then more luminous than the sun which was beginning to rise.

At that moment, when he saw the image of his wife, Victor Frankl gained sudden insight into the meaning of life.

> A thought transfixed me: for the first time in my life I saw the truth as it is set into song by so many poets, proclaimed as the final wisdom by so many thinkers. The truth—that love is the ultimate and the highest goal to which man can aspire. Then I grasped the meaning of the greatest secret that human thought and belief have to impart: *The salvation of man is through love and in love.*

Frankl saw an eidetic image of his wife that had an "uncanny acuteness" and with the image came sudden insight on how to survive the inhuman abuse he was receiving from the Nazis. That insight kept him alive in the darkest days when others around him perished. Watching those around him fall, Frankl concluded that many could have survived if they had had the sort of meaning in their life that he had gained insight into.

Sadly and unknown to Frankl, while he survived Auschwitz, his wife was murdered by the Nazis at another camp.

THE HEART IS THE KEY TO MEANING

The heart is the key to experiencing love and a deeper meaning in life. Many of us have closed down our hearts due to painful experiences in the past. We do not trust, are cautious, and protect ourselves from expressing the love we feel inside. We do not allow others to love us. We are afraid that we will be hurt again. However, by shielding ourselves, we make ourselves more vulnerable and isolated. We are robbing the vital energy and strength of our hearts. We lose the ability to connect with others. When we dare to open our hearts again, magical and powerful things happen. The heart has its own wisdom and when we follow it a natural inner knowing unfolds from within. Potent energies come to the fore.

In order to discover the power living in your very own heart, try this image to discover how your perception of life changes when you bring your heart into all that you do.

IMAGES OF YOUR HEART

By no longer responding through the heart, you have accepted a negative orientation toward life. There is a slow voluntary dying of your life force. The real heart is made of *essence* (a feeling of the heart) and *flesh* (the physical organ). If your performances and relationships in the world need improving, your whole heart must be brought back, both in essence and in flesh.

How do you go about it? First, you concentrate on where your heart is on the left side of your body. You become aware that the heart *exists*. Then you see or sense the image of your physical heart and experience the essence of the heart and the physical heart *together*. Initially, you may feel some discomfort, but soon this gives way to a transforming effect.

1. See your heart that is beating inside your chest on the left side of your body.
2. Now imagine that you are doing things with your whole heart in it.
3. Become aware that your heart is made of essence (feeling of the heart) and it is made of flesh also (the physical side). When you put the essence of the heart and the flesh together you have the feeling of the "whole" heart. Pay attention to this whole heart feeling, with the essence and the flesh both in the feeling.
4. Now see that you are doing things with your "whole" heart in it.
5. See yourself doing other things with the "whole" heart in it.
6. Now see that you are putting your "whole" heart into being with a person with whom you want to relate better. How are you with them? Allow the revelations of your heart to unfold.

From early childhood on we learn to allow just so much heartfelt emotion to be felt. We get used to lesser participation from our hearts. So, we squelch our desires and limit our potential. We get afraid to go for what we really want. The following image brings our passion back and our ability to follow our heart's desire.

HEART AND DESIRE IMAGE

1. Think of all the desires you have.
2. Let all of these desires come into your mind and let your heart beat with these desires.
3. Let the world know your desires and let your heartbeat know the world. Go with your desires into the world.

Lewis, a man in his fifties, felt alienated from his teenage daughter. When she was young she was "daddy's little girl." Now that she was sixteen, they barely spoke to one another. Their relationship had become guarded.

"My daughter is growing up and I don't feel connected to her. She is critical of me and so I feel angry with her. She makes a face like I am an idiot anytime I say something. I feel shut down and I hate to admit this, but I have distanced myself from her. When I think of it, it feels sort of sad and empty."

I asked Lewis to see the image of his heart in exactly the same steps outlined in the directions above.

See your heart that is beating inside your chest on the left side of your body.

"It beats faintly," Lewis said. "The heart looks whitish. It has a steady, slow beat but it is not strong. This tells me that my heart is not fully feeling. My heart is not beating as strongly as it could."

Now, imagine that you are doing things with your whole heart in it again.

"The heart feels more energized. I see energy going into my heart. There is definitely a force that is beyond the heart, energizing my heart. My heart gets electrified gently and starts to beat more and look more vibrant. I feel good. I feel more alive."

Become aware that your heart is made of essence (feeling of the heart), and it is made of flesh also (the physical side). When you put together the essence of the heart and the flesh, you have the feeling of the "whole" heart. Pay attention to this whole heart feeling.

"It feels content and steady. My heart beats rhythmically and faster. There is a feeling of happiness."

Now see that you are doing things with your "whole" heart in it.

"When I am doing things, I am more joyful. I see I am picking up a baby and tossing her playfully in the air. I feel joyful and exuberant. My heart feels really good. It is more red. It's beating stronger."

Now see that you are putting your "whole" heart into being with your daughter. How are you with her?

"I see my daughter. My whole heart is beating strongly. I am being affectionate with her, kissing her on the cheek, hugging her and smooching her. It feels really wonderful and really good. She is laughing and it feels really good to her. Bringing my heart into the relationship with my daughter bridges the gap and makes me closer to my daughter."

After opening his heart to his daughter, Lewis realized he was struggling with putting his whole heart into his work and also into his relationship with his wife. Since he had been deeply hurt as child, having cold and critical parents, he had learned not to trust others and to keep his heart in check. This affected the vibrancy of his connection with the world. In protecting his heart he realized that he could not express the best of himself. I asked him to see the Heart and Desire Image.

Think of all the desires you have.

"I desire to express myself more freely at work. I want to begin to teach new topics at the university where I often lecture, but I am afraid of being criticized. This holds me back. I am often plagued by the fear of not being good enough.

"The other desire is to feel I truly love my wife. Feeling that openness to her on a more consistent basis is what I desire. My heart shuts down. So I am affectionate to her for some moments and then I close down and become cranky and distant. She complains about it, but I just can't remain consistently open. I think it scares me."

Let all of these desires come into your mind and let your heart beat with those desires.

"First, expressing my work. . . . I feel the desire and when I let my heart beat with the desire, I am excited and energized. I feel a positive anticipation of connecting with my students and other faculty and I am having fun. No worry about being judged. It is all a full-hearted expression of me. How powerful!

"Now I am thinking of connecting more openly with my wife. I see my desire and allow my heart to beat with this desire. I instantly move closer to her. I see that I am more affectionate to her and I am happier. I kiss and hug her and express my love. She is responding positively to me. There is warmth and it is sweet warmth. It feels really good."

Let the world know your desires and let your heartbeat know the world. Go with your desires into the world.

"I am like a soldier marching along full of life and fun. I am exuberant and full of playful energy. This is the expression of my real essence."

Lewis had been waiting for something to change in his outer world—when his daughter would finally appreciate him or when the dean of his university would acknowledge him. What he realized was that the power to make the changes he needed and to find the fulfillment he sought was a secret mystery locked in the very recesses of his own heart.

10

Relationships and Fairy Tales

Fairy tales usually end with the white knight riding off into the sunset with the beautiful princess in his arms. Unfortunately, relationships and marriage are not fairy tales. Romance in the social-sexual revolutionary times of the past several decades has often been a battleground as the traditional roles of men and women in relationships and the marketplace underwent dramatic changes.

But anyone who hasn't kept some magic in their relationship or marriage is probably not going to have many ever-afters.

Somewhere between eternal love and the marriage from hell lies the true spirit of love and marriage.

What makes for a successful marriage? When you care as much for your spouse's well-being as you do for your own. The first task is to get to know yourself, then learn to know the other person and have wisdom in how you relate to them.

To be able to love truly is to understand the other person, putting yourself in their shoes while not compromising your own self or loosing your own identity.

Many try to change their partners in some way or another. I have learned that you can never make someone change unless they are a willing participant in the process. You cannot *make* someone change or achieve *their* best potential. For example, you can't make them stop drinking, stop smoking, lose weight, or lose their anger. You can express the desire that they do, but if they don't, you have to be accepting and let go. The key is to go for the best in you. If there is a strong connection in the marriage, the other person automatically changes in relation to you.

Ultimately, you can only change yourself. I used to think that I could "heal people," but after working with so many people for so many years I discovered that unless they want to make the change, it isn't going to happen. I can offer the best techniques, inspirations, and information, but the true transformation occurs only when the person chooses to be transformed.

The same is true with our marriage partner. We can yell, scream, lecture, but it won't work unless your mate is willing. So, when you're yelling to no avail, it is best to focus on yourself.

And that may mean little more than expressing yourself authentically with no attachment to the results.

It's important to be your own unique person in a relationship because your individuality can influence your mate in a positive way. This is different than controlling someone. You can express your desires. You can show the way. If the person is moved by your example, he or she may make the change. It is up to each person in a relationship to do this for himself or herself. Each person is responsible for his or her own growth.

Once you change yourself, you are no longer part of the same old dynamic and your partner will respond differently to you, often automatically changing in the process. However, there are those situations in which a person outgrows the partner and the relationship ends naturally.

If a relationship arises out of love, you must work to nurture that love and be committed to it because the first experience of being in love will fade and in time "history," with all its baggage, will come in. Then we have to develop a committed relationship that is mature enough to deepen and last. Most people need to learn how to truly love with all the sacrifices true love involves. Being able to love means first to love one's self. Only then can one truly love another.

We've all heard of love at first sight, what Hollywood moviemakers call a "cute meet": girl and boy see each other across a crowded room. Their eyes meet for the first time. The music stops, the people around them fade, and for one startling moment he and she bond as they're struck by emotional lightning.

Love at first sight may be fine for movies and the people who experience it, but even if love comes quickly . . . it will not last unless it is nurtured. Eventually that first high closes down for all of us because inevitably we become disappointed.

It is hard work to maintain love. Marriage is even harder, and parenthood falls somewhere between agony and ecstasy. All are based on love. None comes easy or stays without hard work. After the initial bliss of falling in love, for most comes marriage. Marriage today often consists of kids, two cars, two careers, a house payment, and several sets of stressors (spouse, children, job). Throw in commuter traffic, TV, the threat of drugs, violence, corporate downsizing, and the stress of numerous life traumas, it is not surprising that so many marriages are ripped asunder. It is surprising that so many marriages survive.

In the midst of the external chaos and pressures of our lives, love *can be* nurtured. We talked about self-love in terms of having inner confidence and fulfillment no matter what goes on around us. That is true strength. Loving another person is an expression of that inner self-love. Loving someone is to truly care about their well-being even if sometimes they do things that you don't like or go against your own needs. You are secure enough that you don't need them to always fulfill you, so you can allow for the emotional gaps when they irritate you and fail to meet your needs.

Often, we get so caught up in our own perspective and point of view that it is difficult to have compassion for our partner. We fail to see how they see things. We don't know how to step into their shoes. Being able to do so can ease the tension of many disagreements and bring enlightenment to our problems with them.

Learning to see yourself through the eyes of others means to give up your ego first—to die symbolically. In exchange you learn compassion—what Joseph Campbell calls "co-passion."

Co-passion, or co-consciousness, is central to eidetic imaging.

Only when you are honest with yourself, and honest with the person you love and achieve "co-passion," the sharing of their passion, can you achieve true intimacy.

Here is a person learning co-passion, learning to share the feelings of a loved one; in her case through imaging.

Barbara Viner is a thirty-five-year-old woman who sought help from imaging when she realized her marriage needed an overhaul. She had been married for thirteen years and had two children, a twelve-year-old daughter and a nine-year-old son.

Barbara works as an attorney in the legal department of an advertising agency and her husband, David, is a CPA employed by an accounting firm.

For the past year she and David have been bickering more and more, arguing over little things and big things, and she's afraid they will end up in divorce. She still has strong emotions for David and doesn't want to put the kids through the trauma of a divorce . . . but she also doesn't want to have them endure the stress and poor example of their parents constantly arguing.

"I don't want a divorce," she said, "but I don't know what to do. We just seem to be moving farther and farther apart. We had so much affection for each other when we first got married, so much passion. But now I'm constantly irritated at him, and at the kids, too. I snap at everyone. It's even rubbing off at work. My secretary says I act like her mother did when she went through menopause."

David seemed to be withdrawing from the relationship. "It's funny, but the only way I can describe it is sometimes he seems to crawl into a shell and when I reach in to drag him out he tries to bite me."

Barbara used the imaging technique of just *"seeing"* her husband David to examine his feelings toward her.

Barbara preferred to rest on a couch and close her eyes when she did the imaging. Some people prefer sitting up; others have their eyes open. The only thing that matters is that the person chooses a place where they can relax and concentrate. To make sure there would be no interruptions, she waited until the kids were out with friends and David was off playing golf. To avoid interruptions, she unplugged the telephone, pulled the shades, turned off the lights, and closed the doors.

While all of these preparations are fine if they make the person more comfortable, the most important preparation is mental attitude, the *desire* to probe the problem. Barbara had never "visited" herself, she told me. "You read about these things, the soul and stuff like that, but I always thought that 'inner journeys and exploring the self' were things Buddhist monks did on mountaintops. I never realized they could be used as techniques to get to the bottom of emotional problems. But it makes sense. Where are our emotions but hidden away somewhere in that dense maze of our mind?"

She was intrigued by the concept of the soul. "I looked up the word in the dictionary. One of the definitions of the soul is that it's that part of a person where feelings, ideals, and morals center.

"I am also intrigued by the concept of the soul and spirit. I know that there is a part of me that is separate from my physical body, a place that can't be probed by X-rays or a microscope."

After she was comfortable and ready, Barbara first formed an image of her husband, David, using the Walk-Around Image.

"I saw David in full profile," she said. "Then, as if I was a movie camera, and that's really how I thought of it, I slowly zoomed in, coming closer and closer. From a distance, David stood tall and firm. He's a very fastidious person, in his dress and mannerisms, and he appeared that way in the image."

She realized she was seeing David, as he appeared when she first fell in love with him, that time when she got stung by one of Cupid's arrows. This is the "Idol of Love Image," about which we will go into greater detail later. "I feel overwhelmed, my heart literally aches when I see the image. This is the man I fell in love with, the man I love today."

Up close, Barbara felt his skin and it was warm and familiar to her touch. She laughed. "I felt his male parts. They were very warm, hot, hot, hot. We have always been very compatible in bed."

She looked into his eyes to see the "story" in his eyes.

"I got a jolt when I looked into his eyes. His eyes were a little dull and I got this panic sensation that he didn't love me, but then I realized that was my own fear coming out and not the message I was getting from him. As I stared intently at him, I saw a sort of dazed look, almost like the look of a shell-shocked victim. Drawing back I noticed tight lines in his face and the general weariness of his countenance."

I asked her for the meaning she received from the image.

"It came to me like a flash. I didn't really think about it, it just snapped into place. I realized instantly what the image was telling me. David was stunned by life. He had so many things coming at him, you know, the kids, the house, his job, trying to keep it all together, he just wanted to hide his head sometimes."

She walked around the image of David, viewing it from the back and both sides before coming around to the front again. "From every point of view I saw a lack of vitality, of energy in David."

Barbara did the "Co-Consciousness Image" next, in which she viewed herself through David's eyes.

"I conjured up an image of myself, looking at myself through David's eyes. Oh, God, what a revelation. I thought David looked tired when I imagined him. But in viewing myself through his eyes, I realized that I could have modeled for the 'before' character on TV ads they had about tired blood when I was a kid."

She had seen the same sort of dull look in the eyes and weariness that she had seen in David's image. "I was really surprised by the images of David and me. I would have expected to see two people with anger in their face considering how many arguments we have gotten into. What I saw was two world-weary souls."

The three aspects of an eidetic imaging—the image itself, the emotional response, and the meaning it conveys—all came together for Barbara as he saw her husband in her mind's eye.

"We just have too much coming at us. It reminded me of a book called *Future Shock*. I think the theme had to do with the fact that changes in life are happening faster and faster, that people will collapse mentally because they won't be able to keep up with all of the new contingencies."

I remembered Alvin Toffer's book *Future Shock* from my college days. Toffler coined the phrase to refer to the stress and disorientation that people in our dynamic world suffer from too much change too quickly. He considered it a real sickness, what he called a "disease of change." What has occurred is not just the disease of change, but also a disease of complexity. We live in a society in which *everything* is *overcomplicated*.

"What's happening to David and me is that we just have too much coming at us. We're in an overload condition and we need to download. We need more quality time, with each other, away from each other, with the kids and without them. We haven't taken a vacation without the kids since our honeymoon. Maybe we should do that. If the kids object, well, we'll put them out for adoption."

She was just kidding, of course.

The techniques used in this section, Walk-Around, Co-Consciousness, and Story in the Eyes, were related in an earlier section and are repeated in the Appendix of Images at the back of the book.

11

The Idols of Love

A journey that most of us go through is that of falling in love, feeling passion, and then ending with pain and conflict. The god of love, Eros (called Cupid by the Romans), is often pictured as blind because love is blind in the sense that we are too often blinded by our initial attractions. We just don't clearly see the person we fall in love with. At first, they are like a god or goddess, and then somehow they turn into a frog. One of the most dynamic applications of eidetic imaging is in rekindling beauty, reason, and passion into a relationship after our eyes open to the reality of who our mate truly is.

There are a small number of fairy tale romances in this world, love affairs that have no bumpy roads, dead ends, or hair-raising curves. Most of those occur in movies, TV, and romance novels. For those of us existing in *real life*, romance involves struggle. Fortunately, the rewards can be worth it when we succeed.

In a sense, the romantic part of most relationships that involve conflict (and most relationships certainly have an abundance of that) have three stages: first we have that initial thrilling experience of falling in love; then our "history" and the "history" of the other person taints the relationship and conflict arises; and the third stage is where we end the relationship or move it to a deeper experience of love. Imaging can be utilized to heal the conflict by bringing wisdom to nurture the beauty of love.

We will go over the different stages and review imaging examples before doing self-imaging exercises.

The first time we meet a person, whether it is a potential romantic partner, a child, or someone in business, the sense of that person, the first "hit"—our first impression of the person—is eidetically imprinted in our memory and is available for recall at a future time.

In a romantic framework, that first hit that registers inside us is a glimpse of the ideal aspects of the person. In a sense, it is this "image" of the person that we fall in love with. I am not talking about love at first sight but that initial stage when the romantic chemistry connection ignites between two people. At this point we haven't brought any of our negative attributes to the relationship and we don't see the negatives of the other person.

This initial stage in a relationship is the "Idol of Love," that idyllic period in which the birds are singing, the sun is shinning, and the Pied Piper hasn't shown up at our door with his bill. Like Eden before the Snake, it gives us a taste of paradise. The love is pure because the relationship hasn't been tainted yet by all of the history that comes out over time. At this stage we are in a pure state of love in which Cupid, the god of love, has shot us with his arrow and our hearts are full of excitement and positive anticipation. This stage has been described as the early images of love. All other images of love are the "late" images of love, and it is usually in the later stages of the relationship where the conflicts arise.

These first impressions are a vision of the person in their most idyllic sense. But as time progresses, that ideal image is overshadowed by the many other images that register in our psyche. That first impression that stirred our fires is not gone, it is just in hibernation; ready to be roused when we need it.

First comes the ecstasy—and the agony.

Someplace down the line, something we call history enters the relationship. History is our past experiences in life, and those of the person we are romantically interested in. It is all of the pain and love, or lack of love that we grew up in, the anger and frustrations, the legacy of our relationships with our parents, teachers, and friends. This baggage is the stuff each of us brings into the relationship. None of us are perfect, be it the richest or the swiftest, the tallest or the prettiest. None of us were raised in a perfect environment and those in our histories have molded much of our mental makeup.

All baggage isn't negative. If it were, we never would have gotten that first date, let alone any permanent arrangements. Some of the baggage Karen brought into her marriage was her need for closeness, and ran head-on into her husband's need for distance. Neither of them was right or wrong, they were simply being themselves.

Baggage even affects the raising of children. When we first hold a child in our arms we get a hit of that child's pure essence. Later on we see it when they are outside playing with a ball or chasing a butterfly. Then they do something innocent, like break a dish, and we explode and yell at them, suddenly replicating our parents' behavior. We unconsciously treat our children the way our parents treated us when we broke something and the purity of the child's radiance is dimmed. Of course, the child hasn't changed. We've simply transferred a painful part of our past to our child.

Even worse, if a couple survives their historical baggage, everyday stresses can drive them apart, such as economic anxiety, chronic or sudden illness, political situations over which one has no control.

Our most common problems, however, are personal. As Pogo says: "We have seen the enemy and he is us." Fear and anger, jealousy and possessiveness are ubiquitous. They are not gifts of the gods but baggage loaded on us by the pain of our past. Children create additional stresses in a relationship—especially when the relationship is already troubled. And, as wonderful as children are, the sad truth is that kids do not "save" a relationship.

Nonetheless, the idol of love, that pure idyllic essence that first attracted us, is still there in our mate and in us. We need to use our godly gifts—intelligence and intuition—to restore the love, and this time with wisdom.

The myth of Eros and Psyche teaches us this. Eros was the son of Aphrodite, the goddess of love, and Ares, the god of war. From his mother he inherited beauty and charm, and from his father rambunctiousness. His magical bow had arrows of desire, and whomever he shot fell hopelessly in love. The gods sometimes sought his aid, or bribed him to make those they desired fall madly in love with them.

The youngest daughter of a king and queen, Psyche's name meant "soul" to the ancient Greeks. Arrogantly beautiful, she spurned all suitors and boasted that she outshone Aphrodite, the goddess of love. Aphrodite was offended by this and sent her son, Eros, to shoot her with his arrow. He aimed and shot her with his arrow, but he came too close, looking into her eyes.

Both were smitten. (This was no doubt the original "cute meet.")

Since Psyche was mortal, and Eros was a god, marriage was forbidden. Even so, Eros took her as a lover, but he came to her in disguise, not letting her know whom he was. He led her to a secret palace where servants attended to her every need. After dark, he would come and ravish her, keeping his features hidden. Eros made Psyche promise that she would never see his face. She agreed. This is the origin of the phrase "love is blind." She did not fully see her lover.

Psyche was enthralled with her mystery lover until her sisters arrived, jealous of her fortune. They filled her with doubt. Her lover hid his features. They told her it was because he was ugly and a fiend. Giving her a knife and a lamp, they told her to wait until he slept, then light the lamp and see who her lover was.

Late one night, Psyche sneaked into his room, leaned over his bed, and lit the lamp. She saw the gorgeous Eros.

Startled by his beauty, she tilted the lamp and accidentally scorched one of his wings with lamp oil.

Outraged to find his love leaning over him and burning him, Eros flew away. Behind him, the palace turned to rocks and Psyche was cast into the wilderness. Seeking death she threw herself into a river, but the waters swept her to the other side. By seeing him fully, the love and passion was lost.

A wanderer now, she roamed the wilds, pursued by Aphrodite, searching for Eros and lost love. (When the in-love phase goes, don't we always try to find it again?) Suffering one ordeal after another, she even braved the Underworld. The Underworld means suffering loss, obsession, and sorrow. She survives only through the aid of a mysterious friend: Eros. He still loved her and was watching over her, although she did not know it.

Finally, Eros, who had secretly protected Psyche throughout her journey, implored Zeus (the head god) to reunite them. Zeus granted Psyche immortality and Aphrodite eventually accepted her.

In essence, Eros and Psyche overcame personal baggage and external conflict to recapture that first idyllic love they had felt but this time with more wisdom and awareness.

We will look at several modern situations today involving the idol of love, that pure first impression of love, how we fall from it, and how we can regain it.

Coming back to Karen's story, she examines this process of "first hits" in her relationship with Vic, and the cold water thrown on it as their individual needs collide.

"I noticed Vic for the first time when I was on staff at a business seminar he was attending. My first impressions were positive. Here was someone I would feel comfortable around.

"I still feel that way—as if that first impression was eternally etched in my memory. He came over to me and asked me if I wanted to have a drink with him. He looked handsome. His face was open, a smile on his lips. He exuded warmth and kindness. His eyes were deep blue and in an instant I sensed I could feel very much at home with him. I was 'had.'

"After dating for several months, we got more serious. We began staying at each other's place and finally moved in together. Then all hell broke loose. I loved just hanging out with him, lying in bed or around the house, reading and talking and feeling cuddly. Sometimes on Sunday we'd get up, stay in our pj's, make breakfast, and hang around the house all day just being together. Then on Mondays we'd go to work and come back and experience that feeling of being home and cozy again. I suppose I was looking for the same sense of comfort and familiarity I had had in my own home when I was growing up, the warmth and camaraderie of family and being bonded together.

"However, the reality was changing. He gradually withdrew, became more distant, and even pushed me away.

"At the time he was dealing with his father, and his father's chronic medical problems. I didn't understand this and was hurt, even devastated.

"My history entered into it, too. Because of my own needs, I kept coming back for more punishment, trying to recapture that cozy feeling we once had.

"Despite the explosions, when we came together there was warmth and closeness, as if we were a perfectly matched pair. And then he'd say something hurtful and I'd strike out in anger. Afterward, I'd crawl into my hole and cry.

"One moment Vic would be close and available, the next moment he would draw back, nervous, uptight, edging toward the door, telling me he needed space. It drove me crazy. I thought, how could he do that when we'd been so close in bed, so warm . . . so intimate. This Jekyll-and-Hyde routine didn't make sense. But then he'd be intimate again and again I would melt. And then he would say something, and do something hurtful, things that would drive me away, leaving me empty, angry, in despair. The dynamics were destroying me. I finally told him I couldn't take it. I moved out.

"I soon met someone else. I was browsing in a bookstore and I connected with Gregg straight off. He was a person with depth and spirituality, a kindred soul. I loved talking with him, being with him, and I loathed Vic for being such a bastard. And what did he do when I told him about Gregg? Of course, he had to date other women and he told me about them, so I naturally dated more guys and let him know about it."

This should have ended the Karen and Vic story, but it's like those movies where the two lovers split and go their own way, finding someone else, but then they bump into each other on the street or see each other across a crowded restaurant and all of that chemistry that was ignited during the idol of love erupts and . . . damn, "I couldn't live with him and couldn't live without him."

"So, angry and furious, despite the attraction I felt with Gregg, I found myself living apart from Vic but still drawn to him. He felt the same way, that terrible emotional contradiction where he couldn't be with me, and couldn't live without me. Finally Vic came over to my place and told me that as difficult as it was to be with me, that he couldn't live without me, so let's just get married. Besides, you'd look beautiful pregnant, he told me, letting me know he wanted children with me.

"I know I should have been cruel and hard and ground him under my heel, but I have to confess I was just thrilled and excited.

"Now if this was a movie I would be ending this story with something like, 'and we lived happily ever after,' but despite the fact my white knight was back, there were still a few dinks in his armor. And, little wrinkles in my own relationship skills.

"We got married and things sort of settled down, but we still had a lot of stuff to work out. Marriage and a child didn't take the heat *out* of our relationship, or the heat *off* of it. Our history, marriage, family, and careers brought brand-new stress factors for us to trip over.

"With this framework in mind, the Idol of Love period, the wonderful period of first love during which my spirit was drawn to his, got glossed over as angry words and recriminations erupted because my need for closeness collided with his need for space.

"Putting myself in a quiet place both physically and emotionally, I saw an eidetic image of Vic, not the Vic who fathered my child, but the one I met when Eros/Cupid shot me with his passion-tipped arrow."

12

Idol of Love Image

This "Idol of Love Image" is the image that Karen has of Vic when she first fell in love with him, untainted by the cosmic collisions that erupted later. The image will be set out in detail later. First, we will see how Karen does the imaging.

"Relaxing, I see an image of Vic when my passion toward him was first ignited. The image I have of that early time in our relationship is of his dark brown hair and beard, he was godlike to me with his curly brown beard. I noticed him looking at me and noticed the beautiful smile he had, all bright and shiny.

"There's something pushy about him toward me as if he's trying to intrude himself. Yet there's self-consciousness too, his smile is a little self-conscious, as if he's trying to endear his way into my heart. And there is something inviting about him despite the pushiness, I sensed warmth in him. He exudes a warm and homey feeling that I long for. I can be comfortable with him, be myself. I feel adoration and sexually turned on to him.

"Next, I see another image of us. I see myself in the apartment I lived in with Vic before we got married and my immediate emotional response to the image is that I feel a longing to be close to him. Yet I see his need to know that he is not trapped, that he is free.

"As I look at the image, I realize that the most important thing to him was not the physical distance, but the knowledge that he could leave if he wanted to, that he was not trapped and could escape. As long as he knew he had the freedom, he didn't feel the need to back away. As long as Vic knew he had space, he wasn't panicked about being close to me.

His relationship with his handicapped father, with his father's overwhelming and demanding need for his companionship, and his guilt about leaving home as a young man, made him back away from continuing intimacy. He carried this guilt through college and into our relationship for a decade after college.

Not that he didn't want to be with me, he simply had to know he could have freedom in order to be relaxed and intimate. While he was attracted to my desire for closeness, it also made him anxious.

IDOL OF LOVE IMAGE

This technique brings back the image of the person we love at the time of the "first hit" of love, that time when we fell in love. This tool is good to use when you want to remember what attracted you to them. You can recapture the essence in them that you fell in love with.

IDOL OF LOVE IMAGE

Instructions for image:

1. Remember yourself in love, and the person you touched, or who touched you, the first time you realized you were in love with them.
2. Remember the touch and see the person before you again. This is an early image of love. All other images are late images of love, even of this person. There is Cupid in this early image. The god is present here. The more you look at this image, the more it becomes like an icon.
3. See the image. You have bodily feelings and sensations of the god of love being near you. Keep this image at this early stage. Do not bring to your mind later images of this person.
4. Feel your body relaxing, your bones and muscles relaxing. This is Cupid, the god of love in the image. All other human images of love are late images which only contain the problems between you.

Karen used several techniques to understand herself and Vic. An imaging technique that helped Karen gain clarity on her relation with Vic is called "filtering." With this technique you gain insight into yourself by viewing someone you care for through the perspective, or "filter" of one of your parents.

For instance, by imaging Vic while keeping her father or mother in mind, Karen might be able to gain more insight into how she is reacting to Vic. She could see the patterns of her history that she was bringing into the relationship from her mother and father.

Filtering commonly involves a parent because our parents have uniquely affected most of us, and we automatically react and act just like they did in our own relationships. It's a tool where we bring the influence of each parent to the situation we are in.

Karen shows us how to use the filtering tool to get more insight into how her upbringing is contributing to the trouble between her and her husband.

"I evoked the image of Vic in our first apartment. I saw him cuddling with me in bed, and then becoming nervous and jumpy, leaving me with hurt feelings.

"Still imaging Vic jumping around emotionally, I kept my father in mind. As I kept my father in mind I felt a detachment as if I couldn't reach Vic.

"With my father in mind, I felt alone and rejected as if I didn't have the wherewithal to go after Vic.

"Next I kept my mother in mind while I saw the image of Vic being all jumpy. There was an interesting difference from when I used the filter of my father. My father had given me a detached feeling in the situation while my mother was pushing me to get closer. What came to mind with her was, *don't let him go, press him, speak up, meddle, meddle, meddle.*

"But this wasn't completely negative. My mother's influence was telling me to stay involved, to get active and expressive, which was all right because at that point I needed to express my own feelings more and not withdraw. 'Keeping mother in mind,' I pressed him to talk to me and to interrelate with me.

"Eventually I learned that if we talked it out, and I listened to him and became sensitive to his feelings, and he to mine, our relationship improved. In that sense my mother's influence was positive. I didn't sit back and sulk or give up. I didn't let Vic absorb all the guilt he felt at seeing me hurt.

"In a way, my father's detachment also helped. I learned not to let my feelings get scraped raw every time Vic backed away because it felt similar to my father's distance.

"Once I realized his need for emotional space, I respected the need and I backed off, not intentionally acting distant toward him but consciously containing my own needs and giving him the space he needed.

In that way I developed a new self-image. I felt more secure. I saw myself acting a bit aloof and unavailable, and I saw Vic coming closer. When I stopped being the pursuer, he became the pursuer.

"This imaging gave me insight into our relationship. I needed to stop being something I was not and stop trying to make Vic be something he was not."

FILTERS

In order to see how our parents have affected our development, and how they still affect us each time we are up to bat in life, on the job, in a relationship, performing physical activities, or even in the way we rear our children, we can use the technique of "Filters." By keeping them in mind while seeing a situation we are facing today, we get revealing images of their influence on us. This image will quickly demonstrate our sources of power and blocks to our success.

An example is to keep father or mother in mind while seeing a problem or person.

IMAGING WITH FILTERS:

Instructions for image:

1. See a person or difficult situation in your mind's eye.
2. What do you see? How do you feel as you see it?
3. Keep mother in mind and see the problem or situation. This means to think of her as if you can sense her presence.
4. What happens in the image, keeping mother in mind? Let the image unfold without interference.
5. Now, keep father in mind and see the problem or situation. This means to think of him as if you sense his presence.
6. What happens in the image, keeping father in mind?

EMANATIONS

There was another step Karen needed to take in using eidetics to gain understanding and strength in her relationship with Vic. She utilized the technique of *emanation,* the process of revitalizing herself and overcoming her obstacles.

Emanation is an ancient concept. The dictionary definition, stemming from old Latin, means "to come out." And that is what the imaging technique does; a "new you," your true self, comes out from where it had lain dormant under a pile of negative self-images.

You may have heard professional athletes talk about being "in the zone." This phrase, or one analogous to it, is also used by trial attorneys who battle in court, doctors doing complex surgery, salespeople closing deals, executives conducting business meetings, and the butcher, baker, and candlestick maker doing "their thing."

In a sense, *emanation puts you in the zone.* It does this by drawing on your own powers. We all have those powers. Don't think that the power to rise above your present circumstances (i.e., to be all that you can) is limited to the gifted few who have been training to be ice skaters since four, or had their parents groom them for Harvard. It's not true.

We use emanation to change the way we deal with a person we are having a problem with. The process involves freeing our real self that has been buried under negative images of one's self, and discovering inner powers to deal with the person or situation in a new way.

Karen will now do an emanation.

"I returned to the image of seeing Vic in our apartment, with him acting nervous and jumpy and needing space. His attitude in turn made me feel insecure and agitated.

"Feeling insecure, I see a wind come around me and it feels cooling and refreshing. *I see another me jump out of me.* I see that I grab Vic, expressing my agitation. I yell at him. I tell him he's driving me crazy. Stop it! I shout. We have to get a handle on this, you and me, you're driving me crazy, and I can't take it anymore. It's too disruptive. This 'other me' is able to take control of the situation and put a stop to it, not my usual withdrawing self.

"He stops and looks at me like he's seeing me for the first time and says, Okay, and really listens. Then he tells me his fears. (The 'other me' is strong enough to truly hear him.) When he feels heard, he relaxes and feels closer to me. This other me is the 'real me' that is inside, untainted by my history.

"I can see that it's hard for me to hear him and I realize that my inability to listen to him exacerbates our differences. I have not felt secure enough to hear him out and understand him. When I finally opened up to listen, at first I felt very threatened because I didn't want to hear anything negative. Love was an idyllic and spiritual state for me and I hated to drag the practicalities of life into it. I can see how much I needed to grow."

As Karen learns, a strong relationship has to have that intimacy where two people are secure enough to communicate with each other. This means to be able to hear the other person out, to understand them and be able to deal with their fears, doubts, and deepest anxieties, even if those anxieties are about us. We have to have the ability to have enough sense of our own self so we can be there for the other person without getting shattered by the negatives. In that way, these traumatic passages in a relationship strengthen rather than destroy the bond of intimacy.

As Karen sees the image, she understands that she has been having difficulty "hearing" Vic's needs. She felt so desperate about her own needs that she never thought about why he was backing away and demanding space.

This "I-don't-want-to-hear-anything-that-doesn't-fit-my-own-needs" is a form of narcissism. Narcissus was of course the beautiful young man who got so caught up with his own self that he turned into stone. We can't let the other person's expression of fear or disappointment threaten us. We have to open ourselves up and work with them. If *both* sides are willing to listen, to hear the message from the other, to open up to the other's pain and disappointment, there is hope for a relationship. It's also possible to have a one-sided relationship in which one loving, caring, sacrificing partner takes all the blows and keeps on smiling. While it's possible, the sacrificing partner needs a wake-up call rather than a medal. Resentment keeps building inside.

What Karen learned from the imaging was that the more she opened up to Vic's concerns, his fears and needs, the more he came towards her. She saw that she didn't need to feel threatened when his need opposed hers. Before she could obtain the connection she desired, she had to do some soul-searching and learn about herself, be totally honest with herself and find her inner strength.

This technique allows you to draw upon your own inherent powers to deal with any situation in which you feel powerless or stuck. It is a transforming, metamorphosing experience that puts you "in the zone" to deal with a situation.

EMANATION IMAGE

Instructions for image:

1. Relax and clear your mind. Close you eyes and go inward.
2. See an image of a person in a situation in which you feel stuck, powerless, or that you are unable to deal with effectively.
3. How does the person appear to you in the image?
4. How do you feel as you see the image? Allow your feelings and body sensations to come into awareness.
5. If you could say or do anything to this person, what would that be? Let that desire come into your awareness.
6. Now see a big wind come from the high heavens into the room and surround you. This wind is a gift from the gods.
7. Feel the sensation of the wind swirling and swirling all around you.
8. See another "you" jump out of your image. (For some, it pops right out of their head.) The old you disappears and you become the "new you" in the image.
9. What is this "new you" like?
10. See that this new you does or says whatever it wants.
11. What does it do or say?
12. How do you feel as you see the image? Become aware of your shift to the new you.
13. How does the person now react to you? If the new you that came out does not have enough strength, ability, or power, repeat the process.
14. This new you is the "real you" with your original genetic strengths, powers, and abilities.

If the second attempt doesn't give you the response you want, it can be repeated over and over. Often people find resolution in the first emanation. Sometimes they don't and the exercise can be repeated.

13

The Sensual Spirit

I can't get no satisfaction.

The Rolling Stones

We are born sensuous creatures: warm, lush, delighting in touching and being touched. But too many of us have lost touch with our innate sensuality, the aura generated from within that is so sexually appealing, because of the hammering and brainwashing we have been subjected to about our sexuality.

Sexuality is defined as interest in sexual activity, the act of having sex and procreating, whereas sensuality is the state of "being" sensual. It has to do with our senses and expresses inner emotions.

There are few areas of human existence in which our society has been so ignorant than it has been about both our sensuality and sexuality. Historically, both women and men have been emotionally suppressed by sexually ignorant and frightened parents and misguided religious institutions that have taught that pleasure in one's body is sinful. Today we have been hypnotized into believing that only perfect bodies can make us desirable. I dealt at great length with the subject of sensuality, finding your natural sensual self in our world, in my book *Images of Desire*. In thoroughly researching and analyzing the subject, I am still grieved by how we have been robbed of so much of our innate sensuality, the primal essence that is the real source of sexual depth, pleasure, and fulfillment.

It is no wonder so many of us have many problems with sex considering all of the conflicting signals we get from all elements of society. We learn, practice, and experience our sexuality in an atmosphere of social and psychological chaos: We have been misled about what we do with our natural bodies. In the recent past, classical sexual education consisted of telling young people that they were not supposed to have sex, and sex carried with it guilt. The biggest change that has occurred over the past couple of decades is the nature of the threat. Guilt is out and the real fear, AIDS, is in. Overt sexuality is in too, used on TV, radio, movies, songs, billboards, and books to promote and sell products. Preteen children today have more sexual awareness than they have maturity to understand.

With the entire obsession about sex in our society one would think that we are a nation of sexually *satisfied* people, but the truth is that we are a nation obsessed with sex because we are so unfulfilled. We have been sexually bombarded with superficial images of what is sensual in our media, which does not give us knowledge of how to attain lasting, intimate union with another that is in keeping with our innate sensual nature.

We live in a world of contradictions and cross-signals when it comes to sex. Our society constricts us with sexual taboos, yet at the same time our popular culture tells us we not only should be having it but we are supposed to look like fashion models while we're at it. We are awash with mixed messages that leave us confused and feeling inadequate.

It's no surprise that most of us have lost touch with our natural sensuality. This endless bombardment of false images of sexuality cause women and men to lose touch with the real connection to their sensual nature, the essence that makes them a center of love and desire.

Because of the sexual scarring society has put on both men and women they are usually full of self-doubt and pain about their self-image. The damage to women starts at an early age when young girls begin developing differently from boys. There are two critical times women receive messages from those around that impacts their identity. First, when girls begin to develop breasts, and second, when they menstruate. At first the budding breasts are a private thing with a young girl, giving them a new vision of their body and an exciting initiation of forthcoming womanhood. It's a transitional stage that positively anticipates the future of loving a man, enjoying sex, and nurturing a child. The knowledge of all that is feminine is encompassed in the budding breasts of the young girl's psyche. As her breasts develop, so does she into the fullness of being a woman.

But rather than society viewing breasts as symbolic of love and nurturing, they have become sex objects, icons to be talked about by men, gawked at and displayed for public and private scrutiny and comparison. Soon girls are embarrassed, competitive, or feel inferior about their breasts, and about themselves as women. They lose the knowledge of the feminine essence inside of them. They think their breasts or bodies define them as sexually attractive so that a vast number of women develop insecurities about themselves.

I've taken hundreds of women through images of their emerging adolescent sexuality. When they tell their stories of when they were first developing breasts, rather than a time of natural pride and joy there is usually shame, embarrassment, and tension associated with the process. Often they report being teased or suddenly treated differently by those around them. Each woman has her own unique experience and story.

The way women feel about their breasts as they are developing stays with them and becomes part of how they regard their own feminine identity. Unfortunately, rather than generating images of sensuality, love, and nurturing, the gifts from the feminine side of life, the breasts have become cultural icons of pornography.

A woman's menstrual period, the body's signal that she has entered womanhood, has also been a difficult transition for many women. It's more rare to hear a woman, especially one over forty, say that she was fully prepared psychologically and well educated to experience it naturally as a joyful passage. The precise experience of a girl when she first menstruates also affects her future identity as a woman. Was she scared and did not know what was going on? Was it a nurturing experience with her mother? The emotions of her first menstrual experience live on in her psyche through menopause.

Obviously, a woman's sexual appeal isn't determined by the size of her breasts any more than a man's is related to the buffness of his body or the amount of power he has in the world. A person's beauty is found within, not on the surface. But because of all the glitz, gimmicks, and hype about physical beauty and what it's supposed to be composed of, women feel they have to keep buying the latest makeup products, diet endlessly, and look perfect because society has made them feel there is a void in them. No matter what they do, they feel they are never beautiful enough.

Most of us are caught up in the "beauty trap" where we feel judged by that superficial aspect we call "looks." We need to get back to the complete knowledge of true sensuality and not the body parts image of current media advertising.

Men have been injured in their sexual identity as much as women have. Just like women, they have received many confusing signals while developing into men. On the one hand, they are taught that a man's attractiveness is based on his expression of power. They are supposed to be tough and strong, the victors, the heroes. Yet, on the other hand, they are also supposed to be sensitive and caring to touch a woman's soul. It is tough for a thirteen-year-old boy to understand being tough and sensitive at the same time (unless his father is, which is rare).

Men get messages that they have to "perform" in all areas of their lives, such as competing in their careers, assuming they will be the main providers for their families, and telling them they must be successful and be leaders. They are rarely allowed to look vulnerable or in need. From the time they are little they hear, "Boys don't cry, keep a stiff upper lip, toughen up, don't be a sissy." Their inner sensitivities are crushed with expectations of being tough and in control. This robs them of their wholeness and their ability to dip into a deeper, more essential part of themselves. These social pressures make men more insecure and out of touch with their true masculine nature.

Just as with girls, a boy's sexual identity is most vulnerable to the culture's influence when he hits puberty. This is a time of transition from being a boy to being a man. His voice changes, hair begins to grow in private places, and erections shoot up at the most embarrassing moments. Emotionally, boys are still kids, but there is a man inside struggling to emerge. Just as budding of the breasts and menstruation are key times when the messages girls get from those around her affect her future sexual identity, so does the first string of semen for a boy. Waking up and discovering a spot of wetness on their sheets and how those around him treat this event imprints the boy's future identity as a man. For many, it is simply embarrassing, confusing, or they just don't know what happened. Most keep it to themselves and stay quiet because there are no adults to talk to about it with ease and comfort. So they hide it and become isolated. They don't know how to express their inner feelings. Therefore, how can they grow up and know how to connect with the inner feelings of a woman?

From the culture men get messages that sex is titillation. Movie and television masculinity revolves around power—physical power over other males and emotional power over females. There are no models for expressing the potent feelings of sexuality along with tenderness and love. Thus men suffer and do not open up themselves to true love. Most men are not looking for a one-night stand, but rather for a permanently loving and sensuous relationship. However, they don't know how to reach a woman's inner fire.

Natural sexuality asks that we are open and surrender to sensations and pleasures in our body. We can't be stuck in our heads with rationality, fear, and repression. For a man to have pleasure while lovemaking, aside from the momentary kick of ejaculation, his heart must be open. If he has learned that women are to be controlled, or sex is dirty, then male sexuality is sensation without any true essence or deep pleasure. Then men and women both suffer.

Somewhere along the line, as we became a world obsessed with sex, too many of us lost contact with our innate sensuality. We are part of nature. Inside of us we are whole and complete, and the genetic blueprint of our "whole" sexuality is still inside us. To get back to our innate sensual self we need to tune out all of the hype and the guilt, and rediscover our natural essence by simply going within. It is still there, waiting to be uncovered.

THE SENSUAL BEAST

Fairy tales can tell us a lot about human sensuality. They provide lessons about human nature and the human spirit. One of the most popular, *Beauty and the Beast*, is truly a tale of *sensuality*.

There was something about Beast that attracted the young woman. It wasn't his looks . . . and it certainly wasn't his charm. Beauty wasn't attracted to him just because he turned out to have a heart of gold. Her father had a heart of gold. A puppy dog has a heart of gold. Beauty was attracted to Beast because he radiated sensuality from his inner essence.

Nor was it the fact that underneath Beast's rough exterior there was a good person—one doesn't have to be a "good person" to be attractive to the opposite sex (as a lot of men and women attracted to the "wrong" person have found out the hard way).

Take a look at some of the men and women, past and present, who have been thought of as sex symbols but, like Beast, would not have won a bathing suit contest.

Beast had the same essence that men like Sean Connery and Harrison Ford have. Ford has the rough looks of the carpenter he was before he became famous, and Connery exudes sensual charisma, yet his face is not considered classically good looking. Neither of these men is the stuff of men's underwear commercials . . . yet each is extremely sexy.

Connery, Ford, and Beast all ooze with that mysterious essence called *sensuality*.

Barbra Streisand, Katharine Hepburn, Sigourney Weaver, Meryl Streep, Susan Sarandon—not one of them would win a bathing suit competition; there are a hundred models whose much prettier faces and bodies grace the covers of magazines, but it's a Streisand or a Streep that has the sensuality that turn men on.

That is not to say that a man or woman isn't going to be sexually attracted to a beautiful "specimen" of the opposite sex. But sexual attraction to beauty alone does not make a man or woman sensual. An empty person whose only attribute is their looks becomes boring after a short while. It's inner sensuality that makes great love affairs and long-lasting relationships while beauty by itself is only temporary.

People who are sensual are often charismatic. Charisma is defined as personal magnetism. It is a personal appeal and attractiveness that draws others and has nothing to do with one's looks. The appeal comes from the energy emanating from within.

PASSION EMANATES FROM THE SOUL

There is sex, the physical act, and sensuality, which is a state of being. Sex alone is only a physical exchange, but passion is not. Passion is ignited in the soul. Anyone can have sex—it's a function of the reproductive organs—but it is not the potent passion of great love affairs and great marriages.

The combination of love, sensuality, and passion is the basis for great lovemaking. Isn't that the point about *Beauty and the Beast*? The aura of sensuality that glowed around the Beast was his magnetism coupled with his pure and undaunted, raw passion and love for Beauty.

But many think sensuality is something you can buy in a perfume bottle or off a dress rack. When I asked a friend to define sensuality she told me that she didn't know how to define it, but she knew it when she saw it.

I have worked with many people with sex and relationship difficulties over the years and I have received much feedback about what makes one person sensual and another not. The words I've heard over and over are: *warmth, self-confident energy*, and *comfort feeling sexual feelings in one's body*. Not the warmth of fresh baked cookies or the maître d' at your favorite restaurant, but a warm, assured energy emanating from within a person that radiates out, expressing itself in their body language, how they walk and talk, and most of all, something in their eyes. (The windows to the soul are pools of sensuality.)

When two people are drawn to each other in a potent way, it is called chemistry. Chemistry refers to the way two people mix. Good friends, effective coworkers, and team players all have the right chemistry. The chemistry of sensuality is of a mysterious nature, not a scientific one. Like sensuality, "chemistry" is not natural. It is more a magical drawing of people to each other and creates heat between the two people.

We can think of this internal heat as analogous to that of a house. A cold house may be beautiful but it's neither inviting nor comfortable. Neither is a *cold* bed.

"Inviting" is one of the essences of sensuality. It comes in a look or gesture that says we are available or attracted to someone. Inviting is the sense of the potential for *intimacy* rather than just having sex. Intimacy means knowing another with familiarity, experiencing their essence, sharing friendship, confidentiality, love, and physical pleasure with them.

Where did our sensual essence come from? From nature. It is genetically stored within us. It is a gift nature placed in us for our pleasure. But the reason why the flame glows warmly in a person like Connery, and dim in a *Baywatch* character, is because of what has happened to them in life, in the permission they received from their parents and society. Connery's "history" left him connected to his innate sensuality and the *Baywatch* guy's sensuality got smothered under tanning oil and the superficial images of the culture. We are going to use eidetic imaging to bring to the fore the sensuality we have naturally within us. Some of those techniques are ones we've already discussed (tools like filters, to see how others put a damper on our sensuality with their limitations and fears), but first, I am going to introduce you to the *mythic images* that get right down to the heart—and soul—of our sensual spirit, and explain how they affect our daily lives at home and in the workplace.

14

Mythic Images of Sensuality

True sensuality has heart and soul, mind and body, all working together. Once you feel at ease in your own sensuality, it is an easy step to the passionate and fulfilling intimacy with another.

From their wonderful wisdom, the ancients gave us stories that reveal a great deal about our true sensual nature. *Aphrodite*, the goddess of love, and *Poseidon*, the powerful god of the seas, are mythic images that provide a deep connection between our mind and our body to ignite the essence of sensuality within us.

What do these ancient images tell modern men and women? They help get us back to our basic natural sensuality before it was squelched by society. For example, modern women are a product of thousands of years of cultural impositions and messages about what a women "should" be. Historically, women were not considered sexually desirable if they did not fit the current standard of the era. It wasn't that long ago in China that they bound women's feet to make women with tiny feet sexual icons. That was the imposed standard of beauty, passivity and deformed feet. A modern manifestation of the Asian binding of feet is the spiked heels and pointed toes that go in and out of fashion and damage a woman's feet, legs, and back (not to mention society's pressure to be rail-thin).

Men, too, are products of years of cultural imposition and messages about who they should be. They have lost knowledge of their true sensuality by being told that it is manly to be rational and always in control. How can men emotionally surrender sexually to a woman while being in control? Today, the evidence of the loss of natural sensuality in men is clear. They are emulating women, thinking that looking good means being sensual.

It's a sad state of affairs when we think we have to obsessively focus on our looks and bodies in order to be sexually attractive. The worst thing about it is that reshaping our exterior does nothing to stoke the inner fires of our sensuality. Sensuality flows from deep inside of us. Rather than needing a surgeon's scalpel, we can access it with an image, a mythic image, almost as old as mankind.

APHRODITE, THE FEMME FATALE

Aphrodite is a goddess who appeals to and perfectly connects with the sensual aspect of a male. She is the feminine model for sensuality. She has the whole "package" and is the ideal of womanhood—the glow within that radiates out as a warm, erotic aura sensed by men and a sense of her own fullness as a woman. She has strength, wisdom, and is in tune with her own self. As a woman, Aphrodite knows that she is whole and complete, that her sexual essence is connected to the very foundations of nature, not the culture's current fads. Aphrodite knows the mystery that draws men to her. It is a mystery that all women long to have.

Ellen discovered the mystery of her sexual appeal. She was forty-five years old when she came to see me because she was feeling depressed. She felt old and washed out. Men did not look at her anymore when she walked by, the way they used to. "I am missing the charge of male energy pouring in my direction that I experienced in my youth," she told me. She remembered when she was younger, she would simply walk into a room and she could feel the energy, an electric buzz as men's eyes would stare at her . . . following her every move. She had the type of body and looks that men lusted after. But, something had changed in the past few years. They had slowly stopped noticing her. Ellen felt dejected, unwanted. Now when she walked into a room, no one even glanced in her direction. Well, maybe some of the much older men did . . . sometimes. She wondered if it was aging; were her looks gone, had she lost some inner spark? Whatever it was, she was feeling like an old dried-up hag.

Ellen was right. Although she was aging, she had lost her spark, the "it" feeling from inside of her. She told me that she believed that only movie stars with astounding looks and bodies and young Lolitas had "it." Wrong! Each woman has a feminine essence inside her, waiting to be released into the world. "There is a way to activate your inner 'it' and become a Magnet for Men," I told her. "It doesn't matter if you're shy or a social butterfly. It doesn't matter if you have the body of Kate Moss or Camryn Manheim. As long as you are human and female you can activate your own allure to become your own Marilyn Monroe or Scheherazade. It is something that comes from the inside of you." I showed her how to discover the "it" that was inside of her.

Two weeks later, Ellen came to see me again. She told me that an amazing thing had happened to her. "A few days ago I was in a crowded restaurant. On my way to the bathroom I was feeling *very* forty-five. I was wearing jeans, had no makeup on, and was in my 'dried-up-hag' state of mind.

"When I was in the bathroom, I remembered what you said about a woman's allure; that it is unconnected to chronological age or looks, and that it is secret—a mystery that some women have. There in the bathroom I knew that I wanted it too. So I closed my eyes for a few moments and thought of the image you gave me. I felt a powerful feeling, a force of sensuality and centeredness overtake me from inside of me.

"When I walked back to my table, *every* man in the restaurant turned to look at me. Young and old were riveted on my every movement. The male energy that surged into me felt great. I sat down at the table and I could not believe it!"

What did Ellen do? She tuned into her basic feminine nature.

Here's the secret. Women hold the mystery of all life. The secret of this mystery within a woman is found in the way nature formed her womb. Within it, life springs forth, grows, and emerges fully formed. The shape of the womb contains knowledge of both the masculine and feminine parts. Its entrance is a space formed exactly in the shape of the male phallus. She is designed to house him. Thus, each woman has psychical knowledge of both his and her own parts. By having both the male and female within her, she is whole and already unified. She contains knowledge of the totality of all of life.

Men have knowledge of only their own masculine shape. There is no soft, feminine, life-giving mysterious opening to his body. To know the mystery of life, he must join with a woman. He can only experience the wholeness of life by coming into her. Only then can he know both sides of creation and experience union. This is the secret of her allure.

This is why men desire to come home to their woman. They experience the totality of life through sexual union with her. Men have often described it as a feeling of "coming home." They have an innate drive to join with her. It is a powerful force of nature. She has it *all*. Women make themselves beautiful to attract him to come home to her, but her real beauty is the inner signal of magnetic draw for completion.

Close your eyes and picture your womb and vagina. Yes, they're yours. They are not the property of your gynecologist or your man. They're yours. And they're the place in the world where the process of creation happens again. It's in you.

THE "IT" IMAGE FOR WOMEN

1. Close your eyes, picture your womb.
2. It is soft, dark, and mysterious. Allow yourself to experience the feelings and sensations as you see or sense this image.
3. See its beauty.
4. See how you have both the male and female shapes within you.
5. Experience the sensation of having both and be with this feeling for a while.
6. Be aware of the subtle shift of feelings and sensations that come over your whole being. How do you feel?
7. You have it "All." You're complete, a microcosm of life.
8. Concentrate on this image.
9. Let this whole feminine feeling go with you wherever you go.

THE MALE BEAUTY TRAP

Men too are victims of society's messages about being desirable. For him, power, success, controlling his emotions, and being in charge is what he is taught to be, yet, it smothers his innate sensuality.

Unlike a woman, a man does not have the complete knowledge of the unity of creation through his own body. He has the phallus but he needs to make the connection between himself and the female to experience completion—that's why he makes a beeline for the "temple" where the symbolic nectar is stored, to the place of "home" for his sexual desire. (In ancient times men were drawn to the temples of the virgins and in mythology those temples were symbolic of the vagina.)

I have worked with many men concerning their sensuality and what I see most common in men is confusion about how to use their masculine *power* and *fear*. Historically, the image of masculinity revolves around *power*, physical power over other males of the species, physical and emotional power over the female of the species. They have learned that control of emotions means power. This has robbed them of their wholeness and their ability to dip into a deeper, more naturally sensual part of themselves. They were taught that their sense of identity comes from their acquisitions or positions of power in the world rather than from within. These social attitudes squeezed the life force from them, making men more insecure and out of touch with their true masculine nature. Since men are conditioned by society to express their masculinity in terms of power, physical, or otherwise, they remain, like most women, clueless about what their inner masculine sensuality is all about.

Controlling men are not sexually appealing to women. The men that women find most sexually desirable are those that are comfortable with themselves and are not afraid to show their emotions. They are men who genuinely like and enjoy women. Women are turned on to a man who is comfortable with his masculinity and with himself to the point that he can relax and truly enjoy her. She desires to be enjoyed. That is what arouses her. He is the man who has nothing to prove. Sex is not a conquest or game for him, it is truly a joy. She senses that he desires to savor her, to celebrate her, to love her, and enjoy her fully. He wants to unite physically and emotionally with her. Women soften and desire the men who desire them in a pure and unabashed way.

Men who confuse power and control for sensuality do not open themselves up to true love. Most men are not looking for a one-night stand but a permanent, loving, and sensuous relationship, and too many of them don't find it because they don't know how to be masculine and sensual at the same time, or how to touch a woman's deep sensuality.

THE POWER OF MYTHIC IMAGES

Through years of sociological and historical brushstrokes, the natural sensuality of men and women has been diminished, blocked, and covered over at every turn. The result is that many of us question who we really are in terms of our sensuality. The roles and role models are constantly changing and the connection to the real essence of our sensuality has been lost.

Through mythic images we go beneath the layers of cultural and sociological tarnish that the society puts on us about who we are and are not, whether we should be passive, active, plump, or toned. The current fads and fashions are always changing and to find the true nature of woman, her true essence, a woman can see a goddess, such as Aphrodite, who is a model or template for her. And a man may look to Poseidon, the ideal of masculine sensuality, to discover his essential self.

Poseidon is a mythic masculine image of sexuality, coming slowly out of the sea, naked, water beading and glistening on his body, holding his trident as he moves. Waves hit against his chest as he slowly comes to shore, but he is powerful and the waves can't stop him. He comes ashore, water falling off his body, drying in the air as he moves. He sees the temple of Aphrodite in the mist ahead and he rapidly walks toward it, his body getting warmer as he feels the aura of femininity surrounding the temple. He sees the priestess in the temple and senses the nectar within. He is driven. He feels passion. He rushes to the temple, to the nectar . . .

The image of Poseidon is very sensual even though he has a sense of power about him. Poseidon knows his power is in the purity of his desire. He is very strong, yet open and innocent. He longs for and honors the connection to the female. The strength of his desire is very sexual and appealing to women. Poseidon is not self-conscious or controlling. He is the pure manifestation of male eroticism.

So at a very primal level, men's longing for women is revealed in how Poseidon goes directly for the temple, which is a symbol of the womb, just as the nectar is a symbol for feminine essence.

These images of Aphrodite and Poseidon are not fantasies but deeply ingrained images in the psyches of men and women. Passion and desire are extremely strong forces that once unleashed tear down one's separate sense of self and move us to merge with another in blissful union. Everyone longs for that!

In the search for sensuality, Aphrodite is a symbol of the heroine and Poseidon is symbolic of the hero. Both are wonderful images for us to access and use.

ALL WOMEN HAVE THE IMAGE OF APHRODITE IN THEM

Coming back to our essence means getting away from the sociological-historical impositions that smother our true sensuality. What our natural sensual self is like emerges from the outpouring of rich images from a woman's deep inner sense of being. Through the images, each woman's sensuality is revealed in a unique manner, as the image of Aphrodite is a key central image in the core of woman's consciousness, which can lift woman to her true stature. Aphrodite is dynamic, visionary, and protective of nature, and of all living things.

The nature of woman through the image of Aphrodite is that she is sexual, sensual, nurturing, flowing, and full of wisdom, yet powerful and strong. Femininity has power and softness together, strength and nurturance in one. Can a woman go into a corporation and be nurturing, wise, and still be strong? Can she be a leader in her own style? On one hand women have been diminished at every turn; from the time a young girl's breasts start to develop, she's cut down, boys tease her, older boys objectify her, society says that her breasts have to look like those of *Playboy* models, along with the rest of her body. These false notions, instead of allowing the expression of the great feminine power within, diminish too many women. So can women go into a corporation and be strong and feminine? Be powerful and tender? Yes, women have all of those abilities and powers within, available to lead with both dynamism and compassion.

I have seen women in corporations emulating male styles of power when in leadership positions. They think that they have to be like men to be respected, so they become fierce, competitive, controlling, and push through projects and dominate their staffs. They become masculine and tough, losing their more natural, fluid, and encompassing style. Eventually, they alienate others rather than drawing them toward them because they are harsh and not themselves. So, they turn others off.

However, I have seen other women leaders who are comfortable with their unique feminine way of doing things. They bring another way of operating into the workplace, which is all-inclusive and not competitive, is concerned with the larger picture, not just the bottom line, and cares for truth above all else. These women rule with kindness and wisdom. They are not afraid to be sensual. They have the spirit of Aphrodite in them and they command great love, loyalty, and respect.

Aphrodite's real love of nature and children and animals is very much part of the feminine soul. When a woman has accessed the spirit of Aphrodite in her, there's a feeling of bonding with nature, a promise to heal the planet, and she is strong enough to earn money, raise kids, and be a woman of the new millennium if she is true to her natural essence.

The wonderful thing about Aphrodite is that she is truly herself. Many women in corporations think they have to be tough in the same way that men have been to take on what have traditionally been male-only roles in business, but that's not true because the real power comes naturally in being *women as women*. It is just a different type of power than we have been used to.

MEN HAVE THE IMAGE OF POSEIDON IN THEM

The same process is true for men. The real power for men comes in *men being men*. Poseidon is very masculine as he pushes aside the waves coming out of the sea; he has heat in his body and natural power in his chest. Then when he sees the priestess and senses the nectar, he desires her. Although masculine, Poseidon is able to soften in order to know her. Men are direct, but there's innocence and openness as they are inexorably drawn to the female.

I've worked with hundreds of men and what struck me is that no matter who they were, or what positions of power they had attained, men *long* for women. This is a very deep desire based on genetic signals. I see powerhouses of industry who just long for the softness and femininity of a woman to envelop them. They have told me that they'll work like crazy and make a million dollars just to have a woman admire and love them. That is the power of desire.

Aphrodite and Poseidon emerge from the primordial core of rich imagery structures in the mind, which break developmental and sociological stereotyping. The power of these mythic images can alter and transform men and women's notions of who they are. It can reconnect men with their openness towards women and the forthrightness to just go for her. Women really find it a turn-on when men are like Poseidon, direct, open, and passionate, rather than playing the crazy games many men play, like "I have power," or "Mother me," or "I'm scared to be rejected."

15

Images of Aphrodite

When we look at ourselves in the mirror, many of us see negative images projected back at us—negative images and doubt. Our nose is too big, breasts aren't right, hips too wide, thighs are too fat. You name it, most women probably have had not just one but all of the above negative feelings.

But women also have an image inside of them, one that is not apparent in the mirror, an image of Aphrodite, the goddess of love. They have the knowledge contained in that image genetically instilled within them. The knowledge of sensuous fullness can be recovered again.

To change that negative self-image to a positive image, one has to make a connection to the nature of Aphrodite within and draw her essence to the forefront, through imaging.

Here is her story: In the pearly light of dawn, Aphrodite arose from the sea on a cushion of foam and floated lightly on the waves to the flowering island of Chythera. Three Graces who dressed her in shimmering garments and sparkling jewels attended her. They set her upon a golden chariot drawn by white doves and took her to Mount Olympus, the house of the gods. She was so ravishing that the gods rejoiced in her beauty and set her upon a golden throne. They made her one of them. She became an eternal goddess of love.

Wherever she walked, wildflowers and grass sprouted from under her feet. Wherever she went, the birds sang to her and the wild beasts grew tame as they followed. She offered the promise of sexual bliss if only her essence could be captured. Men swooned at her feet and found her irresistible. She expressed her anger at injustice to nature and to one's inner nature, and she stood powerfully for truth in all things.

Aphrodite is full, lush, and sensual and her beauty emanates from within her in the love and grace she has for all living things. She encompasses nurturance, wisdom, and strength all in one. Her magnetism and essential qualities draw others to her as if by magic. Everyone wants to partake of the nurture and beauty she emanates.

IMAGING APHRODITE (FOR WOMEN):

As with all imaging sessions get yourself into a good place mentally and physically before starting the session. Once you are in a quiet place and have relaxed your mind, you may start the session. Read all of the instructions before starting the session but it is not necessary to memorize them because once you see the image, you can refer to the next instruction and the image will still be there when you return to it.

APHRODITE IMAGE

1. See an image of Aphrodite in your mind's eye. Aphrodite is full of love, warmth, sensuality, wisdom, and power.
2. Now see Aphrodite seeing herself naked in front of a mirror. Her breasts appear sensuous and proportional in the mirror.
3. See her admiring her sensuous breasts. Her breasts are reflective of beauty, power, nourishment, of giving love, of all that is feminine.
4. There is a sensuous aroma of perfume flowing out of the mirror. Experience the perfume flowing in the image.
5. See that the perfume expands your awareness of your own feminine nature.
6. See that the reflection in the mirror reveals your true feminine essence.
7. See that you have the essence of feminine sensuality emanating from within you.

The breasts of a woman encompass all attributes that are feminine. That is why they are such powerful symbols that men long to adore. Breasts have sweetness, softness, nourishment, and beauty all in one. As women connect to the essence of their own breasts they can come to touch their deep feminine self.

As women go through this exercise, the size, shape, quality, and condition of their breasts does not matter. What matters is finding the sensuality that is contained in their breasts. The feelings of love, nourishment, caring, and warmth are in the essential nature of women. There is power in this essence and it is much more magnetic than any outer shell such as looks, because these qualities are the nectar that draws others to women.

It makes her strong in a soft way. She has mystery and power and she can be active in the world with this life-affirming energy.

It gives her confidence to be herself and to give love and to be love.

16

Images of Poseidon

Poseidon, the god of the seas, is the mythic image of male sexuality. He is powerful, emanates openness and sincerity, is wise, and is a man who knows and enjoys women. He generates an appeal to which women are attracted.

Masculinity is inherently strong, and a man who is truly strong doesn't have to prove anything. Yet many men are obstructed from making a sensuous connection to women because their belief that they have to perform blocks their potent masculine spirit from connecting with hers. Others fulfill the sexual urge on a base level, not understanding that base sexuality misses the most delicious ways of sensually connecting with women.

Poseidon is very clear and sincere about his strong desires for her. This combination of guileless sincerity and desire melts women. Women long to be admired, desired, and ravished.

Poseidon is the god of the sea. He is the son of Kronos and Rhea, who are brother and sister. Kronos and Rhea had three sons: Zeus, Poseidon, and Hades. They divided the world among themselves, with Poseidon receiving dominion over the sea. Poseidon was known as the god of mariners, to whom he sent storms or fair voyages. He was the god of waters. There were temples in the southernmost tip of Greece in his name, and freshwater springs were consecrated to him. He was known for his masculine prowess and his oceanic powers.

IMAGING POSEIDON (FOR MEN)

Men can access the depths of their sensuality by seeing images of Poseidon.

The basic instructions are the same for imaging Poseidon as with all imaging sessions: Get yourself into a good place mentally and physically before starting the session. Once you are in a quiet place and have relaxed your mind, you can start the session. As explained before, read through the instructions before starting the session but it is not necessary to memorize them because once you see the image, you can refer to the next instruction and the image will be there when you go back to it.

POSEIDON IMAGE

1. See Poseidon coming out of the sea. He is coming ashore. He's holding a trident in his hand, the symbol of his power.
2. See his chest. It is strong and broad.
3. See that you become Poseidon. As you move towards the shore, the waves crash against your chest but the force of your power surging forward pushes against them as you move through them.
4. See that you have come onto the shore dripping water.
5. See that your body is hot and the cool air dries your body as you move. Feel the coolness against your warm body.
6. See that there's a temple on a hill. It is the temple of the virgin priestesses.
7. See a priestess in the temple. Feel the heat in your body as you walk towards the temple.
8. See that as you move towards the temple there's a warm fire in it and an intoxicating essence of perfume. Smell the perfume.
9. See that you're drawn to the nectar in the temple, to the priestess.
10. Experience the sexual energy flowing through your body.

Men deeply long to immerse themselves in the feminine, at a primal level. Poseidon is a man who knows how to touch the sensual depth and soul of a woman. He knows how to make a woman feel adored, cherished, and wanted.

He is connected to his primal sensuality and he savors the feminine; he knows that he is dealing with something mysterious, something precious. That is why she loves him.

17

What Draws a Man to a Woman?

Come on baby light my fire.

The Doors

Before we turn to examples and practice at using other eidetic imaging tools, I want to share with you the results of many encounters I have had with men trying to define what attracts them to a woman. While this is from the man's viewpoint, much of what they think about women is just as applicable in terms of what women find desirable in a man.

What do men find sensual in a woman? I've explored this subject with hundreds of men and some of their responses were real eye openers. Like the woman I asked to define sensuality, and couldn't, men can't define it either, but they know it when they see it.

I have interviewed men from all walks of life. Their ages ranged from the twenties to the sixties and included physicians, therapists, attorneys, artists, salesmen, taxi drivers, business executives, musicians, entrepreneurs, writers, stockbrokers, and an environmental engineer, among others.

The first thing that strikes me about men and their attitudes about sexuality is that there is a difference between what men in their twenties and early thirties believe and the mindsets of men in their late fifties and older. I find that the younger the man, the more at ease he felt being with a woman who asserted her rights. In fact, most younger men assumed women were their equals. The older men had mixed feelings about this topic. Some still believed in male dominance and others were totally at home with strong, expressive women.

All the men defined beauty in very unique ways, images that are not at all based on the traditional *Playboy* stereotype. But the issue of physical beauty, however defined, was considered to be important. Physical beauty in a woman drew them, but surprisingly what they found to be beautiful was not necessarily what appeared on *Playboy* centerfolds.

When I asked men about their images as adolescents, the results were almost universally the same; it was all sexual images of women mixed with incredible hormonal drive. It was sexual in a physical sense and the universal sex object was a stereotypical centerfold woman with all the right body parts.

However, drawing away from their hormonal, adolescent images, the men's perception of what beauty is in a woman drastically changed. The definitions varied greatly and went from magazine-cover faces to Rubenesque women to sultry or even unusual features. One thing most men stated: whatever attracted them to a woman, physical beauty was *not* the main thing.

Men in general talked about the mystery of what women are made of. Men seemed to be somewhat puzzled about what drew them to a woman yet intrigued by the power of their attraction.

A universal appeal was a woman who was fulfilled within herself in terms of liking herself and had both strength and sensuality.

It was very important to men to have a woman who could give them space and some distance when they needed it. Sometimes they just needed to be by themselves or with their friends.

It seemed important to most men to get "nourishment" from a woman. (I am using "nourishment" in this context to refer to the need of a person to have a shoulder to lean on, to hear the war stories from a hard day's work, for physical affection, reinforcement, all without criticism.)

Many men stated that nourishment was not as important as having a woman understand them, to recognize what they think, feel, and how they view life.

Being "understood" seemed to be of paramount importance.

The issue of "control" was more important to the men in their sixties than the men in their twenties. This is because of the many changes in the sexual revolution of the past few decades. While almost every man I've ever interviewed claimed he wanted a woman who was "equal," there were differing definitions of what that meant. The older the man the more he felt the need to have control. Many of these men admitted that if a woman who was all together in terms of actualizing herself in life, physically beautiful, and sensual came into their life, they would not be able to handle it, that they would feel threatened and intimidated by a woman like that.

Few men I have ever dealt with seemed to have a clear role model or sense of exactly what masculinity is . . . what it means to be a man. The question usually stumps them. I often sense a feeling of loss or a complete lack of knowing what exactly their role model was supposed to be in today's age. The model for masculinity is in transition.

It was easy for them to tell me what attracted them about a woman or how they felt about a powerful woman, but men are commonly stumped when asked to define what they believe femininity is, just as they are in defining their masculinity. The discussion, trying to define what a feminine woman is, captured their attention. It was a puzzle for them to define it. Men are intrigued by the very notion of femininity, but they are not sure why. They love the mystery of it, but they can't define it. None of the men equated femininity with passivity. They saw it more as a mysterious force that drew them in a powerful way. They all admitted a longing to be near it and to be engulfed in it.

Men respect wisdom in a woman. When I ask men in group and individual sessions what they want in a woman, the discussions commonly filter down to attributes of a good mother, soft, comforting, strong, and wise—and then shoots up really fast to include sensuality.

Some generalities about the generalities: men have difficulty defining sensuality, and masculinity—but they know it when they see it. They do not have a strong role model for masculinity. John Wayne is out, but what is in? I hope we don't end up with a society of *homogenized* sexes. We need a society in which women and men are equal but each brings their unique qualities and characteristics to the game.

Here is the best description a man has given me about the woman that attracts him:

"It's the mystery that attracts me."

And, kind sir, it's your love of her mystery that attracts women.

18

Starting Over Therapeutically

How shall I be able to rule over others, if I don't have full power and command of myself?

François Rabelais

One of the most significant aspects of our modern society is the lack of permanency. Jobs, relations, and family life are fluid and constantly changing direction. At the age of twenty, thirty, forty, or even sixty and up, we can no longer rely on everything remaining the same. The rug might get pulled out from under us at any time and we find that we have to "start over" at a time when other people seem to be resting on their laurels.

When we've been ambushed by life and lose our family life, our job, or our security, we can feel inferior and fearful. But we can't let the situation defeat us. Our worst enemy is *fear*. It will cripple us, block our energy, eat at our gut, if we don't control it.

Eleanor Roosevelt was one of the greatest women of the last century. While her husband, the president of the United States, went from wheelchair to bed-bound, she helped guide the country and the war effort during those last frantic days of World War II. She once made a statement that goes to the heart of personal power, that sense of confidence we need within us in order to be the very best we can:

"No one can make you feel inferior without your consent."

And, of course, her husband, Franklin Delano Roosevelt, spoke words of encouragement earlier, during those dark days of the Great Depression and rise of world fascism:

"The only thing we have to fear is fear itself."

These words are from a man who was in a wheelchair when he took the helm of office and fought the Depression and Hitler . . . and from a woman who was a United Nations delegate when she was almost eighty years old.

These people guided their own lives and refused to let others daunt them.

Too many of us are controlled by fear and allow others to make us feel less than we are. We are often as much victims of ourselves as we are of others. We must not let others dominate us. To stop the feelings of powerlessness, we must look within ourselves for the answers and strength.

We have spoken before about the *sense of self*. I often use that expression to refer to the *self-images* each of us carries within us. These self-images may either be positive ones that assist us or may be negative ones. Most often these images are no more than the composite of interaction and experiences of what we have been told about ourselves, by our parents, teachers, siblings, peers, or culture at large. If our parents and others around us nurture us well and acknowledge our special attributes and instill in us the belief that we are something of value, we will come to believe in ourselves. The opposite is true, too.

In many ways, *we believe we are what people have told us we are*. We respond and form our sense of identity by how others treat us. The younger we are, the more formative the years are, the more influence our parents and others around us have in shaping us. Each of us has a unique persona, an individual and distinct personality separate from that of others. Like fingerprints, no two people are exactly alike. And no two of us are affected exactly alike by the events around us.

We are going to look at a couple of situations that demonstrate how negative images within us are created, how that negative "history" will come back and haunt us in almost everything we do. You will also see how through using eidetic images we can retrieve the wholeness that is inside of us that can overcome the influence of our negative history.

In regard to the creation of negative images of self, an illustrative although admittedly somewhat extreme example deals with a family tragedy that generated unusual fear. The situation concerns two brothers I worked with. These two men were raised in the same household, had the same mother (a single parent), shared a bedroom until their late teens, ate the same food, went to the same schools, etc.

They were three years apart in age but grew up to be worlds apart in mental attitude and personal accomplishments.

The older brother started many projects and finished few—he flunked out of college, had two failed marriages, and when he consulted me, in his mid-thirties, he had been unsuccessful at starting a meaningful career and was back living with his mother.

The younger brother seemed to have everything going for him—graduated with honors, went on to law school, became a successful trial attorney, and had a stable marriage.

It is important to note that these two men were of equal intelligence, had duplicate cultural and social backgrounds, and on the surface had equal opportunities and resources, yet one failed at almost all of the important aspects of his life.

When the older brother went through imaging he saw an image of his mother telling him that he could never make it in the world alone, that he would always need her. Going deeper into the images, he came to the root of the constant negative assertions from his mother: when he was four, his seven-year-old brother drowned in a river behind the family home. The mother had heard the cries of the other children but got to the water too late to save her son. The death of the child came on the heels months earlier of her husband's death in a car accident. The incidents emotionally scarred the woman and she become obsessively possessive about her children, trying to keep them close to her. The youngest son managed to avoid most of the emotional trauma, but his brother became a victim of it.

The older brother turned out to be what his mother told him he was—someone who would always need help and would never succeed. In contrast, the younger brother was constantly told that he could succeed at anything he tried.

What was smothered in the older brother by the mother's negative messages was those wonderful "aspects of the self" that were part of his genetic makeup when he was born. These are the "eides" we talked about earlier, what the ancients called the "gifts of the gods." He lost the strong sense of his own self-worth. Without a good sense of himself, he was never able to generate confidence in him by others.

Another example concerns Nan Cullins, a forty-four-year-old woman, who, after coming out of over twenty years of marriage, a divorce, and devotion to her children, demonstrated how one's gifts can be buried by the stress of everyday living and how, through imaging, these innate energies may be awakened.

Nan Cullins was full of fear, fears that many of us share. She came to see me for image therapy sessions. When I met her she was forty-four years old and had been through a recent divorce. After twenty years of marriage and seeing the youngest of her three children turn eighteen, she suddenly had to start all over again with romantic relationships and career. They don't give Nobel prizes for Good Parenthood, and successfully changing two thousand diapers did nothing for her work résumé or her ability to understand the "rules" for relationships in the twenty-first century.

She lived in terror of job interviews, fumbled mentally and verbally during the interviews, and managed to antagonize a man she was attracted to. She lacked confidence, belief in her own self-worth . . . traits that certainly were not going to excite a job interviewer or a romantic companion.

However, Nan had the most fundamentally important attribute for success: the *desire to succeed*. And like all of us, she had inside of her, totally within her, all the necessary attributes to be the person she wanted to be—a woman with a career and a loving relationship. The attributes, these qualities of self, are the gifts of the gods that we talked about above. Nan's problem was that they were rusty from non-use during the more than two decades she devoted herself to raising a family and maintaining a home. Life is full of trade-offs—Nan made choices in life and assumed responsibilities, trading her own self-development in terms of a career for child-raising and providing a nurturing home for the family.

But now the sands of life have shifted and she faces other choices—to be everything that she can be or to take a drab job that she hates and hole up as a recluse because she had little courage for a romantic relationship.

She tried to face the world by buying a new car and some expensive clothes, but *things* only gave her brief moments of elation not the long-term confidence she needed to reach her goals. She wanted to perform well at job interviews and she wanted to save a relationship that began at the gym. She met a man about five years older than she while working out at a gym and they began dating. She was attracted to him, but sparks flew and there was friction between them after they were together for a few hours. Yet the attraction was there . . .

Nan needed to make the *journey to her inner self*, to find and dust off those empowering abilities inside her to take on the challenges the world was giving her.

Those traits or energies that were already inside of her and that she now needed to find were her abilities to interact with new people and situations in her life without fear, awakening the confidence and belief in her own self that she had before she spent two dozen years out of circulation.

Keep something in mind while we examine Nan's situation: It was not that Nan did not have the gifts she needed or lacked the abilities she needed; in fact, she was born with many. She didn't lose them; they were merely buried. There were positive aspects about her that made her a successful mother and homemaker. Those aspects were still there. She just needed to pick up and dust off those gifts that were waiting already within her for the new demands in her life.

Nan is going to use an image we haven't dealt with yet, "Crossing the Road," and several other images with which we are already familiar, first from the point of view of a job interviewer, and second from the shoes of the man she had met at the gym.

She will step out of herself and look back at herself through the eyes of another using the "Co-Consciousness" technique. Utilizing this tool of imaging, she is able to gain insight as to her own state of being by seeing how others see her. Co-Consciousness is rich in sensory perceptions because stored in Nan's own mind are the perceptions of others about her. Those perceptions of others come to us through everything we observe during our interaction with them, their expressions of affection or anger, their passion or indifference, their admiration or contempt, their compassion or prejudice, their subtle or overt body language, their facial expressions. These emotional states are conveyed to us by their looks, body language, verbal responses, even the inflections in their voices.

We are able to clearly see these emotional nuances when we evoke an eidetic image of the person. The process can be uplifting, or it can tell us things we may need to change. Regardless of what we learn about ourselves in this illuminating exercise, we will gain insights about how to handle the situation or deal with the person.

The second tool Nan will use is "Walking-Around." In this technique we see many things about another person that we were not consciously aware of, things that help us understand them. We can see deeply within them to see what makes them tick.

We can also see how they feel about us. As we've discussed, a person's feelings toward us have been communicated to us and stored in our brain. By seeing an eidetic image of the person, we have reached into our memory filing system, into the data we have stored in our minds about the person, and are able to gain insight and understanding about how they feel about us.

Nan will also do an "Emanation." This is the exciting tool that lets you light a fire under your present state of powerlessness or being stuck.

Perfectly ordinary people have the power to accomplish their goals. The goals are possible to accomplish and already lie in their imagination. That which impedes our goals may be subtle.

Emanation coalesces and synthesizes the gifts of the gods we were born with and unleashes them in a powerful concentration of emotions that give us new feelings of power and drive.

19

"Starting Over" Images

After relaxing in a quiet place, Nan starts with the image of "Crossing the Road." The purpose of the image is to cross the road in your mind to reach a shop on the opposite side of the road. Crossing the road is an ordinary, routine action on our part. We do it almost unconsciously. And that's exactly why it makes a good image to probe because when we change this routine everyday event by using our parents as a filter ("keep mother in mind, keep father in mind") we can clearly see our automatic attitudes and feelings that we were not aware of before. This image shows the influence in our life our parents have on even our most ordinary daily chores. It clearly reveals to us our stumbling blocks to success as well as our best potentials.

CROSSING THE ROAD IMAGE

The instructions are:

1. Think of the front of a shop that you often go to. Consider the picture that comes to your mind's eye. See the overall appearance of the shop from the opposite side of the road.
2. Picture in you mind that you are crossing the road in order to go over to the shop on the other side. Describe how you cross the road, what images you see, and what happens until you reach the shop on the other side of the road.
3. Think of your mother. Keeping mother in mind, see the image of yourself crossing the road again. Describe how you cross the road, and what happens until you reach the other shop on the other side. Let the image unfold like a movie.

> 4. Think of your father. Keeping you father in mind, see the image of yourself crossing the road again. Again, describe how you cross the road, and what happens until you reach the shop on the other side.

Nan did the image and made a personal discovery.

"I was very cautious crossing the road. I saw myself at an intersection where there was a traffic light. Before I crossed I waited for the green and looked both ways. As I crossed, I kept my eye on the traffic and moved rather slowly."

Then she kept her mother in mind as she crossed. She said, "I felt very cautious and even fearful of crossing."

Using her father as a *filter* when she crossed, she discovered that she was more daring in her crossing. "I seem to have picked up most of my conservative 'don't get too adventurous' attitude from my mother."

What Nan learned was that despite her love and affection for her mother, her mother had instilled traits in her that worked to block Nan's efforts when she needed to go out and take on the world. Once she had this insight, she could change her fearful response. She now understood that the caution and fear generated by her mother would overtake her when she needed to be assertive. From this moment on, by consciously keeping her father in mind, she realized that she could find the daring and courage within to move forward with confidence. Whenever fear would rear its ugly head as Nan initiated new activities, she kept her father in mind and shifted from fear to daring. Just thinking of her father created an instantaneous shift in her perception.

Relaxing and clearing her mind again, she next saw an image of the job interviewer she had interviewed with earlier that week. The job was an entry-level position with a large corporation. She would be notified by telephone as to whether she would be hired, but she was certain that the interview did not go well and that it would be another turndown.

The interviewer had been a woman quite a bit younger than she, little older than Nan's own twenty-two-year-old daughter, and Nan had not felt comfortable with her. Looking *back at herself from the eyes of the interviewer (Co-Consciousness)*, Nan saw herself as presentable in terms of dress and makeup. She had consulted a job interview expert who had helped her choose a dark, well-cut suit that enhanced her complexion, modest jewelry, and a medium-sized purse. Her black shoes were stylish and her purse complemented the suit and shoes, but did not stand out.

So far, so good. The clothing left impressions of modesty and reliability that the job counselor had encouraged.

But as Nan watched the image, watching herself respond to a question from the interviewer, she heard the lack of confidence in her voice, the slight hesitation and inflection in her voice that exposed the fact that she had the jitters. Not that it was necessary to hear her voice to realize she was not comfortable with the job interview, she could see that her features were frozen and she knew that under that thin stoic veneer was just plain fright!

"She could see right through me," Nan said. "I let my fears take control at the job interview and that woman sensed it like a shark senses blood."

She relaxed again, putting aside her feelings about the job interview, and saw an image of the man she was romantically interested in. Out of her own fears and insecurities, she pretended to be "cool" toward the man when they went out on dates. He responded by acting indifferent toward her and soon they were playing emotional Ping-Pong.

When she was centered in terms of seeing a new image, she brought forth the image and began the process called *"Walking-Around."* Again, what Nan was seeing was not just a picture of the man, but an *eidetic image.* She was reaching into her *inner vision,* to bring forth a visual picture of the man. Unlike the image of an apple, the eidetic of the man coalesces her emotions, her feelings, about him.

"I experienced a physical reaction, literally an electric jolt when I looked into his eyes."

This experience of Nan's, the somatic/physical response she describes as a "jolt" is not an uncommon reaction to looking into the eidetic image of the eyes of someone we have strong emotions toward. What was it that St. Jerome said about the eyes? "The face is the mirror of the mind, and eyes without speaking confess the secrets of the heart."

"He wears a mask!" she exclaimed. "He's just as scared as I am, but he hides it behind a shell of masculinity. It really threw me for a loop. But I'm supposed to be the one who's afraid. My fear has been the problem with our short relationship. Every time we get together my fear that I am no longer desirable crawls out and makes me angry. Naturally, that doesn't make me the greatest companion on a date."

After looking into his eyes, Nan mentally walked around the image, viewing it from one side, the back, the other side, and then the front again.

"I sensed the lack of confidence in him. This is my problem, but I saw it in him too. I think he just manages it better. He's a man and more used to hiding his emotions than I am. He told me about his divorce. He took it pretty hard. Although his kids are grown, he believes they took his wife's side. Viewing the image, I realized that he feels even more insecure than I do. It struck me that I'm so caught up with my own problems that I didn't recognize that he had problems too."

The sensitivity, the fear, and lack of confidence she saw, were transmitted to her by the man's subtle interactions with her. Even though her mind registered the data, as it does everything that goes on around it, she had been so wound up with her own problems, so focused on her own feelings, that she had not opened herself up to see why the man was acting the way he was. In a broad sense, Walking-Around and Co-Consciousness are a process of opening old albums of life that we have stored, pictures, emotions and meanings, but we have left closed because we are concentrating on other things.

"I had no power," Nan said about the job interview. "I thought that word, 'power' was one of the overworked buzz words of this generation, but after seeing myself in the eyes of that job interviewer, I realized that that inner flame that some people have just wasn't there. There's a woman at the gym, she isn't any younger or in any better shape than me, but I sense an aura of power emitting from her when I'm around her."

When asked to describe the "power" she was referring to a little more, Nan said, "I guess it's going around in life sure about who you are, confident in your abilities, whether it's at work or in a relationship. There was a time when I had that sort of power, that sort of confidence. Before I got married I had a job and a romantic relationship, but after two dozen years of working in the home, the fire went out. It's like that song, how does it go? Something about 'light my fires'? I need someone to light my fires again."

"You're wrong," I told her. "You need *you* to light your fires. You have all the power within you, you just need to find it."

"What I need is an overhaul," she told me. "When a car or your clothes wear out, you fix them or buy new ones. I need a new set of skin."

A new you, I said.

She clapped her hands. "Exactly, a new me. Can you give me one?"

I couldn't provide Nan with a new Nan . . . *but Nan could*. She just needed some guidance in using the eidetic imaging technique of "Emanation."

Nan's innate abilities to interact with others, to take the initiative in life and explore new situations, had been dulled by a couple dozen years of nonuse. She needed to activate these qualities within her, to bring them forth in that synthesis we talked about.

The emanation process involves seeing an image of a situation in which you feel powerless or stuck and having a "new you" come forth to deal with it. In a sense, the new you is simply the *real* you because in the emanation process those unique strengths you were born with come forth to deal with the person or situation on which you are focusing.

During the process, you are asked to image that a "wind" swirls around you. This imaginary wind is a symbolic dynamic life force, an energy that helps inspire and expose the new you. It is part of the process of rejuvenation that we all need occasionally. Even the Mona Lisa and other great works of art get it—technicians delicately use cleaning materials to remove the tarnished layer that has gathered over the years. The wind that wraps around us is symbolic of that same sort of process in which the tarnish on our innate qualities is wiped away to expose the brightness.

To use the technique, Nan once again got herself into a quiet place where she could relax and concentrate, getting herself centered so she could focus on the image she would evoke.

She then called up an image of a situation in which she felt powerless. "I chose the situation with the job interviewer," she said.

Seeing the image, Nan experienced the same sense of powerlessness, the lack of confidence in presenting herself that she had felt when she was actually in the room with the interviewer.

"She had all of the power in the room," Nan said. "Her voice was firm and her features radiated confidence. I was just chopped liver as far as that situation went. I felt intimidated and my voice and body language showed it."

At this point she generated power from within.

"I imagined a big wind flowing by my image, the wind wrapping around me, swirling around and around. Then I saw another 'me' pop out of the old me."

The transformation Nan experienced was startling to her.

"I was energized, ready to take on any situation, especially that interviewer. I hadn't felt this way since I found out I was pregnant with my first child. When I learned I was pregnant, I sensed a power in me, the power of a creator, because that's what I was. I felt that same sort of radiant power when the new me jumped out of the image. The first thing I did was call the company where I applied for work and made another appointment to see that interviewer. I wanted to explain to her that I had something to offer a company, that I was hardworking, and reliable, and that *they* would suffer a loss if they didn't hire me."

In our grandparents' time, being thirty-something was considered being middle-aged. Over forty and you were ready for the farm. That is no longer true. It's probable that most of us will be expected to keep working until seventy, and many of us find ourselves starting over at forty or fifty.

In the imaging sessions, Nan did bring out that very important point none of us should ever forget: We are the same people we have always been, the same ones that had the strength, enthusiasm, and energy; we just have to reach down inside a bit deeper to find the sources of those gifts within ourselves.

The Walk-Around, Co-Consciousness, Emanation, and Crossing the Road images are all found in the Appendix of Images.

20

Keeping the Love Connection

We have talked about that "history" that covers and conceals those natural gifts and qualities we were born with. Sometimes the coating can be so cold or abrasive that we lack a positive connection with the rest of the world and just don't seem to flow with life. The next example we are going to look at is that of a woman who had everything going for her but couldn't keep the current of love flowing in her life. Imaging gave her insight into why she was turning away men from her life.

Many of us suffer an emotional meltdown from the sheer number of situations we have to deal with. Kate Meyers is one of these many victims of modern life.

Kate is truly a modern woman. She has a career and family responsibilities. When her grandmother was born, women did not even have the right to vote in America and most European countries did not grant the right until her own mother's time. Women were expected to stay at home and be submissive. Much has changed since then.

Like millions of other men and women, Kate has brought a child into the world but has not been able to establish an enduring relationship with someone of the opposite sex. She has not been able to give the child the benefit of learning from both parents and give herself the benefit of having a helping hand in two of the most difficult tasks people face today: earning a living and raising a family. At thirty-eight years old, a single mother with relationship problems, Kate needs to take a deep look within.

Much of what Kate has experienced, we have probably experienced ourselves at some time. We may be married or divorced, we may not be a single parent or a parent at all, but Kate's deep-rooted problems are not her marital status or her parental status—*her problems stem from within her*, from the emotional and personality shaping experiences she underwent since birth. And she will have to journey *back into herself* in order to conquer the problems she faces today.

About five-foot-six, she has recently put on nearly twenty pounds of extra weight. "I'm a binge eater," she told me. "I'm okay as long as I'm busy, but when I'm home with Dillon, my daughter, tucked away in bed and I have to face another night alone, food seems to be my best friend."

Feeding an emotional hunger from the refrigerator is of course almost epidemic in our society. The "eating problem" generated a weight problem, but she knew that overeating was a symptom of deeper issues.

"I just don't understand men. I see women all around me who are not as smart or even as pretty as I am in permanent relationships, but every time someone comes into my life he seems to fade out in a few months."

"Why are they 'fading out' as you put it?"

"Because I'm too much for them. Men like women who are going to give in to them and pick up after them. I expect a man to carry half the load and respect my rights."

I'm sure that there are plenty of men that fit Kate's prototype of expecting a woman to be a kitchen maid and sex slave, and plenty of women who treat men about the same way, but from handling thousands of relationship situations, I had long ago learned that the vast majority of people have acceptable expectations about relationships. This mindset that the rest of the world is off-kilter usually stemmed from the person trying to justify why things weren't going well for them.

"The longest relationship I ever had with a man was with my ex-husband, Ted. I was twenty-nine when I met Ted at a party and we clicked right away. Ted had a great body and I was in the best shape I've ever been in. We could feel the sexual excitement coming at us like sound waves as we looked at each other across the room. We made love that night and moved in together in a week."

"What happened with Ted?"

"We had an on-and-off relationship for over a year, then stopped seeing each other for nearly a year, and finally got married. About a year after that I got pregnant with Dillon, and I suppose if it hadn't been for that we wouldn't have lasted as long as we did. We split when Dillon was one. That was six years ago."

"Why didn't the relationship stick?"

"You can't build a relationship on sexual attraction. Outside of bed, we were miles apart. I was much more ambitious than Ted. I mean, he was the type of guy who liked to be a couch potato on weekends and watch games on TV. Ted was really a bright guy, he could have been anything, but I just couldn't instill any ambition in him."

"How did Ted take your attempts at changing him?"

"It went in one ear and out the other. If he had just been willing to change, to meet me halfway, we could have had it all because we had a terrific sexual attraction. Someone at work summed it up quite nicely—Ted was beer and hamburgers and I was red wine and angel-hair pasta."

I asked Kate about her relationship with other men who have been in her life.

"My first long-term relationship started when I was twenty-five. Gene was a guy I met in college and dated a few times. After I left college and went to work, I bumped into him a few years later. We dated pretty heavily for a while and then moved in together."

"What happened with you and Gene?"

"He just couldn't get it together. Here again, the sex was okay. Not like Ted and me, but you know, okay. But it really wasn't a sex thing. Gene was a floater, you know, a guy who floats in and out of relationships and jobs. He had lived with three different women before getting together with me, and during the year we were together, he changed jobs twice. I told him that he was wasting his life by not putting his nose to the grindstone and staying there."

Ted and Gene had been Kate's only long-term romantic relationships. Since the split with Ted six years ago, Kate had been busy surviving financially and emotionally as a single mother and had had little time for a man. "I get up early to get Dillon off to school and me off to work, I work all day, and pick up Dillon after work. By the time I've made supper and gone over Dillon's homework and maybe watch an hour of television, I've got just enough energy to crawl into bed so I can start the same cycle all over again tomorrow."

Kate did not resent a single moment with Dillon. "She's a great kid and is going to be a real woman. I know that a woman can raise a child alone; hell, I've been doing it. I don't need a man for that, but it would sure be great to have a man around just to help carry the load. That way I could have more time with Dillon. And I would like to have another child and it's getting late for that." She laughed. "I wouldn't have any problem finding a sperm donor, but that wouldn't be fair to Dillon because I'd have even less time for her. Not to mention the money. Not unless I got married."

"Do you want a permanent relationship with a man?"

"Of course I do. But not just any man. It's hard to raise a child alone and it's lonely, but I can't just bring any man into my life. I have to have someone who would be a good example for Dillon besides being compatible with me."

In terms of her early life, her family lived in a house in a suburban area of a metropolis until she was ten and then moved into a larger house farther out as the city encroached.

Her father was an engineer for highway construction projects, a college type who wore a hard hat and made a great deal of money. He died about ten years ago. Her mother, who is still alive, was a schoolteacher who quit teaching with the birth of her first child and stayed home to raise the family.

Kate has been with her present employer, an insurance company, for twelve years.

"I'm considered to be smart and fast, but I admit that I'm not always that easy to deal with at work."

"What do you mean by 'not easy to deal with'?"

"I don't have a lot of patience for people who are screw-ups. Too many people use their brains to sit on. I make the employees in my unit do their job right the first time and I expect the other units do their job. My unit has the best performance record in the company, but the evaluations I've gotten over the years have not recognized that."

"Are the evaluations from the same supervisor?"

"No, I get a new boss each year. If you want to know the truth, people around me keep getting promoted and I don't. It started about four or five years ago when I started being criticized for being hypercritical of others and each new supervisor says the same thing, like it's a script or something they're reading. It's kind of funny if you think about it— I'm constantly being criticized for being too critical of others."

As Kate related her problems at work, it became clear that she was able to quickly get down to the bottom of other people's problems but had a difficult time seeing her own situation.

Kate was obviously "turning off" people around her with the way she spoke to them, the way she criticized them, and in many other ways. Our body is an external shell but it radiates our inner feelings to the rest of the world. It's pretty obvious to see from one's body language when one is angry or depressed or tired . . . but what most of us don't realize is that we convey so many other emotional states with our bodies—feelings from our inner self that tell others that we like them—or don't, that we want them close—or that they should back off, that we have respect for them—or ooze with contempt.

One could say that Kate was so "full of herself," so caught up with how bright and smart she is that she didn't know how she was affecting others. There's some truth in the full-of-one's-self critique, but the larger truth is that Kate was so busy battling her own confused emotional states that she wasn't able to see the whole wide forest around her and saw only trees.

Kate's journey of discovery was first to gain revelations about the people and situations she is confronting . . . and of course, about *her own self*. She doesn't have to ask others to tell her what is wrong—the answers are all within her. In fact, Kate is the type who would probably reject the opinion of others about her personal situations. The most powerful insights into the problem are not going to come from others, who probably only have small pieces of the information, but from Kate herself, who has all of the pieces to the puzzle.

There were several imaging tools Kate could use and she started with part of the eidetics Parents' Images. It revealed some surprising, even shocking aspects about Kate's family life.

She got into a comfortable place and relaxed her mind. She chose a time when Dillon was off to bed and she had a few minutes alone to sit in her living room and find the space to work out the problems dogging her. She turned off the television and all of the lights in the room except the lamp next to the chair where she was sitting.

She began by seeing an image of a home that she remembered from childhood. (This is the Home Image we used before. It's also found in the Appendix of Images.) Like most of us, Kate experienced more than one home during childhood and the one that came to mind was the home of her adolescence. Why that house rather than the home she experienced in her early childhood? She can in fact see a vision of the earlier home, but the reason the later home came so quickly to mind was because of the significance of that particular house to her present problems.

Remembrance of the family home can be a purely pleasurable experience, or a painful one. Most people find mixed feelings when they remember their homes. However, regardless of whether the home evokes sensations of love or repulsion, or even more neutral manifestations, the home is an eidetic image full of *meaning* and significance. It is not just a physical place, so long, so wide, rooms with furniture and walls, but a repository of emotions . . . the walls and ceilings and furnishings are not inanimate things but are imbued, permeated, with the emotional essences of the people who lived there. Kate lived in the house, interacted with the others living in the house, she shared and experienced the love and anger, the trials and tribulations, sometimes even the pathos of the people in the house, and while it may be difficult to evoke every moment of the thousands of days she lived in the house, the sum of those experiences are still there, waiting for her like ghosts in the attic.

When Kate drew from her memory bank a vision of the house of her adolescence, her first vision was of the hallway that ran the length of the bedroom wing. The hallway was dark and cold chills ran through her and tears came.

Getting her reaction under control, Kate looked down the dark hallway. Her mother and father stood at the end of the hallway, a little shadowed by the dim light.

She *felt* the hallway, mentally experiencing it and found that despite the cold chills, the area was not cold, but was more neutral in temperature.

She looked at her parents standing at the end of the hallway, seeing her father and mother neither very young nor very old, but cast in a rather "generic" agelessness.

She first viewed her father's image, in a full-length close-up, "walking around" the image. He had lost a portion of the front of his hairline and grew one of those bushy mustaches so many men do to distract from the receding hairline. His features were not cast in stone, but there was a stoic quality about them, and she remembered that he was not a man who showed his emotions, at least not in public. He had been a very bright man, an engineer, quick with figures and solutions, and she believed that she had inherited his intelligence.

As she explored the image of her father, his features remained carved from stone. There was no weakness, no pain or passion, in his being. Whatever passions—or anger—dwelled within him he kept secret, locked within him. There was neatness to her father, a sense almost of perfection, and she recalled how neat and orderly everything about him was. The home was always spotless, not just because he demanded it of her mother, but also because of the things he did, painting and repairs and yard work, maintaining the house in the same condition he had kept his spit-polished army boots when he was in the service.

She reached out to "touch" his skin and it felt warm, not a burning heat, but more like tepid water. There was love in him for her, but like everything else about him, it was kept in reserve. As she touched his skin she realized that she could not recall a time when her father had told her he loved her or initiated a kiss. Kate knew that her father loved her, she could sense it in the image, feel it within, but she knew it was a reserved love, the kind he doled out in small qualities when he felt like it. And she sensed something else in her father, an aspect she had never put words to before but that now revealed itself to her: *her father was angry.* The strength of the emotion surprised her because she had never identified a strong emotion like anger with her father, but now she saw that the calmness, the stoic features, were a thin veneer hiding a boiling anger under it.

Next she viewed the image of her mother, and she immediately felt an anger arise in her. As she moved closer, her mother moved back, refusing to meet her in the eye, shying away. She walked around her mother's image and her mother's face glowed with shame. The more she viewed her mother's image, the angrier she became, and finally she drew away from the image, back down the hallway. Her mother and father faded and instead she saw herself as a young teenager. She was sitting by the door to her parents' bedroom and she was crying.

Seeing the decades-old image of herself, tears welled up again in Kate and she had to work again to take control of her emotions. Looking at the image again, she saw herself sitting at the door speaking the same words over and over again, "I love you, Mother, I love you, Mother." Her mother's sobs came from the bedroom where her father was beating her.

Kate didn't know when the beatings started; her older sister told her that they had been there ever since she could remember. They weren't public beatings and the damage wasn't noticeable, although she could remember once when her mother had a black eye. The beatings had driven her sister from the house to get married while in her third year of high school and had traumatized her younger brother to the point that he became a drug addict in his early teens.

The worst things about the beatings were the sadistic quietness of them. They were not precipitated by angry words but by her father's cold fury. They never occurred outside the master bedroom and always behind locked doors. The police were never called and the neighbors never knew. But Kate knew, listening to her mother's sobs and the blows, telling her mother that she was there for her.

With the revisiting of the scene the anger she felt toward her mother brought her a revelation: *she was angry at her mother for not fighting back,* for being passive in the face of adversity. She remembered the times she had tried to talk to her mother about the beatings, how her mother had refused to talk about them and refused to do anything about the situation.

My mother's not like me, Kate thought. I would not let a man deal with me that way; I would not let someone get away with taking advantage of me. I am too smart, too all-together.

Kate got another revelation: *she had picked up traits from both of her parents that were affecting her life.*

She didn't have a sick anger that would cause her to bully and beat someone, but she had refused to be weak like her mother and became extremely assertive in her dealings with other people and relationships, making sure that they did not tread on her. She "turned off" romantic interests and people who had to deal with her by never backing down and by being overly assertive and demanding. And, in doing so, she developed her father's habit of being precise and demanding perfection, taking it to an even greater extreme.

She realized that in her dealings with men who were attracted to her romantically that she had driven them away out of *fear*; fear that bad things happen to people in relationships who don't stand up for their rights. Kate didn't just stand up for her rights, but carried her fears to a greater extreme, trying to change people around her, bend them to how she wanted them to be, putting them down in order to gain dominance over them.

"Viewing my parents and our house, I gained immediate insight into how I dealt with others. I saw—and felt—my fears and knew that I was so wrapped up with my own pain and anxiety, that I was letting it escape me and affect me in my dealings with others. When I saw how much negative energy I had within me, I knew that I lacked the compassion to love. If I wasn't comfortable with myself, how could others enjoy being with me?"

How indeed? Remember that expression about having to walk on eggshells around people. Who wants to be around someone who you have to be careful of what you say and how you say it. To some degree, we have to be careful about what we say—obviously, you don't want to tell your boss her clothes make her look matronly and unattractive. But when it comes to relationships, the prime criteria are to be able to *relax* around the other person; to let one's hair down and be one's self.

Modern life is stressful enough just surviving financially and morally without having to suffer through a relationship in which one cannot completely relax and be one's self with that special other person. When those barriers to meaningful relationships are up, they need to come down.

The Parents' and Home images have been previously presented and are contained in the Appendix of Images at the back of the book.

21

Love and Fear

We'll now take a look at a romantic relationship problem involving a man who found it impossible to commit to a relationship because of unexpressed fears. Words that flowed from Tony Fontes' situation were "space," "commitment," "sharing," and "trust."

Tony got involved in relationships—and ran when things got just shy of real commitment.

"I like the person, we get along great, have a lot in common, but when I see issues of commitment arise, you know, no more dating others, talk about living together or even marriage, I slide out of the relationship. Something won't let me bond permanently with the other person."

But the process was wearing down on Tony. He felt like he was cheating the women he dated and was cheating himself out of one of the great pleasures of life.

"And there's Maria. I really like her, want to be with her, and I know I'm going to lose her and never be happy if I don't get this monkey off. of my back."

The first eidetic tool Tony used was Co-Consciousness in which he took a look at himself through the eyes of Maria.

Getting himself into a good "space" mentally and physically to journey into his self, Tony evoked an image of himself from Maria's point of view. We discussed this process earlier, delving into how one can see themselves from the point of view of another person. It relates to the fact that our minds register all the stimuli around it and store it in the form of images, visual imprints that each of us has the ability to access. Tony's mind maintains the entire history of his interactions with Maria, every body movement, every expression of her emotions she has revealed, every nuance of her behavior that she has exposed to him.

In that storehouse of information obtained from her are Maria's impressions of Tony himself, as revealed by her reactions to him. By looking at ourselves through the eyes of those with whom we are in relationships, we are able to gain insight about our own behavior and how we affect others. Even the most self-assured people must sometimes face this inner-learning process, these revelations of self-awareness.

Co-Consciousness is a mirror image of ourselves, not as we see ourselves, but as others see us. In the story of Narcissus, this handsome youth of Greek mythology was doomed to pine away for love of his own reflection until finally he was changed into a flower. When Narcissus knelt beside that stream and looked into the clear waters, he saw a perfect reflection of his beautiful image—or so the Greeks said, but he really didn't. What he saw was only the reflection of his physical features. Had he seen himself as others saw him, a vain youth with well-formed features so caught up with himself that he didn't realize he was turning off people around him, the insight might have turned him into a loving person instead of a flower.

This tale may be a classic example of beauty being only skin deep, not to mention that Narcissus obviously never saw the forest for the trees. Had he been a bit more interested in his spiritual nature instead of being obsessed with his physical appearance, he would have been able to access those wonderful tools of the gods he possessed.

Tony admitted that at first he was afraid to see himself as others see him.

"It's intriguing, yet it's a little scary. Who knows what I might find out about myself," he said. "But I guess that's the point. I need to find out about myself, and no one's going to do it for me. There's no happiness pill. Either I take a look inside and find out what makes me tick or I just give up and be unhappy the rest of my life. And it would be pretty stupid to give up."

After seeing the image of himself through Maria's eyes, he moved closer to the image, examining the details of his features, the emotions he saw there.

"Panic, that's what I saw. I could almost smell the fear I oozed. And I was stiff and kind of stoic, like I was trying to hide my emotions—the panic and fear I felt. When I saw the image I realized that at some point in a relationship I freeze up, the sort of thing that happens when you're scared but you're really not sure of where the danger's coming from. I call it 'free-flowing anxiety' because my feelings don't seem to be related to anything except a vague sense that if I don't get out of the relationship I'm going to be smothered."

Tony decided to continue his journey to his inner self by going back to find the source of his fears. "I knew I had to go back to my parents," he said. "I think someone said 'give me a child until the age of five and you'll never change him.' I guessed that somewhere in my early life my fears began and I had to go further to discover the source."

He did that part of the "Parents' Image" in which he saw an image of his mother and father. *His mother was on the left in the image and his father was on the right.* Mother on the left is an *inversion.* We discussed this situation when I first introduced you to the image of our parents. An inversion indicates that one parent is dominant and the other parent was not available—either through absence or lack of interest or because they were more passive than the dominating parent. Most commonly, it indicates an imbalance in the parental influence that the child experiences. Thus Tony felt he was getting strength from his mother but was drawing little support from the other parental sphere, his father.

"There was a difference in contrast," he said. "My mother's image was much brighter than my father's. I realized that was related to the fact that my parents had divorced when I was only five and I was primarily raised by my mother. We lived on the other side of the state from my father and I rarely saw him.

"I barely saw my father when I was a kid," he said. "When I was old enough to fly by myself, my mother would put me on a plane a couple times a year to visit my dad, but my most significant memories of my father are of the mailman delivering presents on Christmas and birthdays."

Tony moved in closer to examine his mother's image. "She was unhappy. I could see it in her; it came across at me like a flashing neon. She never really got it all together. She was a product of the sixties, not drugs and radical stuff but the feminism. She wanted to be her own person, but never knew how to handle it."

His mother went through three marriages, moving through relationships like a Gypsy. "They fought a lot, my mom and her husbands, all three of them. It always seemed to arise out of my mother wanting to maintain her freedom and rights as a woman and her feeling that the men in her life were trying to make her conform."

Tony's revelations about his mother were not unfamiliar to other situations I'd experienced and other patients I had dealt with. Tony's mother was a victim of the war between the sexes that went hot and heavy from the sixties into the eighties. As he described her from the image that unfolded for him, I got a picture of a woman who never quite got a handle on her feminine power, the powers suddenly granted to her in terms of equal opportunities.

Some people handle power poorly, especially if they lack confidence in their own self worth. Because Tony's mother didn't know how to use her power, she misused it and made her femininity an issue in her relationships.

"Not that it was all her fault," Tony said. "I remember one of her husbands, the second guy, he didn't cut her any slack. He had real old-fashioned ideas on what a wife was supposed to be. He thought he should have control; you know, where we live, how we live, that sort of thing. He expected my mother to put her paycheck in their account each week, but he was the one who wrote the checks."

As he viewed the image of his mother, Tony gained insight into his own adult behavior. "I saw the fluidity of her relationships with men," he said. "When she broke up with a boyfriend or filed for divorce, she always told me that she had made a mistake, that she should never have gotten involved with the guy."

What Tony saw was a person who was never able to fully commit to a relationship. It didn't matter if his mother was right or wrong in terms of the relationships; the lasting impression on Tony was that relationships were hell and that he had better run before he got too bogged down in one.

We cannot blame our parents for our problems in life, though too often they are the roots of many of the problems. Blame accomplishes nothing. We need to acknowledge the heritage we got from our parents, good and bad, and go on from there. As humans we have a wonderful ability to change and adapt. As Joseph Campbell put it, we can "throw off yesterday" like a snake sheds its skin. Only the "skin" we need to shed is the wrapping we have left over those wonderful attributes that each of us were endowed with at birth and that just need to be found.

Through the imaging techniques, Tony got beyond the effect of his mother's inability to be intimate. Kate, unlike her mother, found her strength. The Co-Consciousness Image was related previously and is contained in the Appendix of Images.

The imaging that Tony and Kate utilized told them that the shaping of their personalities by their parents had not left them fully empowered to deal with the world. In a sense, they were out of step, out of rhythm, with the people around them.

There is a rhythm to life. You see it in nature and in people. The rhythms include peaceful, sun-drenched days, as well as storms and sometimes catastrophic events. Some are able to maintain equanimity during crisis and keep moving along the stream of life. Others fall apart and find that life's events overwhelm them. We all know that our emotions can be as devastating as anything Mother Nature can send us.

The key to weathering personal and global storms is to look within, to take an inward journey toward self-enlightenment, to keep an eye out for the signposts along the path and find the core of strength within.

In the end we must trust our own instincts, and the great light which each of us carries within.

> *"Truth" is within ourselves; it takes no rise*
> *From outward things, what e'er you may believe.*
> *There is an inmost center to us all,*
> *Where truth abides in fullness; and around,*
> *Wall upon wall, the gross flesh hems it in,*
> *This perfect clear perception, which is truth.*
> *A baffling and perverting carnal mesh*
> *Binds it and makes all error; and to know*
> *Rather consists in opening out a way*
> *Whence the imprisoned splendor may escape,*
> *Than in effecting entry for a light*
> *Supposed to be without.*
>
> The Historic Buddha, *ed. by Dwight Goddard*

22

Images of Our Children

We love our children. We want the best for them. But parenting is so hard. No one trained us to do it. How do we go about it? The secret of good parenting is to maintain *intimacy* and *connection* with our children. One might think that's easy, that it's the natural consequence being a parent, but the truth is intimacy between parents and children doesn't come automatically with feeding and clothing the child, but is something that has to be nurtured. Our modern life and its stresses have disrupted the emotional bonding between a child and his parents. When we don't mend the break, the child is hurt and the parent is anxious, confused, and feels ineffective.

Parenting today often involves working parents, rushing home to get dinner on the table, and then collapsing in front of the TV. It is difficult to be fully present for our children because we are tired or preoccupied with other matters. The television set thus becomes an influential source of shaping our children's sense of self. Need I ask what sort of intimacy our children get from television?

Many parents I have seen have given up. They have opted to permit schools to take over the function of being the main source of teaching values to their children. Unfortunately, it is a task the schools are not equipped to do. Schools simply cannot provide the continuing context of intimacy, of being connected, that a child needs. Schools are too large, impersonal, and inconsistent to provide it. Teachers are too transitory in a child's life to give a child the deep and close relationship the child needs.

In addition, recent studies show that children are as likely to have been influenced by their friends as by their parents. When children don't get a solid foundation from their homes, they fill the void by imitating the behavior of their friends. And of course the whole thing is a vicious circle in which children imitate their friends who, in turn, are learning their behavior from television, magazines, movies, and the current culture. This process of learning from friends has always existed, and no doubt many of us picked up valuable pieces of information from the kids we spent time with. However, the basis of a solid foundation within children is rooted in their relationship with their parents.

To raise children with healthy minds and emotions, children who are able to resist the constant assault of drugs, premature sex, and other destructive behaviors, we have to bring back the warm bond between our children and ourselves and connect with them so that our values flow to them. A child is like an egg that still needs the warmth of the mama's (or papa's) body to hatch properly. Parents who are emotionally present in the child's life accomplish this. By "present" I mean attention that includes giving care, time, and unconditional love.

When there is an injury to the relationship, the flow needs to first be from parent to child to restore the break. Children learn from stories that parents tell them, from their life experiences, from being close to their parents, watching them, learning from them, and imitating them in countless ways. A teacher can't have that kind of feeling for each child to make the child feel special. And a child's exposure to an individual teacher is very limited. TV and other media are impersonal and try to capture children's minds, fill their emotional voids, through superficial commercialism and exhibitionism, loading them with unreal images. Unreal images are not the building blocks for creating "real" people.

Divorce is epidemic in our society and children can become the biggest losers in the process. Parents who are divorcing are often unaware of what their children experience during the divorce because parents get so caught up in their own pain. About half of the marriages entered into today end up in the divorce courts, and while divorce may be inevitable, there is a need to protect children from the loss of parental unity, the loss of emotional security, and the loss of intimacy with one or both of the parents due to the separation. Children naturally desire to see their *two* parents existing harmoniously, side by side, but will experience fear and insecurity as the family unit disintegrates. Children's emotions have to take precedence over the emotional needs of the parents. When a woman or man's emotions are being shredded in the divorce process, their children's emotional stability will be shredded too. Children need much sensitivity and care during this time to heal what is being torn up, and they need time and attention paid to their feelings.

The pace of our busy, frantic modern society makes it easy to compromise the connection between parents and their children and the result has led to loss for both. In order to heal, deep, nurturing, ongoing, and meaningful interactions become the prime foundation that can restore our relationships with our children. If we don't give that to our children, they fall apart and become superficial and fragmented in their thinking. They end up not deeply rooted within their own selves and lack a strong center to draw from. It is important to remember that children imitate their parents' behavior. When parents have no time for them, they don't know how to "be there for themselves" or anyone else, thus, their relationships with others also suffer.

I see this scenario with so many of the children with whom I work; children who feel very alone, children who end up doing drugs and feel lost and insecure because they lack a strong sense of identity. They feel empty and isolated. They try to find their identity with images of the culture through movies and current fads, but things outside the home are artificial, unwholesome, and can't fill their emotional void. They become alienated and suffer greatly.

Aware parents with two careers and little time can make good parents. At times, economic necessities are such that both parents have to work to support the family. Even if this is the case, the important factors are the parents' "intent" and priorities regarding their child. Parents whose priority is the well-being of their children are naturally present for them. It is this quality of presence and genuine concern that makes for bonding. Children intuitively sense their parents' "intent" and feel secure. Conversely, a stay-at-home mom who is totally self-involved does not impart secure feelings to her child. If she does not know how to be there for her child, she leaves the child feeling emotionally isolated.

One working mother told me, "Even though both my husband and I have busy careers, our kids are *number one*. We are always there for them. Even today, with them at an age when they can be somewhat more self-reliant, my husband and I schedule our business activities as much as we can so there is always someone on the home front for the kids."

When kids don't have strong bonds with their parents, they can't develop fully within themselves. When they become adults, they have little feeling of attachment for others, lack rootedness, and don't have a nourishing internal base from which to draw. They feel an inner void, a vacuum. This lack of connection cycle is then repeated with their children.

I remember a fifteen-year-old whose parents were not present for him. The parents were the type of people who frequently partied. Their social lifestyle was important to them, but it resulted in a lack of intense, continuous nurturing needed by the boy. His material needs were fulfilled, but not his need for closeness with his parents.

The child realized that he was not as important as the work and pleasures of his parents. He felt emotionally abandoned and unimportant.

The result was inevitable—drugs and trouble at school, trouble at home, trouble on the streets, shoplifting, alienation, anger by the child, fear and powerlessness on the part of the parents.

In today's climate, most kids will be offered every type of drug available under the sun. They will also be expected to have sex early on. They aren't going to resist the temptation and know how to be true to themselves unless they have the deep roots that give them a sense of self, of being whole, and the feeling of belonging to something strong and stable. When children feel connected to their parents, they have a core strength within and are not as easily influenced by outer sources. If there is a void, drugs, sex, and acting out will rush in to fill it.

If we don't fill our children with our care, time, and presence, who will? It is not that we sit them down and lecture to them, but rather, it is that we truly hear them and give them our time and our energy. Kids learn first and foremost from example. They know hypocrisy when they see it. The do-as-I-say-and-not-as-I-do syndrome bounces right off them. They intuitively pick up on the truth of our intent and actions. If anything, they are often faster, smarter, and more imaginative than we are because their minds are still innocent and more open. It is important for us as parents to be honest about our motives and clearly look at ourselves because it is what and whom we are that we pass on to our children.

Emotionally unstable parents produce emotionally unstable children, who, in turn, produce more emotionally disenfranchised children. Loving and caring parents produce caring children who feel secure and give back to others. These "sins of the father" (and mother) and blessings are generational, passed along like gifts or defects to the next generation.

The negatives and positives we get from our own parents we pass on to our children. Whatever is not worked out with our own parents, we automatically "do" to our kids. How many moms say "I yell just like my father did," or "I always kiss them good night just like my mother did with me."

We can gain insight into our parenting by looking at the images of our lives with our parents and images of our lives with our children.

The way children's personalities form in relationship to their parents occurs in several ways. First, children *imitate* their parents. That starts very early on. Children adopt attitudes and emotions existing in their parents without realizing they are doing it. This is great if we have wonderful parents and we can imitate great behavior, but sometimes parents have less than desirable traits, traits that can be very subtle but also very negative. The child of an angry father imitates the angry behavior and lashes out at his playmates. He learns from his father that to act angrily is the way to express one's emotions. He is simply imitating his father. On the other hand, a child seeing his father being comfortable and open, talking to people in the shops or stores they visit, imitates him and develops a friendly, warm style of interacting with others.

Unfortunately, children are not in a position to evaluate the behavior of their parents and they will imitate the behavior they see in their primary role models in life. So it's critical for parents to keep in mind that it's not what you say but what you do that's important.

Another way a child's personality is formed is *attachment*. Attachment is the basic biological need a child has for his parents for survival. It is the natural biological and emotional dependence children have for their parents. Early on it is seen as warm holding, feeding, and loving a baby so it can thrive. Later on children need to know their parents are "there" until they feel ready to begin separating emotionally and become independent. Children have both biological and emotional attachments to their parents. However, when children are not properly attached to their parents, they may grow up feeling insecure and develop a false sense of self. Feeling loss, they end up looking to other people or situations with which to fill themselves.

Children need good role models to emulate. When I have heard young women talking about feeling an emptiness or a void within, not knowing who they are as they step into the world, further probing has revealed that these young women did not have good role-model mothers. They lacked the experience of a strong and loving mother who passed on her secure sense of self to her daughter. Men of course also suffer the same type of deficiency from deficient role-model fathers. If the attachment is proper in children, they will operate with the feeling that they have incorporated the goodness of their parent inside of them in a positive way.

The third way children's personalities form is in reaction to their parents; behaviors directly *opposite* to the parents' behavior towards them. Opposite reactions are seen most often in teenagers, and the traits may last a lifetime. For example, a parent may be very religious and the child rebels saying he is an atheist and refuses to go to church. Or a parent may be very neat and the child opposes the parent by being sloppy, keeping his or her room a mess. Or a parent who is very politically conservative sees his child espouse left-wing radical views. In trying to find his own sense of identity, the "radical" is so caught up in not being like his parents that he does not come close to knowing or being himself. Parents' behavior also shapes children's attitudes and behavior in more subtle forms. A parent who is overly probing may produce the opposite, such as a child who is secretive. I have worked with kids who don't want to tell me anything because their parents are so intrusive.

There are many subtle ways parents shape their kids. For example, if a parent is very critical, the child can be very passive. If a parent is very critical, the child may become indecisive for fear that his decision will be criticized. Or children become fearful for life because they have violent parents.

When children have negative personality traits, we have to determine which parent may be creating the reaction. One child I worked with always wanted to do everything her own way, which didn't endear her to schoolmates or her teachers. In teaching her to take another's point of view into consideration, it was vital to know the source of the behavior. What I found was that she imitated her father, a man who always had to be right and have things his way. She was unable to "have it her way" with him, but ended up imitating him in her dealings with others.

A child can also develop personality traits through *neurotic projection*. This means attributing one's own subjective thoughts to other people. For example, if a parent isn't around a lot, the child can come to doubt that the parent really loves him. The truth may be that the parent works day and night to make a living and that in the parent's mind it isn't a question of love but economics. However, the child forms an inaccurate perception of what his parent feels for him. Neurotic projection creates an inaccurate image or feeling in the child in relationship to his parent. Kids do that automatically, getting the wrong impression, and assuming all kinds of false ideas about themselves and the world. It's important to communicate openly with your children, find out what they really think so inaccuracies in each child's mind are found and corrected.

Parents can use eidetic imaging to gain an understanding about what their children are going through. The same imaging process can be used over and over to make discoveries in new situations. We can image our children and gain insights about their experience because our interactions with them are stored in our visual memory bank.

Also, to know your own self better as a parent and see how you were shaped, you can start the process by imaging your own childhood. Use the images from the eidetics parents images we discussed earlier (Home, Parents' Left and Right, Warmth, etc.) to know your own self better as a parent.

Following is the image we use to gain more perspective about a child and our relationship with the child.

IMAGING A CHILD

To discover what is going on emotionally with our children, we can use the following image. It allows us to see them in a deeper way, understanding nuances that we may gloss over in our daily interactions with them. This image gives us insight. We begin by seeing them in our mind's eye, in the home environment (you can see them playing outside, in the home, in their room, or wherever the image takes you spontaneously). After doing this one even more information about the child can be obtained by seeing other images we have talked about such as walk-around, seeing the story in their eyes, co-consciousness, and vague and vivid (an image you will soon be provided).

IMAGING A CHILD

1. See your child somewhere in the home.
2. Where is he/she?
3. What is your child doing?
4. Notice his/her mood, actions. What do you see?
5. How do you feel as you see your child?
6. Look in the child's eye. There is a feeling or story there. What do you see?

A five-year-old girl who was having violent tantrums from the time she was two was driving the family crazy. She would draw a picture, get frustrated, have a tantrum. Or if she wanted a new toy and the mother said no, she had a tantrum.

In imaging her child, the mother saw her child in motion, running from room to room. After a while, she saw her get interested in the mother, come to where she was, make demands, then go back to playing, running back and forth, back and forth . . . the image of a child in constant motion.

"I felt like pulling away from her, like she's always a whirlwind, back and forth. I lose my temper because she's so demanding of me and I have work to do. She's in constant motion."

Remember, there is a story in the eyes. Seeing into the eyes of the image reveals feelings and emotions in a person that are not often conveyed in words. This is exceptionally important when you are dealing with a child because a child is often unable to verbally express his or her feelings.

"She has so much she wants to tell me, that there's a great deal she wants me to know and understand. I see her frustration."

What the mother saw was a well of emotion in her child that her child couldn't express, but acted out instead by being in motion.

The mother gained real insight about this behavior by imaging her child. Her daughter couldn't express what she really felt, and the mother saw it in the image. The mother's insight into her daughter's needs resulted in the mom spending more quality time with her, talking to her and playing with her. By her behavior, the mother was able to fulfill the need in the child that was unexpressed.

I also had the child's father do imaging of her.

"I see her playing with me, her brother, and her mother in the den. I see her competing with her older brother for her mother's attention," he said. "She tries to become a wedge between her mother and her older brother. She's jealous of her brother and the attention her mother gives the brother. She creates hassles because of it."

This insight from the father, that the child competes for the mother's attention, is right in line with the mother's realization that the child became agitated because she felt she couldn't express herself and wasn't being heard.

When asked to see the child and himself somewhere in the house, the father replied: "I see we're playing hide-and-seek all over the house, I tickle her a lot, she giggles and laughs. I feel very close to her, but I only spend the mornings with her. I come home late at night, so I don't see what goes on during the day."

Looking into his daughter's eyes in the image, he said, "I see that she's really happy and joyful with me, but there's a little sadness in her eyes; she's sad when I leave, she doesn't want me to leave, I think, because she feels comforted by me."

You can see more clearly what is going on when the mother's and father's images are compared. The child had a strong bond with her father, but he wasn't there all day to spend time with her. The mother was busy and could not give her daughter the attention she needed so she became hyperactive to deal with emotions that she was too young to express in any other way.

Seeing their daughter in an image helped these parents see and understand their child in ways that their ordinary eyes could not. Sometimes what is most obvious totally eludes us. Seeing with our inner eyes brings "insight" and clarity.

23

Special Children

Children who are easily distracted and have attention deficit problems are usually very sensitive and bright children. Eidetic imagery research has found that their learning problems are due to faulty social interactions, which occur in the process of learning. As these children are learning, something happens that blocks them, stresses them, and makes them feel insecure in their ability to learn. In other words, they shut down and their learning abilities are paralyzed. Although sensitivity is a gift, it can also be a problem. Sensitive children deeply take in stress from their environment and it affects them more strongly than a child who can brush off things. Simple things such as a teacher or adult who is too rigid and who does not follow the child's own pace and style of learning can stress a sensitive child. The child feels pressured to follow the adult's pace and learn in the adult's style. This constricts the child so that he distrusts his own abilities.

I worked with a man who had been taught math by his father. The lessons came in an authoritative and controlling way because the father was very rigid. As a child, he couldn't absorb the math lessons in the style his father was teaching and he would get very frustrated and finally have a tantrum. The father would then punish him for the tantrum and send him to his room.

Is it any wonder that he lost his feeling of confidence to learn? His natural ability to learn froze learning with his father and was still frozen when he became a man. His father's teaching style created a negative response to learning in him.

Many children with learning problems have had interactions with adults, like parents or teachers who have been negative while they were open to learning. When these children get too much negativity, such as criticism, hurry, pressure, or lack of the proper support, etc., they are left unable to use all their mental and emotional resources while learning.

The boy learning math from his dad also experienced humiliation and developed an overall learning problem in school. He lost confidence and literally shut down his learning capacity in many areas. And that's what we're seeing with a lot of kids: while learning, they're losing confidence in themselves, becoming anxious and distracted by events around them that are often subtle and sometimes overt.

Children learn spontaneously by relating to objects in their own way. They learn by playing with something, propelled by natural curiosity. Have you ever watched children *learn* all by themselves out in the backyard? They may pick up a rock or a stick and play, creating games in their imagination, and just feel totally free interacting with the simplest things from nature, things we take for granted. Children enter into a dialogue with these objects in their imagination.

Real learning happens as the child interacts unobstructedly with objects and people. Children are active searchers. Just as they can turn a rock or a stick into an infinite number of things, they can play with a toy car in a million different ways. Their minds are open. They make many connections—a stone thrown in a pond causes ripples. A stick becomes a magic sword and can poke holes in wet mud. This active, searching, imaginative process is how true learning happens—an active, searching child learns spontaneously while playing and interacting with the world around him in a pleasurable, curious, and spontaneous manner.

Children also need warmth and caring to learn well. When one works with children it is important to be nurturing and not critical. Having pleasurable interactions with adults helps children learn, and when learning is pleasurable children don't feel pressured and isolated (as did the boy being taught math in a strict, formalized manner).

Children remain open to learning because the warmth of the adult nourishes and encourages them. They have a safe base from which to learn and explore. It feels "good" to learn.

Children have a lot of curiosity and learn naturally by satisfying their curiosity. They really get into learning in a very natural, organic way that adults can squash. Sometimes stress in the environment is the cause. I interviewed a boy who was labeled ADD and ADHD. Working with him, I discovered that the reason he was having trouble at school was because he was being subjected to taunts of racial discrimination. The kids in class were making fun of him and talking behind his back. He was stressed, anxious, and getting headaches at school because of it. He could not concentrate and became distracted. In essence, the environment around him was making him tense. He was an adopted Korean boy living in an affluent white community. Once we got to the root of the problem and helped him deal with the real stress he was experiencing, his ADD and hyperactivity went away.

This "freezing up" process happens to many children whose learning abilities shut down. There is a belief that they must suffer with ADD symptoms for their entire lives, but this is not so. Their learning abilities can be restored and flourish again.

Children who are hyperactive are very difficult for adults to deal with. They seem to never settle down to learn. Hyperactivity is goal-less activity where the child is constantly moving and interacting with all kinds of objects in an uncentered and unproductive manner. Hyperactive children end up seemingly "all over the place" because they have no stable center from which to direct and process their experiences. Hyperactivity is found in children whose spirit and primal imagination have been thwarted or blocked. Their inspiration or passion for learning things has been crushed somewhere along the line. Hyperactive kids cannot calm down because something is bothering them; they cannot find peace inside of themselves, so they remain restless. When their inspiration is brought back, they calm down, can learn again, and go forward having confidence in themselves. When they are emotionally nurtured and their imagination can flow, their real sense of self begins to return. They relax. They are then able to absorb knowledge.

Kids become defeated in learning because their self-esteem and sense of security in themselves and their world leaves them. Parents of children with learning disabilities are often very caring, concerned individuals. They may not be aware of what caused their children to shut down. When their children can't learn or are distracted it often means that something has made them that way. For example, I have worked with several children who were distracted by noise to the point where they were unable to sit in a classroom and learn. One child was so sensitive that just the sound of a pencil snapping in a quiet classroom would distract him. I found that the source of the distractibility in him was that his parents fought all the time at home and he got scared and felt very alone during the loud noise and fighting. It got to the point that any sound bothered him. He literally brought the trauma of the sound of his parents' fighting into the classroom, and when a pencil broke it triggered the emotion of his parents fighting without his realizing it.

Kids with learning issues feel isolated. They need nourishing adults to interact with them while learning in order to break their isolation. They may seem to be around a lot of people, but their inner experience is one of isolation. They may not feel deeply heard, or seen, or feel that their genuine expressions are not welcomed because of some situation that went on in their past, or is currently occurring.

So children need to learn by interacting with the world. They need to be warmly taught. They need to have a lot of freedom to allow their minds to learn freely as they do. They need to interact with objects, learning materials, and people at their own pace and absorb knowledge in their own style. They need warm enrichment around them so their confidence in themselves grows.

We may help children to build their confidence by allowing them to follow their own curiosity, make their own discoveries, and, ultimately, by allowing them to teach the adults in their lives about the things they are discovering. When a student teaches their teacher, true learning has occurred.

Leslie is a mother who was worried because her daughter Jessica was having problems focusing in school. Leslie used imagery to see what was going on with her daughter. I asked her to see Jessica somewhere in the house they lived in to get a closer look at what might be bothering her.

See Jessica somewhere in the house you live in now. Where does she appear?

"In the TV room. She is watching TV, totally in her own world. She rejects everything else, not wanting anyone to bother her or to be bothered. She looks ISOLATED. I can't reach her."

See that you can't reach her. Tell me about it.

"Just very sad. I feel very sad that I can't reach her."

So you desire to reach her?

"I have been very close to her throughout her entire life. She was the child I worshipped until . . . I don't know what happened. She changed, but I don't think I did. Don't know what happened."

(I asked her to use the Co-Consciousness technique in which she can access her daughter's impressions.)

See life through Jessica's eyes. She is seeing the house you live in. What does she see?

"She does not find peace or comfort. Everything is tense, no safety there for her."

What is going on with her? What are you sensing is the problem?

"Her father yells all the time. She is trying very hard to be close and please him, but it is not possible and she winds up crying and she ends up feeling badly. He cannot be empathetic towards her. He is yelling and impatient and cranky, and does not want to be bothered with her. She finds no peace in the house. She seems anxious."

What else do you see about her? Let whatever information unfold.

"She has very high expectations. She can't fail. She feels she has to be perfect for her dad and for me. She has given up trying. She just sits there now in front of the TV and she tunes out all of us. I think she has given up."

Now look into her eyes in the image, there is a feeling there. What do you see?

"Pain. I just see pain and isolation. She does not feel good about herself. She wants help but does not know how to reach out."

What does she want?

"She does not know how to express what she needs, can't get out what is inside her appropriately. She feels all alone. I want to fix it. Do whatever it would take."

What do you see that she needs?

"She needs contact and understanding . . . not being yelled at and criticized all the time. I see that I am hugging her. She puts her arms around my lap, and clutches me, squeezes me tight."

How do you feel now that you have seen all this through the images?

"I feel much better. I have a handle on what is going on with Jessica, so I know what to do. I need to reach out to her. Then I have to deal with her father. I have to educate him and see if he can park his anger. He is clueless about how it is affecting Jessica."

Seeing an image of your child somewhere in the house and noticing where they spontaneously appear is important. It will give you additional information about your child. For example, you might see them isolated in their room because they are feeling alienated from the family or glued to TV because no one is communicating with them.

Here is how a mother used images to figure out how to get her unresponsive teenage son to pay attention to doing his chores. "I see an image of my teenage son in the house. He's in his room on the computer, he's really into the computer, reading his e-mail, having conversations, instant messaging with his friends, and doing homework. I see that he socializes with his friends in this fashion, and as he does homework, he is in a world of his own.

"In the image I see that the computer connects him with people, friends, and ideas. When I come up to him he's completely glued to this computer and I say, 'Please feed the dogs.' He completely tunes me out. He seems to have shut out the rest of the family as well and is not involved with us. He wants to do what he wants to do. He tunes me out if I make demands on him when he's on the computer.

"In the image I say, 'Come feed the dogs.' I see his attention slip away from me. He says, 'I'm doing my homework; go away.' I see in the image how hard it is for him to break his concentration. Yet, I know he must do his chores and relate to us.

"I see him again in the image and this time I see that I reach out and touch his shoulders as I speak. That breaks his focus and he looks at me. We make contact.

"I say, 'You must feed the dogs now, they are hungry.' With this, he complies. The image shows me that touching him is the key. To connect with him words are not enough. They pass over him. I see that I must connect physically for him to respond."

VAGUE AND VIVID IMAGES

Not all is apparent to the naked eye. Much lingers in the vague, soft nuances of our experiences. I am now going to use an eidetic imaging technique that has not been introduced before. The tool is called "Vague and Vivid." It is a very simple technique to use and which brings to light subtle distinctions of knowing.

The purpose of the Vague and Vivid technique is to allow more information from the image to come to the fore. What is hidden comes to light.

Vague and Vivid is another image that taps into the storehouse of information that we have about other people. We use it to learn more about a person, whether it is our child, spouse, lover, or boss. We tend to get stuck in a fixed perception about the people in our lives and make assumptions about them. "Bobby is kind. Sam is a snob." In this manner we put people in a "box" and relate to them from this limited perspective. We miss so much!

With the Vague and Vivid process we can start by seeing the person as we usually do—that's the *vivid* part. But to keep from being fixed about how we see them, we then relax our intense concentration and make the image of the person *vague*. By relaxing the intense concentration we've had about a person or a problem, more subtle information will readily come to the surface. This gives us much more awareness.

With more awareness comes more power and ability to deal effectively with them.

The reason we do a series of alternating, vivid (focusing on the person) and vague (relaxing our focus) images is because the dynamic interaction between the two polarities of focusing and relaxing allow a continuing flow of information to surface from our minds.

The way the technique works is that you image yourself with another person. As an example, you see how Kate imaged her daughter Annie and herself. She will alternately make her image "vague" and then "vivid" (when the image of herself is vague, her image of Annie will be vivid).

Kate was having trouble communicating with her fifteen-year-old daughter Annie. Annie had become more and more remote and unreachable. Kate tried to reach Annie by getting more authoritative and telling her what to do. . . . "Annie, don't be on the phone so much. . . . Annie, come and spend time with your brother. . . . Annie, come out of your room and be with the family. . . ." Kate's strategy was not working. She felt frustrated and at a loss.

She decided to do the Vague and Vivid Image to see if she received any clues as to Annie's behavior. First Kate saw an image of Annie as vivid and she saw herself as vague.

"I see my Annie. She turns her eyes away from me as I see her. She does not want me to know something or see something in her eyes."

Next, she saw herself as vivid and Annie as vague.

"I see that I am feeling frustrated. I want to pound down her barriers. I want to smash the walls she has put up to keep me out. I want to be let in."

She switched and saw Annie as vivid and herself vague.

"I see anger in her eyes. Her eyes are telling me, 'You don't understand me and you are always telling me what to do.'"

Kate then became vivid and Annie vague.

"I feel an interest in what is going on with her. I did not realize that she felt misunderstood. My pushing her and yelling at her has only pushed her away. I now want to know what is going on with the feelings inside of her."

Next, Annie becomes more vivid—Kate more vague.

"Kate sees Annie tell her, 'Mom, I want to tell you my feelings, but I don't trust you. You are always lecturing me. Chill out!'"

Now Kate is vivid—Annie is vague. Suddenly Kate has a new realization.

"I feel fear. I am afraid of connecting with Annie. I don't know how to. I am afraid of seeing her pain. I am afraid of seeing that I am a bad mother or have failed her in some way. My fear is what has kept us apart."

Annie now becomes vivid in Kate's image. Kate begins to see into Annie's hidden feelings as the imaging progresses.

"Mom, I am lonely over here. I need you to reach out to me. Please . . . I need someone to talk to. I am lonely over here. I need you."

Kate is now vivid and her own inner emotions pour out into awareness, and tenderness for Annie comes forth.

"Oh, sweetheart, I thought you did not need me or like me anymore. I thought I failed you as a mother. I thought I was old-fashioned to you and you were shutting me out. Yes, let's sit down. My heart opens to you. I want to know you."

Kate's understanding of Annie came through the vagueness of the image. She felt wiser. She did not yell at Annie anymore or tell her what to do. Kate's attitude had shifted. She next approached Annie in a sensitive manner with understanding in her heart. She asked Annie how she was. Annie immediately sensed tenderness in her mother's voice and that something was different about her. She was not yelling at her anymore. Annie felt drawn to her mother's warmth. She felt more at ease being herself with her mother. She began to open up and talk to Kate.

In time they began to heal their relationship through talking and building a renewed trust. All Annie needed was to be understood. All that Kate needed was to see the truth revealed, to simply be there with an open heart and ear for her daughter.

SPECIFIC INSTRUCTION: VAGUE AND VIVID

This image is used to gain more and more perception about a person. The technique is to see yourself and a person you want to know better . . . alternately seeing them vivid in your mind's eye and yourself vague . . . and vice versa.

Vague and Vivid Image

1. See an image of a person you want to know better.
2. See that the person is *vivid* and you are *vague*.
3. What do you see?
4. How do you feel as you see this image?
5. Now see that the person is *vague* and you are *vivid*.
6. What do you see?
7. How do you feel as you see the image?
8. Switch again and see that the other person is *vivid* and you are *vague*.
9. What do you see?
10. How do you feel as you see the image?

You can keep going back and forth, *vague* and *vivid*, until you have gained all the knowledge you need from the images.

24

Parent-Child Images

We will now go through an imaging session that a father had with his teenage daughter. The imaging reveals a great deal about how we treat our children in very much the same way we were treated as children by our parents.

It begins with George seeing an image of his daughter Sally. I have set the session out in a question-and-answer technique to make it easier to follow. You will find as you go through the session that there is much to learn about the subtle interactions in the parent-child relationship—and how negative and positive traits of a parent get passed on from generation to generation without the parent ever being aware of it.

The session uses several of the techniques that we already discussed. It will show you how the "sins of the father" (and mother) come back to haunt us as we raise our own children.

The first image George will do is "Walk-Around." As you know, this is the eidetic imaging technique that requires we image the person and examine them from the front, sides, and rear. Looking at a person from various angles enhances our knowledge about the person. (This image is, like all the others, found in the Appendix of Images at the back of the book.) George wanted a better relationship with Sally. Since she turned thirteen, Sally started to talk back sarcastically to George, which hurt his feelings.

I ask George to see an image of his daughter Sally.

Where is she and what is she doing, in your mind's eye?

"Right now I just see her, she's in her bed."

How do you feel as you see her?

"I feel very sweetly toward her, loving and tender. I adore her."

Now see a time when she's got that sarcastic voice, when she upsets you and hurts your feelings.

"Right, it's not hard to see; it's in the car when we're driving."

What do you see?

"She snaps back at me impatiently."

How do you react in the image?

"I get mad, and I want to really put her down, attack her back for doing that."

And do you do that in real life?

"Yeah, sometimes I do."

And what's the result?

"It's no good, she gets hurt, she gets upset, mad, and she'll get angry back, and it doesn't go anywhere."

George, see Sally in the car as she snaps at you. Look into her eyes as she does it—there's a feeling or story there. What do you see?

"She's feeling rejected by me when I say anything at all critical."

So, you've said something critical, is that why she snapped?

"Yeah, usually it's either critical or she senses that underneath my question there is a critical tone or I'm trying to control her."

So, what did you say was in her eyes . . . ?

"Rejection or feeling criticized."

How do you feel towards her, as you see that?

"I feel a little badly about it, yeah."

Do you feel that there is a good reason for her reaction?

"Sometimes I feel there's a good reason, sometimes I don't."

See a time when you feel you are being critical. Now look into her eyes.

"Right, she still feels criticized or made wrong in some way. Sometimes I wish she wasn't that sensitive. It's a pain in the ass."

Do you tell her that?

"Yeah."

How does she react? Look into her eyes again.

"Well, I tell her she's a pain in the ass. She feels criticized again for being too sensitive."

So as you look at her, is she sensitive?

"Very, yeah."

Up to this point, he has been seeing Sally from the front and looking into her eyes. We will now shift the perspective in order to gain even more information about his relationship with his daughter.

Look at her from the right side, her profile, what do you see?

"Beautiful young girl, very, very beautiful, and proud in a way."

Now we will shift the perspective again.

Go to her back and look at her.

"I see a lot of pride there too, self-assurance."

How do you feel about her self-assurance?

"I love it."

Now go to her left side. How does she appear there?

"She's a little younger, more vulnerable, she's real cute, and I feel very affectionate towards her."

Now come back to the front, how does she appear now?

"Well, she's got a mouth, but she's really hurt underneath it, I can see that."

Now that you see she's hurt, how do you feel?

"I can now see the reason for her hurt. I'm being critical and she's reacting to the criticism. When I get angry, she gets angry back. I hate to admit this, but it doesn't matter to me sometimes that she's hurt. I still want her to be different."

Can she be different?

"No, not at that moment. When she's feeling scared or weak, that's when I have the most problem with it. I want her to be respectful and I get angry with her. I don't want to deal with her hurt, I just want her to be more respectful."

See her feeling hurt.

"Well, I see her hurt. I see her hurt and I get annoyed at her."

What's your annoyance?

"I'm not compassionate with her because it's a weakness in myself. I get hurt, too. I hate that I get hurt, so I don't want her to get hurt either."

So see that you get annoyed at her for being hurt. How does it feel?

"That feels terrible."

How does she react?

"Well, she reacts defensively. It's not right, it's not fair, I'm not seeing her separate from me in that moment."

So in the images it shows you're having a hard time with her dealing with your criticism?

"Yeah, but I just saw it, that her hurt feelings remind me of the hurt feelings in me. Why would I be annoyed at her pain? I mean, my defense is that I don't want her to suffer, that I want her to be respectful. So I'm annoyed at her that she gets hurt. You know, that's highly judgmental and critical of me. I hurt her and then I can't take it that she's hurt because I can't deal with me being hurt."

Okay, see her hurt again.

"I feel more compassion for her."

He has completely "walked around" his daughter. In doing so, he got new information about his relationship with Sally and in the process he gained compassion for her. He will now return to the front of her and look into her eyes with the knowledge that he has gained.

Now look at her again. What do you see?

"She feels more connected with me, she doesn't feel so criticized, and some of the fear and hurt is gone. She's open to hearing what I want to talk to her about; she doesn't have to defend herself against me."

So, your just being compassionate actually makes her feel stronger?

"Yeah, no question. I don't know, but I can see that it's the thing I really need to do."

Next we will use "Filters" to gain even more information about George's own past in order for him to understand the present situation with Sally.

By imaging his own parents against the backdrop of his problem with Sally, George will be able to gain knowledge about his reaction to her.

He will first look at Sally while "keeping his father in mind" and then do the same with his mother.

See Sally again when you see her feeling hurt.

Keep your father in mind and look at her. How do you react with your father in mind?

"I'm depressed if I do that, I get depressed if I keep my father in mind with her. If I see her hurting and keep my father in mind, I get depressed. I just see my father and she's not even in the scene anymore. He was abusive and I see his belt."

Now keep your mother in mind and see Sally.

"If I keep my mother in mind, I get angrier. I'm angry with my mother because she didn't stand up to my father. He had explosive rages."

Now see just your father standing in front of you. What do you see?

"I see him red-faced, explosive, angry. He is critical. I flinch back from him. I am scared of him. I feel young."

So you're scared of your father's anger?

"Right."

How does that feel?

"My feelings are hurt. I'm scared and I feel weak being afraid of his anger and his constant disapproval."

Like Sally?

"Yeah, like when she feels hurt and gets defensive around me."

So your relationship with Sally is a whole re-creation of what happened between you and your father? Your father was overly critical of you and you in turn imitated his behavior in your attitude to Sally.

"Right, so at the base of it, it is my own fear of my father's anger."

George, can you now face his anger?

"Yes."

See your father is angry. How does he appear?

"Well, he's screaming, ranting, impatient, loud."

And how do you feel when you see that?

"Small, I want him to shut up and stop yelling, it's scaring me, like my hands are over my ears, I feel small and weak."

George will now do an "Emanation" exercise. This is the exercise we do when we are feeling powerless with a person or in a situation. What George will be doing is reaching deep inside of himself to find his unique strength to deal with the problem.

I asked George to see a wind come down from the heavens and surround him. It is a gift from the gods just for him. Then I asked him to "see another you jump out of you."

He went through the steps and reported:

"This new me, I'm like a bullhorn, I scream back at him. 'Shut up, shut up.' I take a deep breath and say 'Shut up' from the depths of me, really like, it's fear but it turns into power, I'm still feeling a little afraid, but . . ."

Keep seeing blowing the bullhorn and feel the power.

"It's not like I'm blowing a bullhorn, its like from the depths of me, 'SHUT UP! SHUT UP! Don't treat me like that, don't you treat me like that, Shut up,' you know, 'SHUT UP!' "

This is happening in the image?

"Yeah, it's in my chest like the release has to come. 'Shut up—don't you talk to me like that.' It's just screaming, 'DON'T YOU DARE TREAT ME LIKE THAT—SHUT UP! SHUT UP!! *SHUT UP!!!*' I have my hands on his neck."

And what's he doing?

"I shake him. 'Shut up! Don't you treat me like that, you will never treat me like that again, I won't let you, and if you do I will shake you till your head comes off.' "

Does he hear you?

"I'm just seeing him, like, looking at me, 'Don't you ever talk to me like that again, don't you talk to me like that again, you sonofabitch,' in that condescending tone, damned demeaning voice . . . Oh, I see I do this to my Sally."

You're having a realization now that you do this to Sally? What do you mean?

"I take my tension about my father out on her."

So you see what your father did to you, and you do it to Sally in a milder form. You don't get as angry as your father did, but you are critical just like he was.

"Yes."

So now see the image of your father and your hands are on his neck—

"On his shoulders, like, and I'm screaming at him, 'Don't you ever talk to me like that again.' It's funny; I know I'm more powerful than my father, he can't physically hurt me. I'm feeling rage and there's still a little fear in me."

What's the fear about?

"Well, it's like a break in the connection with him."

You don't want to break the connection.

"I don't like that I'm doing this to my father, who I should love, you know what I mean, who I should love, and yelling this way is meaning that I don't really love him."

So there's two things going on with you now, there's the anger and the feeling of fear of breaking the connection, there's a desire in you to be connected. . . .

"There's still a fear that maybe I can hurt him or something or maybe I'm even more powerful than he is, now, but I don't know why there's fear, but there's fear in my chest."

So share the fear with him. Tell him you're afraid.

"It's like, 'I don't like talking to you this way. I don't want to have to be talking this way. I don't want to hate you, it doesn't feel good to hate you.' "

How do you feel now?

"I feel sadder, I feel that's the truth, I don't feel frightened anymore, it's like I don't want to be enraged with him anymore."

So how does he respond?

"He just starts to cry."

In the image he cries?

"Yeah, he starts to cry, he starts to break down and cry, his head is down, and I just start to hold him and I start to cry with him."

See that the two of you are crying.

"Yes . . . it's like a real healing kind of thing."

What's the healing for you and for him, what's going on in the image?

"I'm just crying and he's crying, we both know that, you know, we don't want to hate each other, we don't want to fight, you know, there's love."

You feel the love between you?

"Well, it's sensitive, it's like years of a battle that has been over, both of us are a little uncomfortable with it."

With the tenderness?

"Yeah, with the tenderness, yeah, uh . . . so I tell my father that I really love him, I tell him that I really love him . . ." (George begins to cry at this point.)

Now see Sally and see her when she feels scared and weak around you. What happens now?

"I just am very loving toward her, the other reactions right now are not there. They are gone."

How does she respond?

"She responds positively towards me, letting me hold her and feel comforted by me, and then I can talk to her, yeah."

And is she better now in the image?

"Yeah, yeah. . . . Right, I'm feeling sad now, just feeling really sad, it's about me and my father, I mean, I never got to that place in life with my father, he died."

How do you feel now?

"More peaceful. In my own mind I feel more resolved, softer. My hard edge is softened. I am so sorry I hurt Sally. But, I had no idea. Now things can be different."

The insight George obtained from seeing the direct correlation of his relationship with his father and the way he treated Sally was startling but not unexpected.

The starting point in healing our relationship with our children is to know ourselves.

To know ourselves we can start with imaging our own home as a child and seeing our relationship with our parents. Every one of us grew up surrounded by families who affected us profoundly. We carry the legacy of our histories into the future lives of our children and down into their children's lives. We have the power in the now to break the chain of negative emotions by looking within and bringing out our best. In doing so, we have a hand in changing the direction of future generations.

25

Career and Success

When you follow your bliss, doors will open where you would not have thought there would be doors; and where there wouldn't be a door for anyone else.

Joseph Campbell

Imaging techniques can find the "high" in what we do and bring it onto the job.

When working with CEO's of "brand name" corporations, companies that produce products that are found in most of the homes in America, I learned the secrets to their success. Some of these top executives are household names in industry and government. I have also been brought in to work with employees at all levels who are responsible for planning, creating, and marketing products worth tens of millions of dollars. One of the most important things I have learned over the years is that success in business and professional careers require that we maintain a "high" state within ourselves about what we do and how we do it.

Examples of the "high" state are the positive emotions that drive us: excitement, love, passion, and exuberance.

I am going to share with you the source, force, and spirit behind the men and women at the top of the power structure of business and government and how to one extent or another these successful people at all levels use the same techniques.

One thing that became obvious from working with brilliant people is that despite their success they were open to learn more about themselves and, in turn, have their staffs gain insight into their own success patterns. Successful people know that they must have highly efficient staffs in order to carry out their vision. The imaging process that I shared with them gave them insights into the source of their successes (and failures) and offered solutions to current and future business problems. The images are similar to those we have been using up to this point, although the focus is different.

When we see the images of our career situations we can discover the spirit that truly motivates us by making a connection between our work and our passion. The connection between passion and work is the hallmark of successful CEOs.

A key factor that very much affects our ability to elicit "high states," such as those required for success in business, sports, or creative endeavors, is how our parents affected our beliefs that we could be a winner. While imaging, women and men who achieved success can clearly see a relationship between attaining their goals and their parents' attitudes toward them. None of the people with whom I have worked doubted that their parents were a contributing factor toward their ability to succeed. (I am using "parents" in a generic sense here to indicate the people who were the caretakers in the person's life—sometimes the motivation stemmed from another person such as a grandparent or mentor, etc.)

Taking "winners" through eidetic imaging sessions revealed that the automatic way they approached problems and mobilized winning strategies came directly from the psyches of their mothers and fathers. Without realizing it, they continuously fell back on the inspirational and motivational base that their parents gave them, and utilized it daily in their dealings at work and with their competition. This "daily" flow of potentiality was applied to a wide range of situations, from problem-solving specific issues to using unique strategic methods of negotiating, to gaining loyalty from their staff, and to enhancing their style of leadership with others. I worked with one household-name executive who used intimidation by yelling . . . followed by warmth and love for those who worked for him. The combination created an atmosphere of respect and devotion from his staff underlined by fear. In the imaging session it was revealed that he had gained the traits from his mother and father. His mother was very loving and his father yelled all the time. I told another CEO that his negotiating stance reminded me of a thief who would sneak down from the hill at night to steal your chickens and sell them back to you the next morning. He laughed. The imaging revealed that his mother was very, very clever, a woman who had financial success despite having to raise a family.

REHEARSING FOR SUCCESS

The most effective people *rehearse* their strategies for success. Prior to the event, they do a full mental dress rehearsal, seeing all of the elements they will face. They play a game play by play, try a case in a courtroom moment by moment, or give a sales presentation in the same way. They see beforehand in their mind's eye the situation that they are going into. When they do, all of the emotions they have about the situation arise in the image; emotions that thwart them and those that enhance their presentation. In this way they can strategize before the event and see where they feel confident and powerful and where they have negative emotions or limitations that are going to get in the way. This allows them to face their weak points and enhance their strengths.

The process brings to light the person's abilities and limitations in any specific situation. Thus, they can see how to overcome their limitations and how to enhance their powers before going into action.

In this way we bring our best to any given situation. By doing this visually beforehand, the person "performing" is not going to be caught off guard in any important situation such as presentations or meetings. They have already prepared and seen the negatives that may come at them from someone else, and have developed strategies for victory. They have not only just "seen" the situation, but they have discovered the energies within that can overcome any possible failure. It is little different than an actor playing a role, learning a scene line by line, and drawing from her/his visualization of the character the passion to become the very best character.

When you rehearse, you can use images of past success, filters of your parents, walking-around the person you want most to impress, and the applause tool to gain insight into the situation. (The Applause Image will be discussed shortly.)

CONNECTING THE SPIRIT TO YOUR WORK

Often our work deals with a specific product or service. In making the connection between the products with which we work or the services we offer, and the passion within us, we need to find the link between the product (a toy, a purse, an item of clothing, a car) or service (the lecture we give, the jury we're performing before) and our genuine love for it.

St. Thomas Aquinas said that the self extends into objects. Likewise, we extend a part of our self into the products or services we deal with daily. A good example of this is our wedding rings. If I saw your wedding ring, it would probably not create much of an emotional response in me, it's just a pretty object . . . but my ring carries with it personal feelings of love, sentiment, and loyalty. My identity extends into the ring. It is personal and I am attached to it. It is more than just any old ring to me.

We talked earlier about how incredibly successful people are able to "connect" to a "product" (selling a widget or a dream, giving a lecture, running the four-minute-mile, writing the Great American Novel, investing other people's money) with their passion and imbue the entire project with the force of their energy and power.

We can discover the "high state" at work by making the connection between the product and our positive feeling about it. In this way we project our identity into the product or service we deal with. We discover our very unique drive and passion for what we are doing. It is this genuine enthusiasm that others pick up on and that draws them to us when we offer them our product or service.

The following is an example of how men and women selling insurance plans to individuals were able to find that "high" that excited them and made them successful in their work. Taking several people separately, I asked each to "see an image of selling the plan to a customer." These are examples of the " 'High' in Your Work" Image we will be utilizing.

Each of the insurance agents came up with something unique, but there was a common theme to all of them: imaging their personal feelings about the plan or product they were selling put them in a high state of exuberance, giving them the zest to move through obstacles and keep on going.

One woman realized she was not selling a product but providing long-term security for people. She loved providing security for others! When she saw it that way, it filled her with a sense or purpose for her work. Another man saw himself as selling a lifelong relationship of trust with his clients. Seeing that gave him a deeply rewarding feeling. He felt empowered and had a sense of sacred duty that his clients trusted him with their life savings and their future. Yet another person saw it as his talent to manage couples' conflicting financial needs and to resolve them. It made him feel worthwhile and special to help them.

Each of the financial planners tapped into a unique sensibility of their own that connected them to their work in an emotional manner. They were able to sell more financial services because their prospective clients sensed the genuine passion they emitted.

Visualizing the unique quality of "turn-on" in what they did gave the salespeople energy and passion to break sales records. They were not really selling a product, they were selling a very personal feeling that was within them. The product is the vehicle to express something greater within us.

The same technique used for seeing the personal connection between a product and the salesperson can part a sea of personal obstacles in an incredible number of situations. I worked with a novelist who had writer's block. In a sense he had fallen from grace with the written word and his confidence came down with it. I had him see an image of himself writing, focusing in on what it was about writing that he loved. The connection between the writing and his passion got him out of his block. He told me that he writes because it touches people, that it makes a connection between his vision and others. This connection from his vision with others gave him a sense of elation and inspiration to break through his obstacle.

I have worked with salespeople, writers, designers, and those in dozens of other occupations and the results are generally the same: successful people experience a somatic (physical, emotional) high, filled with excitement and energy when they image the plan and their unique connection to the product or the situation with which they work.

I worked with a team of elite designers of men's suits who were searching for ideas that would increase their sales. One of the most effective eidetic tools they utilized was making a connection between themselves and what excited them about their suits, seeing themselves touching the cloth, smelling it, asking themselves what it was that made them enthused about selling it. One said she got high making people look good in the garment. Another person was inspired by the richness, color, and beauty of the cloth.

Making a connection between a "product" and our genuine feelings for it doesn't just relate to physical products. In my own career when I see someone I'm working with gain potent and enlightening new perspectives on a difficult situation with which they have been struggling, and that look of "I can do this" on their face, I get my own high. There is a deep connection among success, passion, and work. Unless you've been lucky enough to win the lottery or inherit money, you are probably not successful unless you've made the same sort of connection.

People say it is true bliss when they can express the unique gifts within them in their work. Doing so is giving to others the best that is in you. Giving to others and making a difference in someone's life is one of the greatest pleasures we may experience.

Thus "seeing" and "feeling" your unique passion about what you do elicits your natural motivation from within and exudes an aura of sincerity and excitement that others naturally respond to.

"HIGH" IN YOUR WORK

Here is the process for imaging the " 'High' in Your Work" image.

"HIGH" IN YOUR WORK IMAGE

1. See an image of the work you do.
2. See yourself doing it.
3. See what you enjoy about it. Focus on the aspect that gives you the most energy or pleasure.
4. See that what you enjoy gives you a "high" feeling.
5. Feel the high feeling and let it get stronger.
6. This is the high or passion in what you do.
7. See yourself at work in a high state.
8. Let the pleasure, the high state, get stronger.
9. See yourself at work expressing this passion, this high.
10. How is your work now?

Creativity and imagination go together. Of course, so does the discipline to process the ideas as they come and give your inspiration a big dose of perspiration.

In doing this "product or service imaging" you want to take yourself completely away from feeling and thinking of it as "work." Work carries with it many connotations that interfere with the creative process. You need to "play" with the images in your mind, making that connection between the mind and the product or service in order to bring the best of your potentialities to it.

FILTERS

To gain further perspective into your abilities, or into the "blocks" that keep you from reaching your goals, you can use "Filters" to assess the situations. There are a number of different filters that can be used—the most common is parents, because their effects on us are programmed in our brains, but you can also use a mentor or spiritual figure (Christ, Buddha, etc.) as a filter to bring your most profound self to the work situation.

Here is an imaging example of a successful businesswoman using filters to discover and harvest more of her inspirational abilities in dealing with problems. What she is discovering is how her parents affected her everyday business acumen.

The woman was instructed to see herself at an important interview and at the same time *"keep father in mind."*

"With my father in mind, I feel sturdy, purposeful, like I can go out and slay dragons."

Keep mother in mind.

"I feel anxiety. I have tightness in my throat. I still feel a sense of purpose, of getting through the customer's door, but there's more . . . ambivalence." She pointed to her stomach. "Now the tightness has gotten to my stomach."

What were your parents like?

"My father was a real go-getter, a guy who loved a challenge and set out to conquer. My mother was, uh, motherly. She was bright, really smart, in many ways smarter than my dad, but sometimes she hated leaving the house."

Now see yourself making a presentation before a customer.

"I see a man behind a big desk, like the Wizard of Oz, kind of plump. He's listening to me."

Keep father in mind with that image.

"I can charm the pants off the customer, I'm like a tornado, I see myself performing, it's about power and freedom, I feel happy and full of expression."

Keep mother in mind.

"I'm much more careful, demure, more manipulative, not a straight shooter, I'm more concerned with how he views me, with father I didn't care."

Another client I worked with was a man with a more "volatile" attitude than the previous business person. He was having a problem with a coworker. You will see where he gets his aggressive nature.

See an image of yourself at work with your coworker, I told him.

"I see a typical instance with this person."

How do you feel when you see this person?

"Like throwing up."

Okay . . . see the person and keep father in mind.

"I don't want to throw up, I want to beat 'em up. I'm disgusted, but I have to control myself so I'm nauseous. My immediate response is to go after him."

Keep father in mind and see that image.

"I have the same reaction as before. Punch out the guy's lights."

You can see he strongly identifies with his father in the situation, the surge of anger and the temptation to be physical.

See that person again and keep mother in mind.

"I can't win, not with my fists. I have to outsmart him, I can't do it with muscles, have to use my brain, hold back, wait, strategize, if it's a rock in the road you're not going to blast through it, she figures a way around it."

Which parent was best for the situation?

"Clearly my mother."

Did you notice that before I asked him to keep father and mother in mind, his immediate reaction was of rage . . . but of controlled rage? He said he wanted to go after the guy physically, but he had to keep control. It's interesting that the imaging revealed that his parents gave him two different approaches—his father provided a physical and aggressive approach to problem solving and his mother a more cerebral one. He had adopted his father's style without being aware of it, much to his detriment.

Note: "keeping in mind" is like bringing the essence of the person into the situation. Just the thought of them, as we image, alters the context of the image, revealing important information about how we naturally approach life situations.

FILTER IMAGE

Imaging a work situation using a *filter*:

FILTER IMAGE

1. See a problem or difficult situation you are experiencing at work in your mind's eye.
2. What do you see? How do you feel as you see it?
3. Keep mother in mind and see the problem or situation. Let it unfold like a movie.
4. What happens in the image, keeping mother in mind? Let the images unfold without interference.
5. Now keep father in mind and see the problem or situation. Let it unfold like a movie.
6. What happens in the image, keeping father in mind?

RUNNING STREAM

Another valuable eidetic imaging technique for dealing with problems at work is the "Running Stream" Image. Here again, the situations people face are different, but the formula for solving them—gaining fresh perspectives about people and situations and your own emotions and motivations—is evident. The stream is symbolic of your life's energies, and your life force. The way we flow as the stream illustrates how we move through life. As you see this image, two things will happen. First, you will clearly see how you move through the challenges that face you at work. Second, you will discover the energy or spirit within you that is far greater than any obstruction. This image brings the dynamism of your spirit to the fore.

RUNNING STREAM IMAGE FOR BUSINESS:

The *running stream* (from your viewpoint):

1. See that you are a running stream.
2. See that running stream that you are.
3. See something in front of you as you experience yourself as the running stream. What do you see?

4. Now see an obstacle in front of you. When you see yourself as the running stream, see how you run through this obstacle or the problem it involves.

5. Now see your bosses, your workers in front of you, as you see yourself as a running stream. What happens to the stream?

6. See your colleagues in front of you when you see yourself as the running stream.

7. Now see your competitors in front of you, and be the running stream.

8. Now see the world in front of you, and you are the running stream.

9. See the whole world and feel "what will be, will be" and be the running stream.

10. Now see past history in front of you, and you are the stream, the running stream.

11. See the present in front of you, and you are the running stream.

12. See the future in front of you, and you are the running stream.

13. See a negative situation or a negative person and run through it as the stream, and be this running stream.

14. See constraints, prohibition, and other fears, and run through them one by one, as the running stream. Who has the more power?

15. Do not fear anything and be this running stream.

"History" refers to our own history, the events that have shaped us. When we can overcome and defeat our negative history, and allow our pure energy and spirit to surge, we can make the changes necessary to overcome the obstacles life has put in our way.

SWIMMING IMAGE

Another variation of the running stream is the "Swimming" Image. This is an insightful technique to clearly see the abilities of others and understand the people in your life. In a business environment, the technique has been used by an employee to evaluate a coworker competing for the same situation, a manager to evaluate employees for a promotion, a salesperson to evaluate customers and competitors, and so forth.

SWIMMING IMAGE

1. See yourself as a running stream. See that running stream that you are.
2. See your competitor (coworker, boss, employees, etc.) swimming in the running stream.
3. Watch how they swim.
4. How are they swimming (fast, slow, easily, or with difficulty, aggressive, just flowing with the current, etc.)?
5. How do you feel as you see the image?
6. What meaning or insight do you gain about them as you see the image?

Matilda, an editor at a well-known magazine, was feeling confused by a fellow editor. One day the fellow editor would be friendly and then seem cold and hostile on another day. When she saw her coworker swimming, she said, "I see her swimming with hard and fast strokes. She wants to hog the whole river and be number one as she swims. She swims right by me and wants to beat me—get ahead of me. I can see that this reveals her true attitude and it is self-centered and competitive. She's not a team player. I better watch out for her."

WALK-AROUND IMAGE

A technique we have used many times in previous parts of the book is to "Walk-Around" the situation or person, and it is very useful to gain new insights about other people in a work environment. This can be used to assess an employee, supervisor, competitor, customer, etc. I am repeating it here so you can use it to also evaluate the people you compared in the Swimming Image.

WALK-AROUND IMAGE

1. Relax, close your eyes if you like, and see an image of a person that you want insight into.
   If the image is vague just keep looking. The information will come in sense impressions or feelings.
2. Look at the person from the front. What do you see? Notice their body language, the emotions that you can read on their face, and anything that strikes you. Let the information about the other person simply come to you.
3. How do you feel as you see the image?
4. Now move to the right side of the person and look at the person from that side. As you look at them, be aware of how they look, their body posture, the emotions you sense on that side. What do you see about them? Let all of the impressions come forward.
   How do you feel now that you see them from this side? Pleasant? Unpleasant? Neutral?
5. Now move to the back of their head and observe them from that angle. What do you see?
   Again, just let the information come, whatever it is.
   How do you feel as you see them from the back? Pleasant? Unpleasant? Neutral?
6. Now go to the left side of them.
   What do you see? How do you feel?
7. Go back to the front.
   What do you see? How do you feel?
8. Do you have a different understanding of this person than when you started?

Robert, a corporate executive, told me that he was having problems with another executive in his corporation named Joel with whom he was forced to work on several projects. He felt that Joel was constantly trying to intimidate, bully, and outsmart him. Although highly successful, Robert began feeling edgy and nervous every time he had to meet with Joel. He was losing confidence. I asked him to do the Walk-Around Image.

See Joel somewhere at work. Where does he appear?

"He is in the conference room. We are all sitting around a table at a meeting. He is at the end of the table, sitting there, head tilted down a bit."

What does his head tilted down mean to you in the image?

"He is unhappy. Things are not done the way he likes them to be done. He is disapproving of what I am saying. I am sick of being lectured at by this guy. Sometimes I feel that he thinks he should have my job because it has more prestige than his."

Look into his eyes. There is a feeling or story there. What do you see?

"Anger. Frustration. He feels he is smarter and therefore looks down on me."

Move to his side and see his profile. What do you see about him?

"He has a lot on his mind. He is not relaxed at all, very tense."

Go to the back of him. Sense him from the back.

"Same sort of slumped shoulders, not happy. I can see he carries many burdens that have nothing to do with me."

See him from the other side. What do you sense there?

"I hear his voice. I hear a very reasoned argument why something I want is wrong, and why something he wants is right, very competitive. He puts me on the defensive. I always suspected that about him. He is competing with me.

Now look at him from the front again.

"I see a big sneer on his face, like he wants to be one-up."

Look into his eyes again. What do you see now?

"I see that he is jealous. I see insecurity. I see fear. Oh, now I feel sorry for him. I can see that he is really unhappy."

What do you understand from this image?

"From walking around him I see that he is suffering terribly. He can't accept that there is a mismatch between his position and his view of his intelligence. I see that he is really frustrated and has doubts about himself. This is his problem and has nothing to do with me."

How do you feel about him now?

"Much more free and much more relaxed. Once I saw his fear and insecurity, the feeling of him as a threat is gone. Actually, I feel sorry for him. Now that I see what is really going on with him, he does not upset me. I feel more detached, yet a bit sorry for him. I am sure that when I see him again I will not respond to him in the same way."

You can also use the Co-Consciousness Image to see how these people feel about you in a work environment.

There are an infinite number of answers to the above questions and the interesting thing about eidetics is that you don't need anyone to interpret them for you. The insights you gain from the imaging come directly to you. Obviously not every image you see or even every technique you try will be revelatory but most people who try several different techniques find the imaging works like building blocks, with each image adding something to the whole.

APPLAUSE IMAGE

Another eidetic imaging tool used successfully in this area is the Applause Image. This involves keeping your parents in mind and seeing which parent gets in your way of being the very best that you can be and which one enhances you. What you are truly seeing is what inner mental attitudes you have that aid or block your success. I have taken CEOs through this type of imaging and the results have been dynamic.

APPLAUSE IMAGE

The Applause Image instructions are:

1. See that you are on a stage and people are clapping their hands in applause for you.
2. Keep your mother in mind and see the image of people applauding you.
   What do you see? How do you feel as you see the image?
3. Keep your father in mind and see the image of people applauding you.
   What do you see? How do you feel as you see the image?
4. Is there a difference when you keep mother in mind and when you keep father in mind during the applause?

Irene, a corporate executive, did the Applause Image out of curiosity. What she learned delighted her. I took her through the instructions with these results.

See that you are on stage and people are clapping their hands in applause for you.

"I see I am on stage. People are applauding me and I feel a bit shy. Do I deserve all of this applause? I am pleased and I also wonder if I deserve it. I can see that there is a belief in me that I don't deserve having the recognition that I have worked so hard to achieve. Am I holding myself back with this attitude?"

Keep your mother in mind and see the image of people applauding you.

"With mother in mind I crouch down behind a podium on the stage and cover my head. I am surprised by this response. I remember her yelling at me. With mother in mind, I see that I am afraid of being criticized. I hold back because of fear of criticism."

Now switch and keep your father in mind and see the image of people applauding you.

"With father in mind I receive the applause. I stand taller. I feel entitled to the acknowledgment. I stand tall and proud and receive what is coming to me. I remember my father used to come to all of my school plays and sports activities and bring all of his friends to see me. He was so proud of me."

Is there a difference when you keep your mother in mind and when you keep your father in mind during the applause?

"Oh yes! I can see that I am afraid of criticism and this holds back the full expression of my creativity at work. I now realize that that was my mother's influence on me that still limits me. However, when I think of my father, a different me emerges and I feel strong, tall, and able to move through obstacles. I feel confident and deserving. Hey, I am deserving!"

I told Irene to keep her father in mind as she was working on projects, talking to people, and doing the many things she did at work. After dutifully keeping her father in mind for a month, she told me, "I would wake up on the days I went to work and think of my father to get me in the right mindset. Once at work, I simply kept him in mind as I went about my daily responsibilities. I tell you, I feel different. There has been a subtle shift in me. I feel more confident, assured, and assertive at work. Although it is subtle, I can see that others are responding differently to me; they seem to have more respect for me when I speak. I am asked for opinions more often and my boss has asked me to discuss ideas about upcoming projects with him where he never did this before. I must be emitting a signal to others that radiates confidence. Whatever it is—thank you, Dad!"

Using your parents as filters works best because those are your habitual responses that are already stored within you. However, you may find that both of your parents do not yield positive results because your history with them was problematic. In that case, keep in mind a mentor, teacher, relative, friend, or spiritual figure, someone who has been a strong positive figure in your life and who brings out the best in you. This will work very effectively.

An eidetics tool that CEOs and their staffs responded well to was the Emanation exercise in which a wind from the heavens came and a new "you" popped out, giving a fresh infusion of energy, power, and self-expression when they felt blocked. We have used the image before and it is found in the Appendix of Images at the back of the book.

George was a business executive who was being transferred to another city to head up a new division for his company. He did not feel enthused about the move or about his new responsibilities. He knew that if he took this new position for three years, he would then have a strong possibility of being promoted to his "dream job." He was worried because he felt no passion or energy for his upcoming three-year position and he knew that this lack of energy could affect his performance, which would then limit the possibility of getting his dream job.

I asked George to image himself in the three year job position.

"The first image I see is me at work in the new city. I am standing in my office, looking out of the window at the city below."

How do you feel?

"Unenthused. Here I am. I don't fit into the job, I'm feeling passive."

See a wind come down from the heavens and surround you right there in your office. It is a gift from the gods for you.

"I feel calm. The wind relaxes me."

See another you jump out of you. What is the other you like?

"I see someone who is meeting with people, talking about what we need to get done and how we are going to do it; a very active person, very relaxed, but very energized and motivated."

See you become this other you. This is the "real" you. These are the natural energies stored within you.

"I see I am sitting and listening, making decisions. People are laughing as well. It's a good atmosphere."

How do you feel in your body?

I feel great. I am not holding back, not wasting energy thinking that I am ambivalent or I don't want to do this. I am looking ahead. I feel really good in my skin. My body feels very, very light. I feel better physically than I have felt in a long time. No tension."

How do you feel about the move now?

"More energized. I am a leader. It is only three years. I can do it!"

WORKING SMART

One of the most striking characteristics one learns in helping people work out their problems with relationships, careers, and the other walks of life is how much sheer energy people will put out to accomplish—or *avoid* accomplishing—their goals. Unfortunately, I have found people spend more energy doing things that end up hurting them than doing things that benefit them. A lesson I have learned is that whatever venture we are in, we need to *work smart*. Working smart means getting the most done with the least effort. Part of that involves setting goals as high as possible, but keeping our feet on the ground.

Alexandra David-Neel (author, *Mystery and Magic in Tibet*, University Books), who you will learn more about later, relates a story about Buddha that makes a good point about working smart.

It is said that Buddha was once journeying with some of his disciples and met an emaciated Yogin, all alone in a hut near a river in the middle of a forest.

The Master stopped and inquired how long the man had been living there, practicing austerities.

"Twenty-five years," answered the Yogin.

"And what power have you acquired by such long and arduous exertion?" asked the Buddha.

"I am able to cross the river by walking on the water," proudly replied the anchorite.

"My poor fellow!" said the Buddha with commiseration. "Have you really wasted so many years for such trifling results? Why, the ferry man will take you to the opposite bank for a small coin."

26

Enhancing Your Success Potential

If A is a success in life, then A equals x plus y plus z. Work is x, y is play, and z is keeping your mouth shut.

Albert Einstein

The next set of images is designed to permit you to assess your success potential and gain insight about blocks to it.

The sixteen image instructions take you from high school through your present work environment. At each stage you will use a *filter* (keep mother in mind, keep father in mind) to gain perception about how you were motivated to succeed and what the blocks to your success have been. As you go through these images you will notice that they reveal familiar feeling states and attitudes that you bring to your endeavors at work. This test helps you to see your potentials and your obstructions. You may want to take a piece of paper and write down your responses so you can compare them.

SUCCESS ASSESSMENT IMAGE

Education
1. See yourself at high school.
   Keep mother in mind while you are at school.
   Keep father in mind while you are at school.
   Is there a difference in your feelings when you keep a different parent in mind?
2. See yourself dealing with a difficulty at high school.
   Keep mother in mind while you deal with the difficulty.
   Keep father in mind while you deal with the difficulty.
   Is there a difference in your feelings when you keep a different parent in mind?

3. See yourself at college.
   Keep mother in mind while you are at college.
   Keep father in mind while you are at college.
   Is there a difference in your feelings when you keep a different parent in mind?
4. See yourself dealing with a difficulty at college.
   Keep mother in mind while you deal with the difficulty.
   Keep father in mind while you deal with the difficulty.
   Is there a difference in your feelings when you keep a different parent in mind?

Interview

5. See yourself thinking of a job.
   Keep mother in mind while you think of a job.
   Keep father in mind while you think of a job.
   Is there a difference in your feelings when you keep a different parent in mind?
6. See yourself thinking of an interview.
   Keep mother in mind while you think about the interview.
   Keep father in mind while you think about the interview.
   Is there a difference in your feelings when you keep a different parent in mind?
7. See yourself preparing for an interview.
   Keep mother in mind while you prepare for the interview.
   Keep father in mind while you prepare for the interview.
   Is there a difference in your feelings when you keep a different parent in mind?
8. See yourself having an interview.
   Keep mother in mind while you deal with the interview.
   Keep father in mind while you deal with the interview.
   Is there a difference in your feelings when you keep a different parent in mind?

Problem Solving

9. See yourself dealing with a problem at work.
   Keep mother in mind while you deal with the difficulty.
   Keep father in mind while you deal with the difficulty.
   Is there a difference in your feelings when you keep a different parent in mind?

10. See yourself dealing with an obstruction.
    Keep mother in mind while you deal with the obstruction.
    Keep father in mind while you deal with the obstruction.
    Is there a difference in your feelings when you keep a different parent in mind?
11. See yourself working out details.
    Keep mother in mind while you work out the details.
    Keep father in mind while you work out the details.
    Is there a difference in your feelings when you keep a different parent in mind?
12. See yourself implementing a solution.
    Keep mother in mind while you implement the solution.
    Keep father in mind while you implement the solution.
    Is there a difference in your feelings when you keep a different parent in mind?

Success

13. See yourself successful at work.
    Keep mother in mind while you are successful at work.
    Keep father in mind while you are successful at work.
    Is there a difference in your feelings when you keep a different parent in mind?
14. See yourself wanting a promotion at work.
    Keep mother in mind while you want a promotion at work.
    Keep father in mind while you want a promotion at work.
    Is there a difference in your feelings when you keep a different parent in mind?
15. See yourself being promoted at work.
    Keep mother in mind while you are being promoted at work.
    Keep father in mind while you are being promoted at work.
    Is there a difference in your feelings when you keep a different parent in mind?
16. See yourself being applauded for your achievement.
    Keep mother in mind while you are being applauded for your achievement.
    Keep father in mind while you are being applauded for your achievement.
    Is there a difference in your feelings when you keep a different parent in mind?

After finishing this test you will become very clear on which filters give you more energy, ability, and strategy for being your best. It will also reveal those automatic responses that lead you to failure that you may not be aware of. Once you discover which filters work best for you, you can use them as tools.

For example, Mary, a business executive, saw the image of "being successful at work." She saw herself giving a speech to an international group at her Fortune 500 company. She saw herself speaking and feeling somewhat muted, feeling nervous about being judged. She kept her father in mind and saw that she weakened and became shyer. She wanted to run away and not show her face. She recalled that shyness had been something she often struggled with since childhood and remembered how critical her father was.

Keeping her mother in mind, Mary saw herself stand tall, lean forward into the podium to more forthrightly reach her audience. She saw herself speaking with clarity and determination. She felt confident. From then on, every time she gave a speech, Mary kept her mother in mind and felt a surge of confidence come over her.

27

Dealing with Career Problems Every Day

In this section we will take a comprehensive look at a woman named Stella in her business environment. You will see how her personal history, her childhood, and her parents' attitudes in raising her continue to influence her effectiveness at work. You will also see how she overcomes her problems and discovers potent new abilities that help her succeed. In so doing you will gain more insights on how you can use eidetics in your everyday work life to master the subtle obstacles that thwart your success. A number of different images will be used to gain perspective about overcoming ingrained childhood attitudes that are limiting and to unleash the creative power within.

Stella is a forty-nine-year-old administrative manager for a Fortune 100 communications company. She has a Protestant religious background, has been married eighteen years, and has no children. She is a very hard worker, verges on a workaholic personality, and has made it into middle management.

She notices that she has a tendency not to rock the boat with her boss and is suffering an emotional meltdown because he seems to be more and more short tempered with her. She wants to improve her ability to say what she feels, instead of just doing what she's told, and improve her skills at managing her staff better. Her symptoms at work have been distractibility, stress, and difficulty staying focused on projects.

Stella started with her parents' Home Image, the home of her childhood. This image puts into perspective many of our personality traits, our aspirations and fears, because our home and parents are the chief molders of our emotions and personality.

STELLA'S IMAGES

"I see both parents in the kitchen, my whole family is there, which includes my three sisters. We are all having dinner, and it's pleasant. I'm in high school. I'm very comfortable seeing my mother, I feel warm as I see her. I don't feel comfortable seeing my father; he's more strict, more rigid, and an outsider. The women in our family had a clique and he was always on the outside.

"I see that we're around the table, it feels like a home, though I never liked the house a lot. My father was strict, really strict, and sometimes he scared me. He was rigid and authoritarian, not unlike my boss, Ted. My father raised his voice a lot and it turned me to Jell-O inside. As I see the image, I feel like I'm reliving moments with my boss. In the image, sometimes my father mixes with the image of my boss. With my father you never knew what topic would set him off, he could be nice or explode; he was totally unpredictable. My boss is very similar; you never know when he's going to explode."

Now see your parents standing directly in front of you.

"I see them with my mother on the right, my father on the left."

As you see them, do they appear united or separate as a couple? Notice if there is any difference in temperature and illumination in your parents.

"They appear separate, there's space between them, Mother is warmer. They're side by side. I see that the spaces between them clash. That makes me feel uncomfortable down my middle, insecure. I get that same feeling of insecurity when me and my boss clash, that feeling down the middle."

What is your mother doing in the house?

"Mother is much quieter, more reserved, Father is outgoing, knows everyone in the neighborhood. My mother's attitude is 'don't rock the boat,' my father would rock the boat and stand up, he would say 'stand up for yourself, don't let anybody take advantage of you,' but he's always suspicious from the start. Money was a major issue with him.

"This image surprises me. I always thought that my not-rocking-the-boat attitude came from my father because he was so strict, but I can see that my mother was scared like me when my father rocked the boat. Also, I am amazed that the insecure feeling I get when my boss and I clash is exactly the same one I had at home when my parents fought."

Next Stella did a parents' "Listening Image," seeing her parents listening to something she has to say and gauging whether they really listen to her, and, if so, which parent listens to her the best. Through the attentive "ears" of the parents, a child learns to relate to the world and develops confidence in his or her ability to communicate with others.

Some of the images we have done before and I am repeating them here for your convenience. Other images are being presented for the first time.

PARENTS' LISTENING TO YOU IMAGE

The imaging is done as follows:

1. Picture yourself talking to both your parents.
2. Who seems to hear you better?
3. How does the other parent hear you by comparison?
4. Concentrate on how your father hears you in the image.
5. When he hears you, do you feel secure or insecure?
6. Concentrate on how your mother hears you in the image.
7. When she hears you, do you feel secure or insecure?
8. Concentrate on the parent whose hearing creates security for you.
9. Concentrate on the parent whose hearing creates insecurity for you.
10. Which parent do you approach more for listening to you?

"I see my father listening, but he's impatient with me," Stella says. "He doesn't listen well to me, before you tell him the whole story he forms his opinion and makes up his mind. My boss is like that, once he makes up his mind it's set in stone.

"Mother's voice is comforting, she listens, gives her opinion, she's fair, she gives you the benefit of the doubt, while my father is very opinionated. Mother hears me better, Father has selective hearing, hears what he wants; that's the same with the boss. I can see that I am more like my mother when I listen to my coworkers and staff. I am patient and fair. However, I tense up around people who are impatient and have a hard time finding my voice—just the way I would feel around my dad—and, just the way I respond to my boss."

Stella will now assess how well her parents *understand* and give credence to what she has to say. The process of hearing, listening, is linked to the process of understanding. If one hears but does not understand what has been said, or ignores the content of what has been said, one is not properly communicating with the other person. The parents' ability to pay attention to and understand what has been said creates confidence in their child and serves as a bridge to reality.

PARENTS' UNDERSTANDING YOU IMAGE

1. See yourself talking to both of your parents again.
2. Who seems to understand you better, mother or father?
3. Concentrate on how your father understands you in the image.
4. Do you feel understood?
5. Concentrate on how your mother understands you in the picture.
6. Do you feel understood?
7. See father. What kind of ideas would you like to exchange with him?
8. See mother. What kind of ideas would you like to exchange with her?
9. Which parent exchanges ideas with you more?
10. Which parent do you feel should exchange ideas with you more?

"Mother understands me better, in fact with her I feel very understood. My father understands me less than Mother, but he's encouraging me more to rock the boat, he's not as cautious. I can see that I need some more of his rock-the-boat ability because I tend to be a people pleaser like my mother. In my review, I was told that I need to develop my skills as a leader—which means taking a stand, like my dad."

The next image involves "Warmth and Connection" to the parents' bodies. During the child's period of dependency, the parents look after the child's physical and psychological needs, feeding and providing comfort. As a result, the parents' bodies should at best appear affectionate to the child and impart a feeling of personal warmth.

The image reveals the intimacy and connection between the child and his parent, whether the parent was able to express love in a tender and intimate manner to the child.

If a parent's body appears cold, it is usually indicative of a lack of affection and leaves the child feeling isolated and less able to feel confident in connecting and interacting with other people.

PARENTS' WARMTH CONNECTION IMAGE

1. Picture your parents standing directly in front of you.
2. Which parent's body has more personal warmth?
3. How is the other parent's body in comparison?
4. Concentrate on your feelings concerning father's body.
5. How do you feel as you see his body?
6. Relax and recall memories as you concentrate on your father's body.
7. Concentrate on your feelings concerning mother's body.
8. How do you feel when you see her body?
9. Relax and recall memories as you concentrate on your mother's body.
10. Which parent's body do you wish to know more? Why?

A related image concerns feelings of "Acceptance"—or rejection—by the parents. The care given by the parents is reflected in the positive feelings, which their skin generates when they come into contact with the body of the offspring. At best, the parent's skin should appear warm and accepting.

PARENTS' ACCEPTANCE OF YOU IMAGE

1. Picture your parents standing in front of you.
2. Look at your parents' skin and concentrate on it for a while.
3. Does it seem to accept you or reject you?
4. How do you feel as you look at their skin?
5. Whose skin gives you the feeling of acceptance? To what degree?

6. Whose skin gives the feeling of rejection? To what degree?
7. Concentrate on your feelings concerning your father's skin.
8. How do you feel as you experience father's skin?
9. Concentrate on your feelings concerning your mother's skin.
10. How do you feel as you experience mother's skin?
11. Which parent usually touches you more?
12. Which parent do you usually touch more?

"My mother's body gives me a feeling of warmth, my father's is a lot cooler, and it rejects me. That's how he was with me, more reserved. Imaging him I can see he's afraid to feel emotion, he won't initiate a hug. My boss is like that, kind of cold, more held in than my mother.

"When I touch my father's skin it accepts me, but I can feel a wall there. I feel that wall when I talk to my boss, too. I can see that I hesitate expressing myself freely with my boss. I have the same feelings as I had being around my father of holding back and being afraid to contradict him or tell him what I really thought. I do this with my coworkers, too. This problem is what I now bring to the table at work and I want to get over it."

How a person reacts to the images of their parents can show whether the person is at ease or is stuck in places in life. You can see how we imitate our parents or react against how they were. Stella can be either warm like her mother at times, or controlled like under the influence of her father. The knee-jerk responses she developed with her parents follow her into her relationship with her boss.

Another image concerning our connection to our parents concerns the temperature of their "Brain." The brain, like the rest of the body organ, displays a temperature. A parent's thought processes are reflected in the thermal images of the brain, the normal temperature representing normal activity and the abnormal temperature representing abnormal activity. Usually, the parents' brains should appear slightly warm and pleasurable in temperature.

PARENTS' BRAINS IMAGE

1. Picture your parents' brains.
2. Touch each parent's brain and feel the temperature there. Is it cold, warm, or hot?
3. Now touch your father's brain. What is the temperature?
4. Is touching your father's brain pleasant or unpleasant?
5. Now, touch your mother's brain. What is the temperature?
6. Is touching your mother's brain pleasant or unpleasant?
7. What does hot temperature of a brain mean to you?
8. What does cold temperature of a brain mean to you?
9. What does neutral temperature of a brain mean to you?
10. Which parent's brain do you tend to avoid touching?

"Mother's brain is warm, pleasant," Stella said. "Dad's is unpleasant at times, sometimes it's very hot, which can be very unpleasant."

Brain temperature is usually indicative of temperament. A hot brain translates to a hot temper, explosiveness, and that's how Stella's father was—he could blow at any moment and she wouldn't know where she stood. Stella is more like her mother, and she has a boss like her father, who tends to make mountains out of molehills and is quick to anger. "Boy, have I learned to shut up and not respond to my boss blowing up, exactly the same way that my mother dealt with my father. She would just let the storm pass on."

"Parents' Heartbeat Images" are symbolic of the presence of love. An affectionate heartbeat with a regular rhythm is expected to reveal whether the parents are tender in their expression of love. The person one sees in the parent's heart generally has a deep emotional connection to the parent.

PARENTS' HEARTBEAT IMAGE

1. Picture your parents' complete images standing in front of you.
2. Image a window opening in each parent's chest so you can see his or her heart beating there.

---

3. See your father's heart beating. Describe its beat and its appearance.
4. Is there any sign of anxiety in father's heartbeat?
5. Imagine a picture in your father's heart. Who do you see?
6. See your mother's heart beating. Describe its beat and its appearance.
7. Is there any sign of anxiety in mother's heartbeat?
8. Imagine a picture in your mother's heart. Who do you see?
9. In what way do you wish your father's heart to appear different?
10. In what way do you wish your mother's heart to appear different?

Stella was asked to see her parents' hearts beating.

"Dad's beats very fast, it's in a hurry. Mom's is even, slower. There's lots of anxiety in Father's heart, and frustration; some anxiety in Mother's, and she has fears there.

"In my father's heart I see my mother. In my mother's heart I see me. I know there was a greater connection for me with my mother than with my father. I can see that I have turned out just like my mother. My boss is just like my father. Am I replicating their marriage dynamics here at work? I am afraid to admit that it may be true. Yet now that I can see how I am bringing my childhood responses to work, I have more knowledge and objectivity. Now that I can see it, I can do something about it. This gives me a good feeling of hope and more possibility."

Next Stella explored the issue of being distracted at work. She sees an image of herself at her *office*. Just as the home environment can provide fresh perspectives about the sources of our behavior, imaging one's work environment can provide insights into how we function at work and where our strengths and weaknesses lie.

"I see myself at work. I go into my office and look around. What do I feel? I am bored. But I feel something else, fear. I realize that I get distracted when I don't know all the answers. I realize what's happening is that I avoid getting started on projects because I'm afraid of my boss's reaction, of his criticism. I get the bulk of my work done in a timely fashion, but I can see that I procrastinate when I am nervous about the results."

She sees herself working on a project and uses her boss as a *filter*. (Remember, a filter involves imaging a situation while keeping someone else in mind. In this case, Stella sees herself working and keeps her boss in mind.) When she keeps her boss in mind, she immediately experiences nervousness.

"I get a black feeling in my gut," she says. "I realize that I'm fearful that he will change his opinion about me. He has a good opinion of me, but he's the type who if you screw up once he never forgets it, just like my father."

She uses her father as a filter while she's working and gets the same reaction.

"I had a hard time finishing things around him, too."

Stella saw herself in the office, her boss coming toward her, annoyed. He's coming to criticize her.

"I feel the emotion of anxiety and I'm nervous in the pit of my stomach. He's very annoyed and his face is red. We are all dumb; obviously he's right and we are wrong. That's the attitude of my boss."

Stella can clearly see that she has a problem dealing with her boss and she can see that the source of the problem is that she reacts to his temperament much like she reacted to her father's. The Stella reacting with fear and indecision to her boss is a product of her "history." She will now do an Emanation to go beneath that history and bring forth a "new Stella" to deal with the situation.

EMANATION IMAGE

1. Relax and clear your mind. Close your eyes and go inward.
2. See an image of a person in a situation in which you feel stuck, powerless, or that you are unable to deal with effectively.
3. How does the person appear to you?
4. How do you feel as you see the image? Allow your feelings and body sensations to come into awareness.
5. If you could say or do anything to this person, what would that be? Let that desire come into your awareness.
6. Now see a big wind come from the high heavens into the room and surround you. This wind is a gift from the gods.

7. Feel the sensation of the wind swirling and swirling all around you.

8. See another "you" jump out of your image. (For some, it pops right out of their head.) The old you disappears and you become the "new you" in the image.

9. What is this "new you" like?

10. See that this new you does or says whatever it wants.

11. What does it do or say?

12. How do you feel as you see the image? Become aware of your shift to the new you.

13. How is the other person reacting to your new self? In the image when you see the new you—with your new strengths, powers, or abilities—interacting with the other person, notice how the other person reacts.

14. How does the person now react to you? If the new you that came out does not have enough strength, ability, or power, repeat the process.

15. Now see a wind come from the heavens and surround this new you. Feel the wind, this gift from the gods, swirling around.

16. Now see another you jump out of the "new" you.

17. See how this one interacts with the person.

Stella did the Emanation.

"As I see my boss criticizing, I see a wind come down from the heavens and wrap around me. It makes me feel calm and stronger. It blows away the anxiety and there's no fear in the pit of my stomach. I see another me jump out from the top of my head. Now I'm even calmer. I say to him, this project is long, repetitive, and there are problems with it. I don't understand some of it. I am calm and straightforward. When I look in his eyes, I see he respects me when I speak up and tell the truth."

We constantly pick up bits of information about other people through subtle body language, facial expressions, and moods. These sense impressions get stored in the computer of our brain and will reveal to us in an image the reactions of that person when we change our behavior toward them. When Stella spoke to her boss, she saw respect for her in her boss's eyes. When people stood up to him, he admired it. He didn't admire weakness, which was the signal he had been getting from her, making him even shorter tempered with her. Stella realized her boss loved it when she was truly herself and voiced her opinion even if the opinion disagreed with his.

The next image is the "Running Stream." This is the same image tool we have used before, but this time we are going to do it from a new perspective. In the past we used it to deal with a particular business situation. This time we will also get an idea of how we relate to the world at large. The stream is symbolic of our life energy and reveals how we use that energy to deal with problems.

RUNNING STREAM IMAGE

The running stream (from your viewpoint):

1. See that you are a running stream.
2. See that running stream which you are.
3. See something in front of you as you experience yourself as the running stream. What do you see?
4. Now see an obstacle in front of you. When you see yourself as the running stream, see how you run through this obstacle or the problem it involves.
5. Now see your parents in front of you, as you see yourself as a running stream.
6. See your father in front of you, and you are the running stream.
7. Now see your mother in front of you, and you are the running stream.
8. Now see the world in front of you, and you are the running stream.
9. See the whole world and feel "what will be, will be" and be the running stream.
10. See history in front of you, and you are the stream, the running stream. People make the history of the world. Do not fear history.
11. See history and you as the running stream battling each other. Who has the more authentic power?
12. Are you afraid of anything now?

13. See a negative situation, and run through it as the stream.
14. See a negative person, and be this running stream.
15. See constraints, prohibition, and other fears, and run through them one by one, as the running stream.

"I am a fast running stream," Stella said. "The waters are blue and they move quickly; there are rocks and the water flows over the rocks."

When asked to see an obstacle in front, Stella said, "A tree has fallen across the stream; it holds back water; the stream goes over, but it backs over itself; it takes persistence for the water to get over the tree."

The obstacle in the stream and the stream's interaction with it tells how a person deals with obstacles in life and how they overcome them. Stella had persistence and perseverance. She could go forward. Some people can't get over the obstacle, some struggle while others sweep by it. Their actions describe how they deal with problems in life.

Next, Stella sees her parents in front of the running stream.

"The stream slows down, but it feels pleasant."

She now sees her mother in front of the stream.

"It slows down a bit, it's going very slow, a much slower pace than normal, and it's frustrating and annoying."

Now her father is in front of the stream.

"It starts to move faster and is freer. I feel invigorated. He's more open about running and being free, and he's more adventurous."

Stella could see that the influence of her mother has slowed down her spirit and inhibited her energy. Despite the fact that he was the critical one, her father was the freer spirit in the house and gave her vigor and freedom.

Now she is given the following instruction: See the world in front of you and you are the running stream.

"I feel a great expression of joy and freedom and ability to do anything to accomplish things; I can lay back or really go forward. This is a very empowering feeling. I am free and I am me!"

Then she is told: See history in front of you and you are the running stream.

"I sweep over it," she said.

People make the history of the world. People are our history. Nature is more powerful than history and in the end nature wins. She saw that she swept over history. The stream gave her the feeling that she had power over events of her history; that her life force could overcome all obstacles.

Seeing history as an obstacle reveals that whatever happened to a person in their history is not as powerful as their true essence, that history isn't as strong as nature, that one's own inner nature can always come back in full force and triumph. Stella could see that sometimes she would approach a task at work as though she was under the filter or lens of her mother and she felt irritable, slow, fearful, careful to not rock the boat. Keeping her father in mind, she felt more open, more adventurous, and could do more things. But her own life force, which was the third option, would allow her to go soar with all her energies at her disposal.

Some weeks later Stella shared this with me.

"When I start tensing up at work and get distracted or lose track, I just close my eyes and see that running steam. When I do that, I get back on track. I see the stream image and I get back to the project with full energy. If I feel timid and insecure, I see the stream and I feel vibrant and whole again."

STELLA "WALKS-AROUND" JACK

The next image concerns how Stella resolves her problem at work with Jack, a fellow employee. Jack has a reputation in the company for back-stabbing and trying to grab the limelight whether he deserves it or not. Stella is annoyed because she can't trust Jack, who is not a team player.

Stella sees an image of Jack. She will use "Walk-Around" to gain perspective about the man. Remember, this is where we walk around an image of the person and examine the person from different perspectives, learning more and more about the person and their motives as we view the person from different angles.

She starts off with the office image, seeing Jack at work, and then does the walk-around.

"He's at work," Stella said, examining the image. "I see a little child who needs attention. He's afraid that someone will outshine him. He's so jealous, so insecure. Running to our boss to curry favor is important to him."

Next Stella views Jack from the left.

"He's standing there with a smile on his face, happy go lucky. In this image of him I like him. I feel comfortable with him. He can be pretty intelligent. But I can see he's manipulative, too. He'll come to me and pump me for information, and the next thing I know our boss is sending out a memo praising Jack for the information. He's a user. I see he wants to succeed, he's insecure about his knowledge, he wants to please."

She views him from the back.

"I don't get that much from his back."

Then she views from the right side.

"Oh, it's a whole other side; he looks happy, joking, wants to do a good job and get along; its' a lighter side."

Then she looks at him from the front again.

"This is interesting, he's half and half, one side dark, competitive, insecure, pulls information from people, selfish. On the other hand, he's friendly, wants to be team player. He can be very nice and charming, but he's got a dark side to him."

Stella looks into his eyes, for the feeling or "story" there.

"He has insecurities. I don't know, maybe he never got it from his parents or got weaned too early (just kidding). He has a hard time accepting blame. Can't take criticism."

How does Stella feel about Jack now?

"I feel more compassion, I understand his need for approval. We all have that in us to some extent, and I also know what to look out for. I feel I can deal with him now and I am not so charged up about him. I am aware he has a dark side that I need to look out for."

What would she say to Jack in the image?

"I'd tell him to accept mistakes, be more upfront. He feels people don't like him. They would if he'd just be more open."

28

Visions of Creativity

The most beautiful thing we experience is the mysterious. It is the source of all true art and science.

Albert Einstein

My job frequently takes me to work with traditional creative people such as authors, artists, actors, photographers, and filmmakers. While there are certainly different types and levels of creativity, the fact remains that within ourselves we all have a natural ability to be creative, whether creativity is defined in our lives as being a successful stock investor, a good salesperson, a good teacher, or a moviemaker.

Creative people depend heavily on a flow of inspirational ideas that come from within. Many creative people, ancient and modern, have described the inspirational sensation as a "flowing stream." It's interesting that poets and scientists alike have used the water analogy because the first creative act, God's creation of the heavens and the earth, arose from water: As Genesis tells us, in the beginning there was only water, and God divided the waters, making the upper "heaven" and the lower "earth."

Three-quarters of the surface of the earth today is covered by water and our bodies are ninety-eight percent liquid. In a sense, we are all products of the primordial waters that God divided, waters that have been evaporating to the heavens and falling back in a continuous cycle since time immemorial, waters that flow through our veins and nourish our minds today.

Have you ever thought about the wondrous quality of that liquid we take so much for granted—water?

If there is magic on this planet, it is contained in water. Its least stir even, as now in a rain pond on a flat roof opposite my office, is enough to bring me searching to the window. A wind ripple may be translating itself into life. I have a constant feeling

that sometime I may witness that momentous miracle on a city roof, see life verita-
bly and suddenly boiling out of a heap of rusted pipes and old television aerials.

                                        Loren Eisley, *The Immense Journey*

This concept of seeing the stream of creation, of inspiration, tapping into the divine "waters of God," is available to us through the use of eidetic imaging.

Creativity can only come from within us. Information obtained from the world around us may provide us with some of the detail we need in order to create a "product" (whether a painting, scientific discovery, or something we do on a daily basis at our job), but the mere regurgitation of what we have read, heard, or seen is not being creative—rather, it's akin to simply parroting the ideas of other people. (If regurgitating information were the key to creativity, people with "photographic memories" would come up with creative products like the Theory of Relativity and Mona Lisa!)

Eidetic imaging takes us deep into our psyche where our genetic imprinting and the complete history of our interactions with the world around us are stored. When we go deeply into ourselves, we also touch a greater source than our own history. From this place within, ideas flow because the images in our visual memory bank are all from the same source of inspiration. As one image comes, others follow, and soon we have a "stream of creativity" that flows from a pure fountainous source of imagination.

This steam of creativity is a stream of ideas coming forth in a free-flowing fashion from a deep source in our mind. It comes when we allow it to come naturally. Excessive thinking and structuring an idea from the rational part of our mind or from the ego obstructs us. Rather, letting go and allowing whatever to come into our minds without censorship brings about an opening of the tap within, so the creative flow comes.

It is a matter of not judging ourselves and trusting that there is a flow that will emerge. The ego sits and judges, dissects and analyzes everything we do. Approaching creativity in an analytical manner hinders it because we end up analyzing the situation to death, rather than allowing it to flow with its inspirational insights.

We will examine how this stream of creativity is accessed, but first we need to learn more about the general nature of creativity, including some of the more traditional views of it.

Creativity is essentially inspiration, stimulation of the mind or emotions to a high level of feeling or activity. It is the ability to make or otherwise bring into existence something new, a new solution to a problem, a new method or device, a new artistic object or form. Creative people rely strongly upon what they believe is their *intuition* or *insight* into a situation. What they are doing is "letting go" and opening up the gates so an unimpeded stream of ideas may flow.

In his book *The Courage to Create*, psychologist Rollo May talks about how we need "creative courage" in our society. "Creative courage is the discovering of new forms, new symbols, new patterns on which a new society may be built. Every profession can and does require some creative courage. In our day, technology and engineering, international diplomacy, medicine, business, and scores of other professions are in the midst of radical change and require courageous persons to appreciate and direct the change. The need for creative courage is in direct proportion to the degree of change the profession is undergoing."

We need to have the courage to bring a new vision to the world. The ideas that are generated from a new vision imbue us with direction and hope. We need to trust the source of creation within us and allow new visions to emerge and we need the courage to bring these new visions into our existing situations.

We are too prone to think of courage in terms of physical acts and not recognize how much moral courage is needed in our daily life. Even a common task like going into your boss's office and telling her/him that you deserve a raise can be hair-raising.

> *The highest courage is not to be found in the instinctive acts of men who risk their lives to save a friend or slay a foe; the physical fearlessness of a moment or an hour is not to be compared with immolation of months or years for the sake of wisdom or art.*
>
> Joseph H. Odell, *Unmailed Letters*

THERE IS *MANA* IN ALL OF US

Creativity in many parts of the South Pacific is perceived in terms of *mana*, a word of Pacific origin that is commonly used in Melanesian and Polynesian languages to express a power or force that is concentrated to objects or persons. This includes creative energy, which emanates from supernatural sources, rather like those "gifts of the gods" that we have discussed before and are found in each of us.

In Greek mythology, inspiration and creativity were also gifts of the gods, bestowed by the Muses, the nine daughters of Zeus and Mnemosyne. Each of the daughters presided over a different art or science, acting as a guiding spirit and source of inspiration to the artist or scientist.

Mana and the Muses are, of course, just a way people have tried to explain the originality and expressiveness that we each have within us and through which some of us have been able to accomplish a great deal. Creative geniuses know how to tap into, contact the power, and express it better than the rest of us, but these gifts are there for all of us if we make the simple effort of going with it and permitting the stream to flow freely. Once we get ourselves out of the way, inspirations flow.

CREATIVITY THROUGH EIDETIC IMAGING
IS AVAILABLE TO ALL OF US

Early schools of psychology believed that eidetic imaging was the domain solely of creative geniuses and small children. Those theories have been rejected and eidetic imaging techniques and its rewards are available to all of us. Artists, writers, painters, and poets at all levels can employ imaging to create a work of art. Technocrats, scientists, engineers, and architects can build monuments, and millionaires can buy and sell them, gifts from the Muses are to be found in each of us.

It is true that there are a relatively small number of creative geniuses in our society, such as Spielberg in the movies and Toni Morrison, a Nobel Prize winner in literature. But for every Spielberg or Morrison there are tens of thousands of people who operate on a creative level that enhances their lives, careers, and hobbies. In a sense, it's analogous to how we deal with money in our society—there are a few billionaires that dominate the news but there are *millions* of financially successful people.

One of the main things that distinguishes a creative person like Toni Morrison is her ability to go deeply into herself, to tap God's waters and bring them forth in a steady stream, sometimes even as a roaring river. However, like Morrison, most people perform creative tasks on an almost daily basis, tasks that enhance their career and their monetary success without realizing they are doing so.

There is something of a movie-making quality to the stream of creativity that flows from us. Images generate other images and soon images, and the ideas or insights they contain begin to unfold like the scenes of a movie. Each frame of the film is interrelated and forms a part of the whole reel: When it comes time to put the project together, whether we're making a movie or a sales presentation, we have prepared ourselves by seeing the project as a whole, even if all of the answers to all of the possible contingencies have not been anticipated.

The point needs to be emphasized that most of us deal with creative issues on a daily basis. Our results can be enhanced by going deeper into ourselves, tapping into the stream of creativity, with eidetic techniques. Almost anyone in any occupation or profession can see instant results from imaging. The dentist who provides a crown that is not noticeably different than our other teeth, the lawyer who guides us through a divorce that manages an agreement in the best interest of *everyone* concerned, the computer technician who solves a hard-to-analyze problem, the salesperson who comes up with just the right package to get a difficult buyer to say yes—are all being creative. They may not have the fame of Spielberg or the honors of Morrison, but they stand out from the crowd because they have gone deeply into themselves and tapped into the rich flow of creativity we all have available to us.

Everyone has the potential to tap the source of the creative flow that exists within them and to rise to much greater heights than they ever thought possible.

Is age a factor in creativity? Do we get too old to create? The answer to both questions is a definite NO! Most Nobel Prizes have been awarded to individuals for work performed while the recipient was in their forties or fifties. While some highly creative people seem to flame out after their twenties or thirties, most continue on for decades because the flow of creativity is eternal; it never dries up and is always there for us. Once you know how to let creative energies flow, you get better at it and it is much easier to do. Michaelangelo, Voltaire, Tennyson, and Tolstoy remained incredibly creative late in life, often producing outstanding work into their eighties. So did Winston Churchill, Bertrand Russell, Margaret Thatcher, Eleanor Roosevelt, Pablo Picasso, James Mitchner, Harold Robbins, Linus Pauling, Margaret Mead, and Jessica Tandy.

The ability to create is very much centered on the *desire* to create, to problem solve and to allow the solutions to come forth. The desire to create is the *intention* to create. Intention is a very important word in creativity because it focuses our efforts on the objective. We start with an intention to create something. The mind begins to align itself with the intention and bring its creative resources to the intentionality that we desire or prescribe.

If I'm thinking of putting a seminar together where I have to make a presentation, my intentionality is that I'm going to prepare this seminar for businesspeople on problem-solving techniques. Once I start *intending* to create, all of the ideas begin to flow—images, thoughts, feelings, impulses, body states related to the presentation. Creative people, regardless of the field they are in, approach problems in the same way.

Then, you must have the *time*. Leisurely and uninterrupted time to think can be a rare commodity in our frantic society because there are so many demands upon our time, from the demands of our jobs to our domestic chores and to parenting duties. Most of us spend more time just taking care of business and home than our parents or grandparents ever did. We are left with little free time just to *be*.

We need time to put our mind in a quiet place, to still the rational mind, to go within and have a vision for what we intend to create, allowing our thoughts, feelings, and impulses to emerge, and then letting the inspiration flow to our awareness. For example, when I want to come up with ideas to create a fantastic seminar, once I have created the intentionality, the problem will be with me, on my mind or in the back of my head while I brush my teeth, take a shower, feed the dogs, and drive to work. It starts to be there subliminally in my mind all the time, and when I think of it little nuggets of ideas appear. Some nuggets are brilliant and others ordinary. It is not up to me to create, but to let the nuggets of creation come as I focus on the seminar.

Expressions like "on my mind," and "sleeping on it," are used because they are the terms we commonly apply to the mental process that allows creativity to surface. But in truth, while we say "they're in the back of my head," the images connect us to a spiritual source, going deep within our psyche to find that stream of God's creative flow.

If I put my mind into something else, like the demands of my children and their needs, or a discussion with a friend, it momentarily takes away from that focus on my seminar, that loose focus (it's not good to be overly focused), taking away from allowing the nickels to drop. However, once I place my intention on the seminar again, the stream returns. Creative ideas can come any time when we have the intentionality to be creative and any place in which we are psychically able to be receptive. For deep concentration, it's good to have moments of solitude and let the mind ruminate.

Don't try to discipline or control the flow. You may not use everything the stream of creativity brings, but by trying to control the stream you lose the spontaneity that is so important in the creative process. Let your mind have free reign to go plunging into the depths and let the river of ideas flow. Do not criticize what comes because that stops the flow also. Simply observe, note down ideas, and later pick and choose what works best.

Of course, there are enormous demands upon our time and much of life revolves around what we might call trade-offs. If we want to direct our attention to being creative, we have to turn off ourselves from the demands on our attention and carve out an appropriate amount of time for the task, in midst of fighting traffic on our way to work, dropping off the kids at school, and jumping the rest of the daily hurdles.

Eidetic images flow from a creative source and constitute a steam of vision that flow like a river in our mind when we need it. Hits of inspiration, visions of creativity, come in the form of images, and they may be very subtle. We don't sit there and say, "Oh, I'm having this vision," but the subtle images are there—forming in the mind. Like other eidetic images, these have somatic feelings. Seeing the image that carries with it the inspirational solution to our creative dilemma is much like an "Oh, that's what I'll do" experience. It's as if a light goes on and we have an "Ah ha!" experience.

For example, if I'm thinking about a presentation I will be giving soon, I spontaneously see in my mind the image of the people attending the seminar and I experience a flowing of the ideas that I want to communicate to them. I see them understanding the concepts, and when I think of the topics I'm going to speak about, other ideas spark. I have sensations in my body, good feelings and sometimes uncertain feelings; but the feelings and the ideas flow, all interconnected, one image connected to another image, and all of it wrapped in mind-and-body responses that give me insight and provide meaning about the problem I am dealing with.

The meaning or image may come to you first and then, second, the somatic response, or you might get the somatic response first—perhaps as a sudden surge of excitement or emotional high—and then the meaning. The order in which you receive the data doesn't matter.

A factor that highly successful creative people have in common is the degree to which they maintain their focus and intentionality on a problem. They concentrate on it by clearing their mind and thinking about it, directing their thoughts and attention to it. In our busy society, sometimes concentration has to arise in an atmosphere that is more akin to riding a bucking bronco than sitting before a fireplace with one's feet up.

However, no matter how you do it, you have to keep a steady focus on the problem, even if you're "sleeping on it." You don't need to lock yourself in a windowless room and have food shoved under the door; just do what works best for you. One of my clients, an individual who has written both fiction and nonfiction and whose works have been translated into half a dozen languages, is best able to focus while driving a car. Once she gives her mind the order to create, it begins to come. And, as I've said, don't hinder the flow by trying to direct it. Ideas don't like shackles.

Another factor that is common to successful creative people is that they consider all *options*. The options come only after all of the ideas drop—you can go back and analyze them and polish them and put the complete project together once you have all of the data. Again, first comes the flow of ideas; afterward you can judge and criticize them. You can do all that *after* the flow comes, but you can't do it while the flow is coming. That's the point of creativity. Criticism shuts down the flow.

Considering all of the options is the analytical part of creativity. It doesn't matter whether creative people are designing or modifying a product, painting a sunset or composing a presentation for a sales meeting, they approach a problem like a chess master analyzes a move, going deep to let the stream of ideas pour forth, seeing every possible option and only then making a move.

Often the answer to the problem, the key to just the right touch on the artist's canvas or the right approach in a management meeting, is reached after letting all of the ideas come, considering all of the options, dropping some, restructuring others, allowing more thoughts and ideas that are sparked by the ideas that already dropped. When you meditate or refocus on some of the ideas that have dropped, you will eventually see more ideas that in turn generate other ideas that in turn lead to a solution.

An image in the creative process, like other eidetic images, is a *holographic* projection, a three-dimensional experience, full of range and depth. The mind can conceive holographic images in succession where one nugget put forth has many more thoughts, ideas, and other creative bursts attached to it. Out of those, you pick one, two, or three, and again more creative ideas burst. So it's constantly letting the flow come, looking at the pieces, and refocusing on those.

In considering all of the options, we have to stretch our mind, looking at the problem from all directions. Sometimes there is a fine line between the ridiculous and the sublime and we have to walk that line, sometimes letting our imagination roam to the impossible and working our way back to the probable. Do not censor anything.

Taking the time to focus, place your intentionality on a problem, allowing the flow to come, not censoring it, taking the nuggets—the inspiration from the flow—considering the options by picking the ones we like best and allowing more flow to come. That is the creative process.

My dear Mr. Heifitz,
My wife and I were overwhelmed by your concert. If you continue to play with such beauty, you will certainly die young. No one can play with such perfection without evoking the jealousy of the gods. I earnestly implore you to play something badly every night before going to bed.

Letter from George Bernard Shaw to violinist Heifitz

29

The Waters of Creativity
Accessing the Primal Flow

"Images of Darkness and Light" are very exciting concepts that you have not been introduced to yet. In addition, the "Running Stream" Image is a wonderful tool for getting the creative juices to flow. We have used the running stream a number of times and with creativity it is used in three ways: (1) to unblock the creative flow, (2) to deal with specific issues or obstacles, and (3) to open ourselves up to let ideas pour out.

One of the most significant purposes of the images used with creativity is to relax your mind and open yourself up to the flow. The images help us make the connection to our inner spirit and help direct the flow by focusing it on our task.

Some of the work I have done with eidetics and creativity has been with employees of companies involved in designing products. At other times it has had a more individualized focus: working with a writer doing a book, or with a person conducting sales seminars. The process is the same for each. And it is a reasonably simple process regardless of what the objective is. The difference between what one person gains and what another gains is usually in the results since each has his or her own needs. But for most of us, the more we are able to concentrate and focus, giving direction to the stream, the deeper we tap into the spirit of creativity and the more the waters will flow.

It's vital to relax and not try to force the flow. When the flow doesn't come after a couple of sessions, go get a cup of coffee, pick the roses in your garden, call a friend and have a fun chat, or all of the above. Then when you are relaxed and centered again, come back to it.

IMAGES OF DARKNESS AND LIGHT

Imagination begins in the dark. Darkness is the primordial source of all creation. Isn't that how it was at the beginning before God divided the waters? In the beginning there was darkness and the spirit of God brought light to the waters.

It's in darkness that our imagination roams free, when we close our eyes and fall into the darkness of sleep, our dreams, the imagination of the night, come alive.

"Images of Darkness" is an eidetic imaging technique that I have used with great success with people who are responsible for creating and designing some of the world's most popular toys, items of fine apparel, and other products. The context of the activities is that the people and groups responsible for the creative flow of ideas that keep the products fresh and brilliant found themselves drying up creatively. The reason for the drying-up process seemed to be the inherent difficulties in working in a corporate environment in which there were too many demands and too much stress.

The exciting ideas are still there, but they are hard to access because the people who have to produce them have so many demands placed on them to be creative. The pressure to create is tied to a paycheck, and the financial pressure dries up their creative source. When the creative flow dries up, the creative person suffers "creative block."

I will show you how eidetics will extract those ideas in a steady stream. But before I take you through a self-imaging session, I am going to let you get a feel for the technique by briefly summarizing the basic steps as applied by others.

The first step in the process is to get relaxed. I often ask the subject to act and feel as if they are very, very sleepy. The idea is to get the person into a relaxed, almost drowsy state of mind to take away the tension they're experiencing from not producing. Tension tightens the body and cuts off the blood flow, not just to the muscles but also to the brain.

Next, the subject is told to see that they are in a very dark place, and to feel and experience the darkness. Some people have a fear of darkness, but as they go through the exercise they see that it is a place of deep rest and intuition, not an empty place, but one filled with richness. The subject walks through the darkness, feeling that they are engulfed in a source of creation, a place of beginnings.

The third phase is that in their mind's eye they reach out and open a window and see what is beyond the window. They are asked to experience and feel what is on the other side of the window. Commonly, a bright, rich, vivid image comes to mind when they look through the window.

Fourth, they go out and explore the place they see through the window of their mind. During the exploration many different images come. They are asked to breathe deeply as they explore, to let the ideas and thoughts come to them naturally, without straining to find them.

In experiencing the images people go from the "rational" place in their mind, where they are under pressure to perform, to a deep place within themselves, a quiet place where images and the ideas they carry flow naturally like water bubbling out of a spring.

What these people need is a way to open up their creativity that has been strangled by pressure from the demand to perform in schools or the work environment. Children are expected to think and produce in the classroom, but many of them are too nervous because of poor self-images instilled in them by their parents, peers, or insensitive and even insulting teachers, to allow the ideas to flow. Their brains tighten up with fear and they become inhibited, suppressed, and constrained.

With adults in the workplace, the constant pressures of making money, interacting with coworkers, cranking out production, meeting deadlines, putting on dog-and-pony shows for their bosses, takes the cutting edge off of their creative flow. When the creative flow starts to dry up, the person's self-doubts begin to grow; there is a diminished ability to trust one's own instincts and ideas.

But the creative block is all a façade. We are the same creative person we were when we started. We don't run out of ideas. There is a rich vein of primordial images that are always in our minds and accessible through eidetics. The Image of Darkness takes a person to that source, the place of darkness, and then opens the window to let the flow come back.

IMAGE OF DARKNESS

1. See yourself in total darkness, descending into a very dark space in which there is no light—a rich darkness, pitch black.
2. Feel yourself enveloped in the darkness and let a nourishing feeling of calm pass through you. Relax your body and your mind.
3. See that darkness is the source of all creation, that everything starts in darkness; it's rich and full, not empty.

4. Walk in the darkness, feeling the darkness, getting comfortable with it.
5. You can't see in the dark, so as you walk use your instincts to guide you. Your senses can't help you, so let your feelings and intuition guide you.
6. Walk in the darkness, guided by your intuition, with a feeling that you know things intuitively.
7. Let your feelings flow as you walk.
8. Now reach out and open a window.
9. Explore what is beyond the window.
10. Breathe freely and explore that place in an active way.
11. How do you feel about what you are seeing?

Images of Darkness is an eidetic tool that has a similar purpose as a creativity technique that was popular among Hollywood writers and directors in the early 1980s. The technique involved putting one's self into almost total isolation, eliminating the senses of sound, sight, touch, smell, and taste in order to free the mind to tackle creative projects.

"Isolation" was created through the use of a soundproof tank about the size of a coffin. With a few inches of body-temperature salt water at the bottom of the tank, a writer or director would lie in the tank naked as the salt water kept him afloat. The top would be closed and the person in the tank would be in utter darkness and complete silence. The whole effect, from the water temperature to the darkness and feeling of buoyancy, created a sensory-free environment. Creative juices flowed with the mind free of distractions.

As I recall, the tanks were called flotation tanks.

Although these "flotation tanks" failed commercially, the concept of freeing our minds of sensory distractions around us to open the door to that rich stream of creativity within us was important.

The Images of Darkness tool is a way of freeing the mind and letting the stream of creation flow. And it's a little more convenient than going down to the local isolation shop and climbing into something that resembles Dracula's coffin.

BRINGING LIGHT TO THE DARKNESS

Imagination begins in the darkness of our minds but just as the universe, the greatest creation of all, is filled with blackness, out of the black void come the stars and galaxies that excite and thrill us as much as whispered words of endearment or ecstatic poetic zeal. One of the ways of utilizing the powers that are released in our mind when we do Images of Darkness is to give our imagination a base from which the stream of creative images can surface. Just as God brought light to the dark world by illuminating the waters, we can use these waters to bring our ideas to light from the darkness.

We do this by "connecting" Images of Darkness to the Stream of Creativity.

We first go to the Images of Darkness, closing our eyes and relaxing our body and mind and seeing ourselves in a totally black room, a room filled with a warm richness. We open the window and explore what we see, asking ourselves how we feel about what we are experiencing.

Then, with the image in mind of what we have seen, and the insight we have gained from the revelatory experience, we see ourselves as a running stream, flowing, with what we found before us . . . and ask ourselves how we feel now.

What happens when we connect the darkness insights to the stream is that we gain more qualitative and quantitative information about the situation. It's similar to seeing an image of a person and getting meaning from that image . . . and then looking at the person's eyes, side of her/his face, seeing yourself through their eyes, and so forth.

The stream and darkness images are both dynamic creativity tools. Linking them together creates building blocks of information and enriches the meaning we gain from the images. The darkness opens our minds and the stream directs the flow.

One of the things I like about the darkness and stream tools is that they permit us to work at our own pace, in our own style, and to feel through things, bringing ideas to surface that are buried within us that are often a different kind of knowledge and approach than a more homogenized approach of an office or think-tank environment.

30

In Pursuit of Excellence

High Imaging in Sports and Executive Performance

Mark McGwire leads the major leagues in home runs, and in blank stares. Visualization, he calls it. Before each at-bat McGwire will imagine the pitcher throwing the baseball. He will imagine how the pitch will move, maybe a fastball or a curveball, and he will imagine smashing the ball with his Paul Bunyon swing.

Reported in *The New York Times*
(before McGwire broke the home run record)

People who succeed physically as well as mentally—athletes, dancers, runners, and entertainers—are imbued with feelings and states of inspiration that are deeply personal to them. Some athletes, however, are not aware of what inspires them to excel, while others utilize the sources of their inspiration to motivate and propel themselves to enormous feats of achievement. These athletes can typically cite dramatic examples of the deepest kinds of personal inspiration. Take Eamonn Coghlan, for example, the longtime Irish world champion, who in 1994 topped his career off by becoming the first person over forty to run the mile in under four minutes.

Similarly, in 1983, through sheer inspiration, Coghlan became the first person to run under 3:50 in the indoor mile. He broke the record shortly after the death of his father and both his boyhood and college coaches. In visiting their gravesites before the race, he came upon a newly inscribed epitaph on his coach's gravestone. It read: "Don't quit until you're beaten; fight back to an even greater victory, not only in competition but in life."

This filled Coghlan with passion and a sense of mission. He plucked some grass from the grave, which he carried into the race, and went on to achieve one of the great records in track and field.

In the journey of life that we are all on, many of us seek to find the greatest fulfillment by mastering life, either in our personal or professional lives. Deep inside each of us, at our core, resides what I call an

"Inner Athlete," whose passion moves us to be the best we can be, with an intuitive belief that there is more to be experienced—more success, more power, more love, and more fulfillment. For most of us the core contains untapped potentials, skills and God-given talents.

That mastery is available to each of us whether we are interested in improving our tennis game, enhancing our proficiency at work, having a better relationship, helping our child excel at soccer, or just improving our mind and body through exercise routines such as running or working out at the gym. The opportunity to achieve a mastery of life exists in every one of us. The greatest achievers possess genetic talent, for sure, but it's their tremendous passion and desire *in* the pursuit of personal excellence that fuels their greatest performance.

The methods for tapping into the Inner Athlete are available for everyone. By utilizing the tools from the playing fields of psychology and sports, each person can bridge the gap between their potential and their performance, and can uncover their innate, natural ability. Eidetic imaging is the tool that can achieve this end because it links the mind, emotions, and body into one unified force.

A great illustration of accessing the "inner athlete" is the story of John, a corporate executive who wanted to excel and be at the top of his career. He had just received a big promotion and was given added responsibilities, money, and perks. He was thrilled; however, part of his new responsibilities included public speaking, which terrified him. To over come his fear, he decided to take public speaking lessons from a well-known agency. While he received helpful advice which included how to dress, how to stand, make eye contact with a friendly person in the audience and how to use breathing techniques to relax, he realized that inwardly he was still afraid.

He needed to find an inner confidence that would naturally overcome his fear of speaking, not "techniques" that he had to think about. He tried eidetics and found mind-body images that holistically mobilized his energies into ease and confidence as he spoke publicly.

At first he was asked to see an image of himself delivering a speech. In the image he saw that he froze before the audience. He noticed that his heart was held in and it seemed to almost stop beating. He was so tense that he could barely speak.

He was then asked to remember a time in his childhood when his heart was beating strongly with natural excitement and exuberance, an instruction to bring out his natural "high." An image suddenly popped into his mind and he saw himself as a child playing baseball in a little league game. He was up at bat and as he swing, he saw that he hit the ball into center field. He heard the cheering of his teammates and shouts of "run, run, run." He was thrilled, filled with elation; his heart was beating strongly as he ran. Excitement, exuberance, elation coursed through him while seeing the image. He realized that this was his natural high. He had experienced this high before—when he asked his wife to marry him, when he learned to fly an airplane, when he was promoted at work. It was familiar to him when breakthrough-exciting things happened.

Once he experienced his natural high, he was asked to see himself swinging the bat, to feel the high in his body, and to see his heart beating strongly all at the same time. As he saw the image he felt power, excitement, and energy filling him. With this sense of power he was instructed, "Now see yourself giving a speech. Giving a speech is like making a really good hit. See yourself swing the bat, your heartbeat comes forward, let the good swinging feeling of the bat come forward and flow into giving your speech."

He responded, "I see that I have the bat in my hand and I see my heart beating. I swing the bat powerfully. I feel good, confident, powerful. I see myself give a speech. I feel good, strong. I swing the bat. I give the speech. I feel the 'high.' The excitement of swinging the bat is transferring to giving a speech. I can see that they are the same thing, the same potent expression of me."

He practiced this image before his first big speech and reported, "I gave a speech and I practiced the image many times before speaking. When I got up there I surprised myself. There was a tremendous physical feeling which I experienced that came over me in the middle of the speech. I was exhilarated in a way I had not known before. I was relaxed, my heart was beating strongly, and I spoke right from my heart and gut. All the energies I needed were right there and I did great. I mastered my fear and am at the next level of my own personal achievement!"

By bringing back the image of hitting the baseball, he reconnected to a high state of natural exuberance. Adding the heartbeat helped him to focus his power and added physical potency to his ability.

DISCOVERING OUR INNER SPACE

Another helpful part of the eidetic imaging process for success is to discover one's inner space. We are all naturally anxious before the "big game," the sports event, business meeting, job interview, first date, etc. But we have to prepare our mental and emotional spaces so they do not cloud our minds and our actions when we need *everything* we have to perform our best. A calm, concentrated, and rested mind that gives us a feeling of supreme confidence deep within is critical for performance. The Physical Preparation Image, at the end of the next chapter, is a tool to attain this calm state of mind.

High states of physical and mental performance come after we empty ourselves of images of our "history" and get into that eidetic-like state. When our history is unloaded from our back, our genetic energies and powers can come to the fore.

The tools for pursuing excellence are available to us. It is through these eidetic images that science has gained access to our great brain with its complex, ongoing mind-body flow, so that it's now possible to bring forward our best mental, emotional, and physical states. Just like the man giving the speech, through these images we can transform weakness into strength, fear to courage, self-doubt to self-confidence— all from the core of the inner self where our genetic powers lie.

Positive states of well-being and relaxation, and high states of inspiration, are our genetic birthright and provide us with an energetic approach to life. High states are imbued with a spirit of exuberance and imagination, frequently associated with experiences in childhood. These states are often lost due to the demands of adult daily living. For attaining success, these high states, or "expectation highs" that gear us up before the big event and sweep us to victory must be retrieved.

Eidetic imaging can help us not only discover our "high" states but also find what keeps us stuck. For instance, it can be used as a precise diagnostic tool that reveals specific areas of difficulty in performance. Through imagery testing, such as the Vosi Test (at the end of Chapter 31), it is possible to accurately pinpoint the origins of our problematic physical, mental, and emotional obstructions as we compete, perform at work, or physically exercise. Once these are found, they may be overcome with the many tools available to us.

Through the three parts of the eidetic, (I) the image that you see, (S) your somatic or bodily response, and (M) the meaning you gain from the image, a congruent flow of unified body-mind potentials, where you feel in the zone, can be achieved.

The images are not simply a mechanistic training but a deeply holistic one. Rather than using forced training techniques applied by someone telling you what to do or how to do it, its main gift to you is that it lets you access deep, inspired abilities to perform, arising from your own innate knowledge. It also puts your body and mind together so that you are not struggling with tremendous effort.

Very few of us are going to break the four-minute mile, but the mind-body, eidetic-like state in which we can put ourselves to fuel our physical performance with our mind is illustrated by a technique used by a recreational runner, who, without even knowing it, utilizes a technique practiced by lamas for centuries in Tibet, land of mystery and magic.

The connection between the modern runner who keeps trim and fit running but who isn't out to win any world records, and the ancient rite practiced by the lamas, came to me when I heard a runner describing how he had to condition his mind and body to give him maximum stamina with the least possible energy output.

"I always have an image of water," the runner told me. "It's a place I go to for strength and power." Images of water. Remember the "waters of God" we talked about in the section on creativity, that stream of primordial energy that we can tap into with imaging?

"I see myself running," he said, "a very long run. But I am not on hard ground but on a stream; no, actually it's like I am the stream and the water is rejuvenating me as I run, recharging me. The water for me is a place of energy. I see water glowing with different shades of light, of sunshine and brightness, as well as a serene peace to it. I go to the water for strength and power. It's a very calming state."

The runner is connecting through his mind's eye to the image of the stream and riding the energy of the stream much like a sailboat is pushed along by a fresh breeze.

I emphasized the word calming because to people not initiated in the mind-body connection, exercise and running, as well as any sport, are very strenuous activities that put our mind and body into a stressed and stimulated state. But what this runner is telling us is that peak performance for his activity is to make a connection to the stream and flow with it in a calming state. It is that calming effect that will give him the stamina to endure, to make his legs and arms fluid so that they feel lighter and looser.

There was another sensation that the runner experienced that was significant—breathing. The pacing of his heart and lungs were regulated by the sensation of a drumbeat and the sound of the wind as he exhaled.

Often it is the beat of the heart that the mind connects to. When you put the heart and imagination together, you get into a high state. When you add heartbeat to the image, you are focusing your power.

As I mentioned above, the mind-body connection is not a new phenomena and what the runner has tapped into is a technique used since ancient times by Tibetan mystics. In Tibet, the technique is called *lung-gom* and its practice was revealed to us by one of the most daring and fascinating women of the past century, a woman who walked on the Roof of the World, yet is almost forgotten by history.

Alexandra David-Neel was over forty years old back before World War I, yet she had the courage to leave behind an ordinary life and take on one of the most dangerous and adventurous trips ever accomplished by a woman. She trekked from China to India crossing hundreds of miles of Tibet. To understand the sheer courage and determination of this "forty-something" woman, you have to appreciate that Tibet is a *three-mile-high* plateau filled with savage badlands and raging storms. The mountains that ring it, of which Mt. Everest is the queen, are often as high as the Rocky Mountains . . . stacked atop the Swiss Alps. When she made the journey by foot and horse early in this century, there were no trains, planes, or automobiles; there were not even roads!

Alexandra was a superb reporter of the culture of Tibet and returned to Europe to write about her travels and the "mystery and magic" of Tibet. (Margaret Mead, the great anthropologist, incorporated substantial portions of Alexandra's findings in one of her own studies of primitive cultures.) Alexandra spent fourteen years in Tibet and became the first Western woman to be made a Tibetan lama.

In her travels she made an intense and very scientific study of those strange and exotic techniques we call the "tantric arts." She observed Tibetan ascetics and mystics who were able to sit naked in snow and maintain their body temperature, but among the most curious phenomena she's observed were lamas who were able to walk at a high speed for days on end, covering great distances without rest. (You can imagine how valuable this feat must have been in a country where feet and pack animals were the only modes of transportation.)

The first time she saw a *lung-gom* walker moving along in fluid motion she described his feet as if having wings. She investigated the phenomena and found that control of their breathing created by intense concentration and silently chanting gave the walkers stamina. They fixed their eyes on a distant object and then concentrated as they walked, opening themselves up to a stream of energy.

It was startling to see that the *lung-gom* walkers had "perfectly calm" features and a peaceful look to their faces, even when climbing hills. They regulated their breathing with their chant, much the way our runner paced his with the drums of thunder he heard. Alexandra described the physical affect on the walkers as a kind of anesthesia. That anesthesia is of course the physiological effect on the body when the mind-body connection is made by the Tibetan walkers and the American jogger. (The brain generates chemicals for the body to create the anesthetic affect.)

Modern sports stars describe the sensation of opening one's self up to that stream of effortless energy and power as "being in the zone." The zone is available in one degree or another to all of us. People who are exceptionally successful are able to put themselves into a high state of sustained concentration, sometimes with trancelike qualities, a mind-body connection. And it's not limited to sports and other physical activities; salespeople do it, trial lawyers in front of a jury do it, I do it when I am in front of an audience.

It's available to all of us once we learn how to tap it. The mind-body connection is both physical and mental. The images we see are stored in our brains and trigger neurological, chemical, and electric signals that flow to the body. When negative images from our history come up in our minds we get knee-jerk responses that keep us from succeeding. With some simple techniques we can turn the knee-jerk responses into positive responses that make us winners.

When you have attained the positive mind-body connection through an image, the feeling inside you is exhilarating, as if every cell in your body is alive and your nervous system is one-on-one with your mind, creating a peak performance state.

It is these exuberant, surpassing, inner mental states that create the winning edge for an athlete and propel his or her body beyond normal human capacity. These qualities of the Spirit—of being one with one's self—are exactly what creates success; it's the fuel driving the passion to exceed beyond what's imaginable. But it *is* imaginable and possible for all of us through imagery.

Through specific sets of images, people may clearly see how to access energies for excelling that already exist within them, and avoid those that hinder their most potent capabilities.

The techniques and their applications are useful for anyone who exercises or engages in any physical activity—running, walking, aerobics, basketball, baseball, bowling, soccer, golf, tennis, dancing, and a host of other physical activities.

Imagery research over the past quarter century has demonstrated that eidetic images send neural signals from the brain to the body's nerves and muscles, affecting not just our emotional and mental states but our physical body as well. Inside our mind exists a hologram of vast information about life. Our brains are incredibly sensitive, powerful, and complex machines that regulate and affect the functioning of our bodies and the equilibrium of our physical, mental, and emotional states. It is now widely accepted in scientific communities that the body and mind are indelibly interconnected and researchers have concluded that there is no distinct separation between the two. In fact, body and mind, with their mysterious and subtle links, are indeed one uninterrupted flow of back-and-forth chemical and neurological signals.

Researchers have also established that it is not only our genetics but also our developmental history that can enhance or thwart our genetic abilities. Think of the child of an athlete, who inherited the genetic capacity to excel, but who was criticized by his father every time he threw a baseball. The child ends up afraid to make mistakes, begins to lack confidence, and his natural throwing ability is impacted negatively.

The experience of criticism by his father becomes imprinted in his brain in the form of a mental image, which affects his ability to play with joy and self-confidence. As he becomes an adult, he may consciously forget the youthful incidents of criticism from his father. Yet, even though he forgets, his brain remembers. Every time he throws a ball, the negative image is activated as a signal from the brain and he experiences a negative feeling of self-criticism that obstructs his throwing.

Conversely, a child who is given positive messages, such as "You can do it," will trust in his natural abilities and feel confidence.

The young baseball player might not consciously remember his father's criticism every time he threw a ball when he was young, but in adulthood his brain will replay those critical images, and in an automatic manner beyond his volitional control affect forever the way he throws a ball. His body will respond as if his father is right there criticizing him. He will feel a vague sense come over him of not being good enough, an anxious feeling will begin in his chest, and a shakiness in his throwing arm will happen automatically.

However, he can isolate the historical triggers in his brain that unconsciously impede his performance and find his natural genetic capacity.

Do we all have a genetic ability? Of course, we do. We may not all be genetically engineered to win Olympic Gold, but every person can improve the quality of their everyday life by going deep within and finding the basic gifts that will stir them to bring out their most potent abilities.

In a way, our genetic imprinting is analogous to the seed of an oak tree. The tree's seed is innately programmed to be a magnificent, large, and vibrant tree. It is planted in the ground, and as it grows acid rain (father's criticisms, accidents, emotional trauma) falls on it. It ends up being a shabby replica of the original intention nature had for it. We humans suffer the same fate as that oak tree. Our natural gifts are often disturbed by the events of the history of our lives. However, when cared for properly and given pure, clear water, the tree restores itself and regains its original capacities; new leaves and branches spring forth. We are part of nature the same as the tree. With the right "nourishment" we too can regain our natural genetic capacities.

For more in-depth information on the clinical and experimental applications of imagery and sports, read Dr. Ahsen's article, "Imagery in Sports, General Performance and Executive Excellence," in the *Journal of Mental Imagery*, referenced in the Bibliography of this book.

HIGH IMAGING: THE SWEET SMELL OF WINNING

Even though the knowledge of one's developmental imagery (childhood images that help or hinder us) is critical in actualizing one's effectiveness, there is another avenue that accesses *extraordinary* mind-body states. These inherent states are truly our "gifts of the gods" and are known as "High Imagery."

High Imagery brings to the surface our most striking and potent abilities, which aid in going beyond the influences that have limited us. For the athletic performer, these are strong tools that unify mind, emotions, and body for enhanced performance, providing access to a profound synchronized mastery of the mind and body.

While High Imaging is being used here in a sports and physical activities context, it obviously is a factor in almost any area of life where there is a pursuit of excellence. In terms of nonphysical areas, I am often reminded of an image that motivated Oprah Winfrey to excel past normal expectations. As a girl, she saw Sidney Poitier get out of a limousine to go to the ceremonies at which he was awarded the Oscar for Best Actor. The knowledge that a Black man received the highest honor of the Academy of Motion Pictures, Arts and Sciences fired her own ambitions, motivating her to reach deeply into her own "gifts of the gods" to excel.

It is interesting that Oprah's girlhood image of Sidney Poitier survived into adulthood. Too often our very first impression of what we want to do and the success that we want to attain gets quashed. "I want to be president," the child says. And Mommy says, "You can't be president." And guess what? There is now a damper on that young girl's aspiration to be president.

Our perception, especially our *self*-perception, determines almost everything about us. I can look at someone and feel threatened. Or look at Sidney Poitier on the stage accepting an Oscar and feel like I can leap tall buildings. Images are vehicles that change perception when introduced into the mind.

When you have an image in your mind that shifts your perception and brings you into a positive state of mind, you get the will and determination to excel. Images function like keys that open hidden mental and attitudinal powers within us. They provide illumination, direction, and power that emerge from deep within us.

We've all seen pictures of that state of incredible, frenzied ecstasy a whirling dervish can achieve by using his mind to generate adrenaline. In a similar matter, all of us can energize our will power to motivate ourselves to succeed. World-class athletes use images to get a rush of adrenaline and other body chemicals to supercede in their performances.

Images used by athletes are usually of a visual nature, but following the visual image and its body response, other bodily senses can be brought into play.

In his studies of the phenomena of increasing performance, putting ourselves into a High Imaging state by using other senses, Dr. Ahsen found that imagery experience during athletic activity operates in a *multisensory* manner—sometimes High Imagery is accessed through a *visual image and at other times with the addition of other senses*. The studies show that our olfactory sense of *smell*, when brought into play with the sense of vision, can greatly enhance results.

Ahsen's studies found that the sensation of imaging a smell associated with the sport can mentally *reduce the distance* between the *participant* and the *target*. For example, a baseball pitcher normally only relies on his sense of vision from him to his target, the catcher's glove. But when the pitcher images the smell of the leather in the catcher's glove, it brings the target closer to him. The same findings are true in studies with archery (smelling the target), golf (smelling the cup), and other sports.

What the sense of smell does is make another *sensory connection* between you and the target.

A tournament-winning golfer described the procedure as follows. "I paused on the green to make a putt. I closed my eyes and saw in my mind's eye the distance from the ball to the cup. I saw myself swinging the club, it coming into contact with the ball, and the ball rolling to the cup."

At this point he is using visual imaging. Now she adds a sense of smell to the image. "Next, I again imaged the cup visually, but I also imaged smelling the cup. It has a moist, earthy smell. Keeping the smell in mind, I mentally made the shot again." Keeping visual contact while making a visual-olfactory connection between the shot and ball improved the golfer's game.

The smelling image can be applied to any sport. For example, in pitching a ball in the game of baseball, one needs to smell the target, in this case the catcher's glove. However, in baseball the olfactory aspect is more complicated because there are two smell signals that need addressing. One is the catcher's glove into which the ball is aimed and the other is the batter's bat that needs to be avoided and passed through. The pitcher has to reconcile the two smells.

Rick Peterson, the pitching coach who has used these images, finds the rich smell of glove leather to be a powerful stimulus. The ball is also leather and he sees the two pieces, the glove and the ball, being attracted to each other like magnets.

Dr. Ahsen's study of an archer demonstrated a dramatic increase even in an archer hitting the target with arrows when the archer imaged smelling the target.

The imaging procedure for adding the *olfactory sense* to physical activity is (after relaxing your mind and getting yourself centered):

SMELL IMAGE

1. See that you are playing at a sport where there is a target or goal (basketball, pitching, soccer, golf, hockey, archery, etc).

2. See an image that you are ready to aim or shoot at the target/goal.
3. See that you are aiming/shooting at the target/goal while you are only visually looking at it.
4. What happens as you see this image?
5. Now see that you aim at the target while you are visually looking at it and also while smelling the target at the same time. Imagine an olfactory connection with the visual target/goal.
6. What happens as you see this image? As a result the target/goal comes closer.
7. Notice that you become closer to the target/goal when you add the smell.

(Note: Runners can also use smell to enhance their run. They need to smell the end of the line when the run is over.)

REHEARSING TO WIN

As Mark McGwire's philosophy illustrates, rehearsal can be a critical element of winning in sports. I pointed out in the section on careers that top performers in business and the arts "rehearse" their performances, whether it's giving a presentation or negotiating a deal. The most effective people rehearse their strategies for success. Prior to the event, they do a full mental dress rehearsal, seeing all the elements they will face. They play the entire game, play by play, in their mind's eye, seeing their whole performance, the flow of the game, and experience the thrill of the excitement.

The most successful people in all walks of life know that talent alone does not equal performance. Even more, we know from experience that it is possible to outperform one's preparation. The greats know that there are no short cuts and are willing to pay a high price to succeed. The truly successful know that *preparation* equals performance.

PUTTING YOUR HEART INTO IT

The feeling in the heart, where joy resides, is also where the passion resides that motivates us. When joy and exuberance are shut down, we cannot attain our goals. We stop believing success is possible and, slowly, our dreams die. To rejuvenate the passion for our performance in the world, the *whole* heart must be brought back to life so that we can perform from the depths of our *whole* heart and soul. The heart-drumming image at the end of the next chapter brings our heart to our performance.

When we do images, whether it is using our parents as filters to assess the sources of our blocks and inspiration, or to connect our mind with the smell of a catcher's leather glove, in a sense we are preparing and rehearsing for the "big game."

SILENCING THAT VOICE OF DEFEAT WITHIN US

True champions see problems and obstacles as new opportunities to perform to their fullest potential. Eidetic images are effective tools with which to identify problems and obstacles and discover creative new ways to use these obstacles as steppingstones to success.

In the next chapter we will use imaging exercises to see and concretize obstacles to our best performance, finding and overcoming those knee-jerk reactions that limit our performance. To succeed we need to silence the critical voice and understand and face our inner oppressors. We will then do imagery exercises to find our inner power, to overcome the past limitations, and unleash our genetic gifts from within.

31

Excelling by Silencing the Critical Voice

I have worked closely with Rick Peterson, a former professional pitcher, presently pitching coach for the Oakland A's. Rick has coached, worked with, and has been associated with some of the best athletes in the world from Olympic gold medalists to several Cy Young winners, and Most Valuable Players in baseball and basketball.

A remarkable success story on tapping potential is relayed through the progress of former White Sox pitcher Wilson Alvarez (who went on to play for the Tampa Devil Rays). Wilson's major league debut was with the Texas Rangers in which he failed to retire even one hitter, leaving the game in the first inning with no outs. He had setbacks over the next couple of years after being traded to the White Sox. Through intense training using imagery, in which the three parts of the eidetic were utilized (the image, somatic response, and meaning), Wilson restructured his attitudes and habits, preparing himself for success. The type of imagery tool he used involved the act of performing a movement of skill with his eyes closed, using his mental camera to link the image with the feeling of the movement in his mind's eye. This is a powerful tool to enhance performance.

Wilson returned to the major leagues with the White Sox two years later and pitched a no-hitter against the Baltimore Orioles. After establishing himself as a major league pitcher for more than two years, he experienced yet another setback, losing his confidence and going six weeks without a win. He was sent back to the minors to be reunited with his former teacher, Rick Peterson. Wilson went through a brief, intense refresher course to strengthen his attitudes and habits to rebuild his confidence. Wilson returned to the major leagues ten days later and began a fourteen-game consecutive winning streak, including a win in the American League Players Championship Game.

"Every time I talk to Rick Peterson, he makes me feel good."

White Sox Pitcher Wilson Alvarez, on his longtime coach,

after pitching a no-hitter

Rick has actively studied the biomechanics of pitching at the American Sports Medicine Institute. He studied applied psychology at Rutgers University in a graduate program, cowriting workbooks and manuals as well as producing audiotapes on performance enhancement. He produced the instructional video "Mastering the Fundamentals of Pitching Mechanics," with Florida Marlins' pitcher Alex Fernandez.

Rick uses eidetic imagery to enhance the performance of amateur and professional athletes, after working with me and utilizing imaging techniques originally developed by Dr. Ahsen.

"Rick Peterson molds minds."

Larry Monroe, Chicago White Sox Baseball Executive

I asked Rick how he uses eidetics in enhancing the performance of the people he coaches.

"If we want to see where the person is in terms of coaching them, and that's the beginning, we would do the House Image and the Left/Right Parental imagery dynamics because we would know if the person has an inversion and is going to have a problem with their play. People with inversions (mother on the left and father on the right) may have a problem because one parent has become more dominant in the psyche and they may be drawing the gifts of only one parent for success. This often produces an internal mechanism that will get in the way in that they can't get their energy out fully, or it gets sabotaged. Overcoming this is done subtly and informally, working with an athlete's thoughts and feelings."

For more discussion about inversions, see page 47.

Rick is talking about how the people who shaped us—our parents, teachers, and coaches—have left an indelible mark on us. One thing a coach will want to do is find out what negative triggers are in his players. It doesn't matter if it is a Little League player or a major league MVP—the name of the game in every sport and at every level is to keep improving. We've all experienced the criticism of a dominating figure in our life, possibly a parent, a sibling, a teacher, a coach, or a teammate from a peer group. It is difficult to perform, constantly hearing the echo of a critical voice. A simple process silences that voice, and allows us to hear the cheers from our spirit.

"That critical voice from the past has to be dealt with," Rick says, "with compassion and forgiveness. Through imaging we have to change that voice into a voice that will elicit a positive response from the player. If you fail to change the voice, it will sabotage the player's effort. We need to change the mind-body connection, redirect the electronic impulses going from the brain to the physical body so that positive images feed positive muscular responses. It literally amounts to rewiring the mind-body connection."

An example of eidetic imaging that leads to "rewiring" the mind-body connection concerns a college basketball player who seemed to have everything going to become a championship-level player, but he tightened up under pressure.

His first image was to see his parents. He saw his mother on the right, his father on the left. Next, he saw himself making a three-point jump shot on a crowded basketball court from thirty feet back *while keeping mother in mind* (i.e., using his mother as a filter).

He saw himself rise high above the other players, his arms go up, the ball lifting off, sailing across the court to drop in the net. His psyche's eye saw his mother watching him off to the side, a smile of encouragement on her face. "I felt her support and passion. She was always there for me, encouraging me, telling me I was good enough to make it. When I see her I feel like the ball in my hand is connected to the basket, like I'm connected to both of them."

Next he again saw himself trying to make the same shot, only this time *keeping his father in mind*.

"I knew instantly that it was going to be different. My dad was so damn nervous about everything I did that he made me nervous. It was always so important for him that I win. When I missed a shot he would talk about it for days, drive me crazy. He made me feel bad, like I wasn't good enough if I missed a shot. Suddenly every shot of the game became something vital, blown out of all proportion. His nervousness got me nervous!"

He never doubted his father's love for him. "When I touched my mom's body in the image it was warm, and so was my dad's. I know they both loved me and that my dad really loved me as much as my mom, but, man, he just got under my skin with that thing about having to be perfect. *Nobody's* perfect."

What he learned from imaging is that when he was in a tense situation, the nervous, disapproving image of his father surfaced, triggering an emotional response and an electronic neural jump from his mind to his body, causing his body to tighten just enough to take the sharp edge off his shots.

The insight he obtained from the images were that while playing he was having negative, knee-jerk responses triggered by his father, and that he needed to "rewire" the images that sent failure signals to his body when the going got tough.

This happens in all arenas of performance. I worked with a thirteen-year-old soccer player whose father apparently thought he was the Vince Lombardi of teen soccer. When the young soccer player saw an image of her playing while her father watched, she folded under the imaginary demanding shouts of her father.

Not all images of one's parents are going to be negative. As I mention earlier, Rick Peterson was a professional athlete who has coached professional athletes. He shared the following images of himself running while keeping his mother in mind, and then his father.

Running and keeping mother in mind:

"I can feel her compassion and understanding. She has a very calming affect on me, a very warm sensation. It doesn't seem to matter what I'm doing, I sense the strength to keep going. I see the sun setting as I run and there is an eternal peace around me."

Running and keeping father in mind:

"I feel a strong will, a strong pace at the start, although it's difficult to keep up. There's a strong will and determination that the pace must be kept up and the run has to be finished. There's no slacking or backing off, I can feel the power and the determination that the pace has to be kept up."

I told him to keep his father in mind and feel that strong will and determination, to be aware of his body, and asked him what sensations he was experiencing.

"Deep inside, I feel it in my heart, it's a feeling of thunder, thunder in my heart and lungs, there's this thunderous beat that has to be kept up with."

"Now keep your mother in mind while you run," I said to him. "How do you feel?"

"It's an overwhelmingly serene feeling, a serene peaceful feeling, as if I'm immersed in warm water, wrapped in a blanket; it's a sensation that overwhelms my entire being, the feeling I've experienced relaxing in front of a fire."

Rick Peterson is currently a coach and teacher in the major leagues. Is it any surprise that he would have positive images in which his parents come across as positive forces for success? That his images have a spiritual quality to them, evidencing that he operates on a very, very deep level in his profession, that he has a finely tuned mind-body connection with golden wiring from his brain to his body? Rick has tapped deep into those waters of inspiration and determination to develop his gifts. All great performers who tap into their inner images have been able to reconnect the mind/body wiring to its fullest potentials. They practice daily to keep it connected. It is hard to image any world-class athlete who hasn't. By the same token, no matter how great an athlete is, to excel, break a record, or go for the gold like Sarah Hughes, 2002 Olympic women's figure skating gold medal winner, they are constantly working to improve themselves and silence the negative triggers that hamper their performance.

As Rick puts it, "Imaging helps me gain a perspective about myself and see where my strengths and weaknesses are. Players I coach need this too, to go deep to their sources of energy, the source of light within them, and reprogram the wiring of the mind-body connection allowing the light within to shine its brightest."

The bodily response you experience and the meaning that provides insight will be highly personal. To quote Rick, "Guiding a player to become their own best coach is really what it's all about."

• That "light" Rick talks about reminds me of a metaphoric image of glorious illumination which Dr. Ahsen uses to describe that source of high energy and ecstatic power within us: that within each of us is a beautiful cut diamond that has the power and potential to illuminate the being to its greatest achievements. Dr. Ahsen has called it "glorious serotonin."

What he is saying is that when our genetic imprinting gets tarnished by all the negatives that dull it, we can go within and get that diamond to send up a powerful beam of light. Once found, positive chemicals flow into our bodies. Rick Peterson and other successful athletes have a very bright diamond within them.

We all have a diamond within that we need to reach to let the glow of our spirit connect to our physical, mental, and emotional energies and potentials.

Through images like the ones below: "Sports Action with Filters," "Success Assessment Image with Filters: Vosi Test," and "Left/Right Position of Parents," athletes and others involved in strenuous physical activities can perceive the play of energies within their bodies by seeing how the images of their mother and father function to help or hinder them. Through the "Physical Preparation Image," "Heart Drumming

Image," "Swimming in the Running Stream with Competitors Image," and the "High Sports Image," athletes and others may access their most potent and glorious genetic abilities.

PHYSICAL PREPARATION IMAGE

This image gets you prepared to do physical events by putting you in a calm and relaxed state of mind with intentionality directed toward the upcoming activity.

1. See that you come into an empty place. This empty place is where your energies come together.
2. See that you are preparing to launch out.
3. Concentrate on this feeling of coming together in this empty place and getting ready for the activity.
4. See that your energies are coming together.
5. See that you are getting ready.
6. See that you are going to launch out.
7. See that you will do the impossible.

PARENTS' LEFT/RIGHT POSITION IMAGE

1. Picture your parents standing directly in front of you.
2. As you see them, who is standing on your left and who is standing on your right?
3. Now try to switch their positions. Are you able to switch them?
4. Notice any difficulty or discomfort when you switch them.
5. Now see your parents standing in front of you again.
6. Who is standing on the left and who is standing on the right now?
7. Switch your parents' position again.
8. Do you again experience a problem when you switch them?
9. Notice the two different feelings: spontaneous and forced.
10. Notice that you have no control over your parents' spontaneous images.

Sports Assessment Images: Vosi Test

The following is an image similar to the sixteen-element Success Assessment we used in the careers section, only this one is geared toward sports and other physical activities. In assessing our performance, we use parental filters.

1. See yourself thinking of the event.
   Keep mother in mind while you are thinking of the event.
   Keep father in mind while you are thinking of the event.
   Is there a difference in your feelings when you keep a different parent in mind?
2. See yourself preparing for an activity or physical event.
   Keep mother in mind while you are thinking of the event.
   Keep father in mind while you are thinking of the event.
   Is there a difference in your feelings when you keep a different parent in mind?
3. See yourself during the activity, experiencing the event.
   Keep mother in mind while you are thinking of yourself having success.
   Keep father in mind while you are thinking of yourself having success.
   Is there a difference in your feelings when you keep a different parent in mind?
4. See yourself improving in an area in which you need work.
   Keep mother in mind while you are thinking of the task.
   Keep father in mind while you are thinking of the task.
   Is there a difference in your feelings when you keep a different parent in mind?
5. See yourself being applauded for your achievement.
   Keep mother in mind while you are being applauded for your achievement.
   Keep father in mind while you are being applauded for your achievement.
   Is there a difference in your feelings when you keep a different parent in mind?

HEART DRUMMING IMAGE

This heartbeat image can be used when engaging in any sport or physical activity (running, dance, soccer, etc).

1. Remember, your heartbeat becomes stronger during physical performance.
2. Now feel your heartbeat and see that it pumps stronger.
3. See that you can hear the drumming of your heart. There is imagination in this heartbeat. As your heart beats, it goes in rhythm with your imagination.
4. See yourself performing and let the heart beat.
5. You become stronger, your performance is more pleasurable and easier to release.
6. How does your performance change when you add the image of your heart?

SWIMMING IN THE RUNNING STREAM IMAGE— TEAMMATES AND COMPETITORS

This image permits us to compare and contrast our teammates; not just with ourselves, but each other. In your mind's eye, take a competing player through the image. If you have teammates, next take them through the image. The way they handle the stream indicates how they handle situations in the game.

1. See yourself as a running stream. See that running stream that you are.
2. See your competitor (or teammate) swimming in the running stream.
3. Watch how they swim.
4. How are they swimming (fast, slow, easily, or with difficulty, aggressive, just flowing with the current, etc.)?
5. How do you feel as you see the image?
6. What meaning or insight do you gain about them as you see the image?

SPORTS ACTION WITH FILTERS IMAGE

1. See yourself involved in a physical activity (tennis, golf, basketball, jogging, bicycling, etc.).
2. Perform an action in regard to that activity (hit the ball, jog, pedal the bike, lift weights, etc.).
3. As you perform the action, keep your father in mind. What do you see? How does it affect your performance?
4. As you perform the action, keep your mother in mind. What do you see? How does it affect your performance?

The object of performing a physical activity while using your parents as "filters" is to assess where we have blocks to our performance. We may also tap into power and enhanced ability. In most cases, we are not getting full strength from both parents.

HIGH SPORTS IMAGE

1. See an image of performing in an athletic activity you enjoy.
2. See what you love about it, what makes you high as you do it.
3. Let this high feeling envelop you. Feel it in your body.
4. Let it get you high.
5. This is the passion in your performance.
6. See that you perform with this high feeling. This is the power in you.

HIGH EXECUTIVE PERFORMANCE IMAGE FOR PEOPLE IN BUSINESS

There is no difference between sports and executive performance, as I said in the beginning of the previous chapter. Where the executive overcame his fear of speech making by using his childhood images of playing baseball, you may use all the above image instructions by replacing the word "sports" with the specific area of executive performance and skill required. For instance, I have rewritten the above exercise for executive performance by changing just one word.

1. See an image of performing in an executive activity you enjoy.
2. See what you love about it, what makes you high as you do it.
3. Let this high feeling envelop you. Feel it in your body.
4. Let it get you high.
5. This is the passion in your performance.
6. See that you perform your executive duties with this high feeling. This is the power in you.

32

Images at the Periphery
Moving Around the Roadblocks of Life

Sometimes we're so stuck, so blocked by a person or a problem that we feel completely hopeless. We image the situation but the answer as to how to deal with it just doesn't come. The block could be to our creative juices, to a situation involving a romantic relationship or something at work. Going to the *periphery* of an image, the information found on the edges of the image, rather than focusing on the center of it, can often break the blockage.

For many years, imagery researchers felt that the only important part of the image was the central part; that all the action was in the center. There is a therapy in which you focus solely on the central part of the image and the bodily response that it gives you. However, Dr. Ahsen discovered that when you go to the periphery, that vague area on the side of the image, there is a tremendous amount of information and vast healing energies for the person. Thus when someone is stuck, feeling overwhelmed or hopeless, they can go to the vague edges of the image and gain relief.

I used this technique with a woman named Joyce to deal with the memory of personal trauma. When she was seventeen she walked into the house to find her mother sitting across the foyer on a chair, screaming, "He's dead! He's dead!" Her father had died suddenly from a heart attack and the sudden death of her vibrant father affected her life in a profound manner. Joyce's father was her buddy. She was about to graduate from high school and her father was instrumental in helping her identify the right college for her to attend. They had planned several trips to visit the colleges of her choice.

Her dad had shared in all the important decisions and activities in her life. She was the champion basketball player on her high school team and he was the proud father who encouraged her and cheered her on. The loss of her father was simply too much to bear. He would not see her graduate, would not be there to help her find the right college, share her excitement when accepted to it, or inhale the sweetness of her graduation from it. He would miss seeing her grow into a successful young woman, maybe even becoming a mother, presenting him with his first grandchild. This was a loss that overwhelmed her.

Joyce not only suffered through her remorse and grief, she discovered that she felt guilt over his death. She looked back over the last four years in high school and realized that she had begun to break away from her father as she established her own sense of self. Even though she dearly loved her father, she was trying to feel her own independence from him. Sometimes she smoked pot in secret with her friends; sometimes she drank alcohol at parties. On occasion she asked her father to borrow the family car to go to the library when she actually went for rides with her friends. One night she even snuck out a window of her house to meet her boyfriend.

Now he was gone! Never mind the guilt, she was crushed by the profound loss of her father, her ground, her support, and the greatest coach ever. How could she go on without him? The independence she wanted from him never included his death. She could not shake the despondency that enveloped her or see a bright future of any kind without her father in it.

Feeling bereft, Joyce came to see me.

Her mother's words "He's dead!" stayed with Joyce. She tried to shake it, but she was emotionally traumatized and could not get the words out of her head. She could not shake the feeling of despair connected to that event. I asked Joyce to see an image of the scene and she saw her mother screaming the words "He's dead, he's dead." She went to the periphery or edge of the image, to the plateglass window behind her mother. From there she then moved to the next periphery of that image, which put her in the backyard of the house. She saw that it was dawn; the first rays of light were beginning to filter through the dark. She heard the first sounds of morning, dogs barking, car engines revving up to start the day. Then she looked down and saw a single blade of grass shooting up from the ground.

When she saw the blade of grass, a feeling of rebirth, of the dawn, and of new growth came over her. The new day and the new growth were symbols of a new beginning.

At that point she realized that life had cycles of death and rebirth and that although a death had occurred, a new cycle was beginning and life would go on. This gave her a broader perspective and brought her out of the depths of her despair. It gave her a new futuristic vision to be able to deal with her father's death, to keep on going on.

She gained an understanding that even though bad things happen, life still goes on, that there is hope beyond loss. It was a transforming experience for her, and the image of her mother screaming those terrible words no longer was traumatic to her.

Peripheral images are especially helpful with hopelessness and grief because they shift difficult emotions. When using the technique of images at the periphery, one starts by seeing an image of a negative situation. Then one moves to the periphery of the image and notices what is there and how one feels. If it is still negative, the person can go to the next periphery. It can start with a negative focus or feeling at the center, then shift to the periphery to find a positive feeling. One goes from periphery to periphery until one discovers a healing image.

Images at the periphery not only break fixed perspectives and perceptions and the hopelessness that comes with them, but peripheral images carry a lot of healing power. That's why they have been used so effectively in situations involving grief, hopelessness, and despair.

With creativity it works very much the same way. When we get stuck, experiencing a creative block, we can go to the periphery of the first image of feeling stuck and find relief, or keep going on to the following peripheries. After going through a series of peripheral images, the creative juices will start flowing and you will see the project in a whole new light, with a new infusion of ideas about it.

The same with a situation at work, when we are stuck with a problem for which we cannot find a solution, whether it is with a project or person, we can do the same thing. We simply need to see an image of our current work situation, experience the feelings we have while seeing the image, and move to the periphery of the image to get a glimpse of a new perspective on the problem.

A woman with whom I worked felt stuck in a horrendous marriage in which she felt that she couldn't breathe in her house. She felt trapped in a bad marriage with a man she hated. She went to the periphery of the image and ended up outdoors. She became aware of the wind, and of the sun warming her, breathing in the fresh air and the flowers and trees all around her. This brought a sense of breath back to her and with it she gained insights about herself and perceptions about her marriage that allowed her to feel much freer. The tightness and stress generated by the image of her home life lightened and allowed her to see a whole new way to deal with her husband.

A man named Joe had a chronically ill sister. As a teenager, Joe's father demanded that Joe nurse his ailing sister and put his own needs last, not understanding Joe's need to spend time with his friends, to date, and just have fun. Joe felt controlled, and the constricted feelings stayed with him, leaving him scared to get close to anyone later in his life. He feared being trapped if he allowed himself to care for someone. When he imaged being stuck taking care of his sister, he went to the periphery, and found himself outside, in the backyard. Next, he went to the periphery of the backyard image and spontaneously saw himself floating on clouds. For the first time in a long time Joe felt free with an enduring sense of peace and endless spaciousness. The image helped him break the feeling of always feeling enclosed. He saw that he could go back and interact with his father and sister, and not feel trapped, that in his soul he was always free. He understood that he could get away and be free anytime he desired, and this sense of freedom allowed him to move closer to another person. The power was in *his* hands, not his father's.

PERIPHERY IMAGE

1. See an image in which you feel hopeless or despairing.
2. Go to the edge, the periphery, of the image. What do you see? How do you feel?
3. Now go to the edge of the new image. What do you see? What do you feel? Do you feel any different?
4. If needed, go to the edge, the periphery, of this image. What do you see? How do you feel?
5. Repeat going to the edge of each new image until you get a shift in your original, stuck feeling. Allow the relief and illumination to come over you.

I will now take you through a couple of situations involving going to the periphery so you get a feel for doing it.

The first involves a man named Robert who is having a problem at work. He's been on the job for eighteen years and feels threatened by his boss's attitude toward him and a woman hired recently.

"I'm looking for recognition from my boss and I don't get it," Robert said. "There's no feedback, that's how the boss is to everybody, no positive feedback. Things are just taken for granted. I know I do a good job, but I am never appreciated. That lack in my boss makes me angry. I don't know why he's like that.

"It makes me feel paranoid, worried if I'm doing the right thing, cautious. And sometimes I feel jealous if he seems positive to somebody else or gives attention to another worker. Lately it's really getting to me because he hired somebody new and he is giving a lot of attention to this woman. She's younger than me and a hell of a lot prettier. I'm feeling very jealous. But some part of me knows that he never gives positive feedback. He's been meeting a lot with this new worker and I'm hiding my feeling of insecurity, but I'm struggling with this. It's making me realize I'm fifty-two now. I've been there nearly twenty years, and I don't have anyplace else to go. I'm not married, have no kids, no close family, and my whole life is my job.

"When I think of it, I realize my father was exactly the same way. He used to keep secrets at work about the mechanics of how the plant operated as a whole so he would be the guy everybody leaned on. They had to come to him for the answers. He was the head supervisor in the plant. He didn't give a lot to the family. Work was his whole identity. I think I'm like my father because I put so much into work. I know that my self-esteem has to come from inside me, not from my boss. I know I can't rely on him for my self-worth, but honestly I'm feeling very left out and don't know how to feel good about myself without his approval. I'm really stuck."

Robert sees an image of himself at work.

"I see my messy desk, my office, my PC, just an overwhelming mess. I do feel energized to get the work done. Also, I'm seeing people leaving at five o'clock and I still have two hours left because they're all used to me staying behind to get the work done. I'm tired of being the guy who stays behind. I want to go home and just be a couch potato. But, I can't go home like the rest of them because then no one will look up to me."

The image that comes up for Robert is conflicted, reflecting his state of mind. There is no relief in it.

He went to the periphery of the office image.

"I'm in the reception area outside my personal office. I feel apprehensive because I have a lot of work to get done."

This image brought him more anxiety and apprehension to get back to work.

He went to the periphery of that image.

"I'm outside in front of the building," he said. "I feel less stressed, I feel better. I see I'm waiting for the bus to take me home. I am anxious to get home. At home I feel safe and comfortable."

He went to the periphery of the image of being outside and saw himself at home.

"I'm starting to have regrets at home," he said. "There's nobody here for me. And the place is the shits. I mean it's just a place to sack out. The furniture is wasted and just doesn't feel good. It feels like my life— empty."

Going to the periphery broke the focus Robert had on his office and made him take a look at his life, and he didn't like what he saw. The lack of a home life made him a slave at the office, where he wasn't getting the reinforcement or the sense of security that he needed.

"What I saw," he said, "is that I needed to get a life. I've got to do my job, but I've got to fill my life with something else because jobs aren't forever. Neither is life. What I realized is that I can do my job really well without stressing myself out or waiting to be petted. What happens around the office is that I don't just do my own job, but I'm always running around picking up for other people. I do all of this for recognition. I realize I am overly sensitive about my boss's approval. I'm not happy about it, and as I get my priorities right, I will feel better about myself and then it's going to work better at the office and at home."

The next image involves dealing with grief. Terry is a forty-three-year-old self-employed real estate broker. She lives on the East Coast and her sister in Houston is dying of a rare form of cancer. At the time this interview was done the sister was still alive, wasting away in a hospital bed.

Terry is overwhelmed emotionally, physically, and financially by flying back and forth to be with her sister in Houston. She is the last surviving sibling, her parents are dead, and she is all her sister has. Terry is not strong herself and the situation is overwhelming her.

Her sister looks like a skeleton, and each time Terry sees her in the hospital she is devastated by what her sister is going through. To complicate matters, she and her sister were not especially close during most of their adult life; her sister was often mean and confrontational toward her. Now that she is dying, her sister has become loving and open, Terry naturally reciprocates and wants to be at her bedside. But, she doesn't know how long she herself can last because she has to keep returning home to keep her business going.

When Terry sees an image of her situation, she sees herself dragging and tired in the image. She focuses on the image, but it overwhelms her. She can't relax and finds no relief. She is overwhelmed with stress and responsibility.

She goes to the periphery of the image and spontaneously finds herself playing in her bedroom at home with her sister when they were children. She feels a lot of love for her sister and this love releases a flood of loving energy within her.

"I realized that part of my problem was dealing with our history," she said. "My sister and I were really close and loving when we were little kids, but we moved apart physically and emotionally as we grew up. My sister had some hard knocks, a couple bad marriages, couldn't stick to a job, and she resented my career and my relationships. They say when you go through life's troubles you either get bitter or better, and she became bitter. Seeing us playing as kids I realized how much I loved her and how much she really loved me."

Terry was still fatigued after her image breakthrough—she still needed rest and still had financial worries, but she went about tackling them with more energy and determination because she was operating off of a positive base of love. The feeling of stress, which tired her, shifted to love which energized her and gave her hope.

She then saw an image of her sister in the hospital. The pain her sister was in was unbearable to Terry. She went to the periphery of the image of her sister in the hospital.

"I see an end to it all, I see her passing over and see her spirit is released," she said. "I see that my sister will die and her suffering will be over. That's the important thing, that she doesn't suffer. For myself, I have two good feet and I can keep on working. And living. Now that I know she will be at peace and there will be an end to the pain I don't feel so desperate anymore."

She went to the periphery of the above image that she was seeing.

"I see a blue sky," she said, "nothing's in it. It feels like a state of purity, of starting over with clean energy and pure spirit. I realize that I have a lot of energy in me, that I don't need as much rest as I thought. Things were dragging me down and it's my mind not my body that needed the rest. I feel like I can handle what is to come."

As you can see, imaging at the periphery can lead people into profound shifts of perception.

33

Imaging the Future Today

Most of us sense a void within us that needs to be filled—when we get that job, promotion, meet that special person, new Mercedes, win the lottery, buy that dream house, have a million dollars in the bank—then everything will be okay.

What I have just described is an expectation, an expectation that something in the future will fill the emptiness in us and everything will be better. The truth is that few of us win the lottery of life, and even when we do, we suddenly look around and sense an emptiness, and start thinking everything will be better when we find true love, when our health improves, when our book gets published, when . . .

Somebody once described this situation to me as analogous to taking a train ride across the country without enjoying the scenery and instead spending the entire trip anticipating the destination. The problem is, of course, that life is a journey in which the ultimate destination is death. We better enjoy the journey rather than awaiting the destination.

This void, this emptiness in us that we experience and try to fill with an expectation from the future, is a very important aspect to our lives. And it's not restricted to Western culture. Even the Buddhists talk about being empty, about the void before the fullness of creation comes forth.

The Greeks talked about "hypnoia," or the underneath sense of being. In our consciousness there is a bipolarity, or two levels of awareness. The upper level of mind awareness includes all the thoughts and ideas of the social milieu, the things that society taught us. It is where the rational mind exists. This part of the mind says "I need a (Mercedes, movie contract, million dollars, dynamite love affair) to be happy." The lower layer or the underneath sense is where inspirations, intentions, spiritual knowledge, and the deep inner sense of the fullness of life is found.

The emptiness is the space between society's superficial values and our deeper self. That emptiness is a place of void or space that we connect to before the fullness of the underneath sense comes out.

In our modern life the truth is that nothing has changed since the ancient Greeks. We are physically and psychologically structured to experience the sense of needing something to really fulfill us. Naturally, the real truth is that no matter how often our expectations get filled from the outside, we still suffer from the void inside until we fill it with a deeper knowing.

One person I worked with described the process like this:

"When I started college I thought, gosh, if I can just get a college degree, everything will be fine. Four years later after I earned a degree, I looked around and everybody else had one, so I thought if I got a graduate degree I wouldn't feel so empty. Three years later I had a doctorate and discovered that almost everyone I associated with had a doctorate, and it was no big deal! Next I thought if I could just practice as a professional and make a lot of money, have a fancy car and a big house—and a few years later I parked my fancy car in front of my big house and thought, wow, if I could just . . ."

Not all of us are lucky enough to have the fancy car and big house, but it should be obvious that none of the material things in the world will fill our inner void.

What will fill the void is a spiritual sense from the inside, or an image that arises from within that shifts our perspective from an expectation of something happening in the future to one that will fulfill us by bringing the sought-after feeling of future fulfillment to the present.

In eidetic imaging we call this image an "Eidola," an image that brings the future to us today.

We know that real wisdom and fulfillment come from within and that the sense of emptiness within us is a product of interacting with the superficialities of the world in which we live. We fall victim continuously to overt and subliminal types of messages that give us false values and distorted impressions of reality. We hear that when we make more than a certain amount of money we are valued by others, or when we have the perfect relationship we'll be okay, or if our kids don't get A's they are not worth anything, and, for that matter, neither are we. Rarely are we told to march to the beat of our own drummer or to push against the crowd, to hear and follow the messages from our inner self.

This sort of false basis of self is the ruin of us because it pollutes our minds with false images, taints the connection to our own inner being, and the wonderful gifts of spirit that reside within us. It has also been the ruin of the planet, this wonderful wet and green spaceship-earth to which we are bound, yet we have fallen from grace as the result of our arrogant, rational minds.

That tainted upper layer, the social layer, is always with us, but we can use the Eidola to go underneath and find our real selves and awaken to fill our void. When we live in the upper layer, we keep waiting to get to the destination and don't enjoy the journey. The ancient Greeks believed that the inner sense was very powerful, even sacred, and that when we are separated from it, it's waiting there for us to enter, like the doors of a temple waiting to be discovered inside of us.

The Eidola is a special futuristic message which fills the void that we feel, comes from our underneath sense and addresses our past, present, and future. It brings future longing into the present to be filled. Our minds are goal-oriented, so we have an impulse toward action, toward futurism. Since our minds are futuristic (always thinking of what *will* happen), the present is experienced as empty. By going down into ourselves we bring forward an image that fills the void.

The image that emerges fulfills and beckons the person to move forward futuristically into their greater self. In seeing the image, the people sense their own power, radiance, and optimism to move forward.

It is said that the wisdom of archangels and prophets living within the person speak and come forward through this image.

EIDOLA IMAGE: THE FUTURE TODAY

1. There is a past, a present, and the future.
2. The past is way back, and appears remote and covered over.
3. The present has a lack, a void.
4. This void is painful.
5. Something from the future is needed to fill the void.
6. See an image in this void of lights or of a Being who is a visitor from the future.
7. It is beautiful, awesome, with an omen and a special power.
8. This is a visitation that is futuristic. It is a visit taking you to the future.
9. This is called *Eidola*. This is a futuristic visitor.

10. See this image, this Eidola from the future.
11. Now feel its awesomeness.
12. There is a feeling of a message in the image. What is the message? Experience your feelings and vibrations from the Eidola.
13. How does it change you when you look at the Eidola?
14. Let the futuristic message from the Eidola pass through your mind and transform you.
15. Do not resist; become like the Eidola. Experience feelings and vibrations.
16. Become vibrant like the Eidola.
17. Now experience these special feelings within you.
18. There are messages of the future in your body.
19. Experience the energy in your body.
20. Let the energy move you into the future.

The following is an Eidola imaging session with a forty-two-year-old woman. The woman was plagued with a sense of emptiness inside of her, a feeling of dissatisfaction despite the fact that on the surface things seemed to be going well for her. She said that she had set goals in life and that each time she reached one she felt like she had to keep climbing because achieving goals didn't fulfill her expectations.

We began by reviewing the first five points in the Eidola image: There is a past, a present, and a future. The past is way back and appears remote and covered over. The present has a lack; there is a void, emptiness. This lack is a painful one, a void that something from the future needs to fill. Let it come. It is beautiful, awesome, with an omen, and it has a special power. This is a visitation that is futuristic. It is called an Eidola.

Describe the image you see.

"I'm seeing light, it's an oval, nothing really distinct in the middle, opaque, all around it like an amoebae would be, it's full of rays of light all around and it's shimmering."

Feel its awesomeness, there's a feeling of a message there, what is the message?

"I'm just hearing love, peace and love."

Experience your feelings and the vibrations, the energy from the Eidola.

"I can feel it in my body, an energy running through."

How does it change you when you look at the Eidola?

"It's almost like pulsing, the same pulses going through my body, the same flooding, my pulses are in unison with the energy of the brightness."

Let the futuristic message of love and peace pass through your mind and transform you. Do not resist, become like the Eidola, experience the vibrations, and become vibrant like the Eidola.

"My head is shaking and my whole body is like this incredible pulsing going on, everywhere."

Experience these special feelings in your being.

"I've got tears coming now, not sadness . . . my heart feels full, and like pushing against my rib cage . . . I feel warmth all over me."

There are intimations of the future in your body. Experience the vibrations of actions in your being and let the actions flow; let yourself become futuristic.

"I feel like I'm just floating, and light, just like buoyant, like a bubble would float, only all light, just floating away, like there's no pressure on me and I can float away. I feel full of love and peace."

Full of love and peace, that was the message she got from the future, the image that came from her inner essence to fill that void, despite her accomplishments.

Wouldn't this world be wonderful if we could all reach into ourselves and fill our emptiness with love and a sense of peace?

Perhaps we can . . .

34

Imaging Our Genetic Roots

Our ancestors . . . are players on this stage . . . not ghosts who are revisiting but living apparitions in the mind of the person. The ancestral time zone is the place where you go and meet them.

Dr. Akhter Ahsen

In the previous chapter, imagining the future today, we talked about the two levels existing in our minds: the surface level that society has put its paint strokes on, and a deeper spiritual level that comes to us as a birthright. In that cosmic, genetic plane are more layers that can be peeled away like the layers of an onion, each layer a plateau offering a new revelation about who we are.

One of those layers, those birthrights the ancient Greeks called the gifts of the gods, is the *ancestral zone.*

All humans have ancestors. Even test-tube babies are a product of other living tissue. If we go back far enough, back to that "being" scientists call the Missing Link, or back to the Garden of Eden, we will find that we all shared a single ancestor at some point.

From whatever point we started, in the Garden of Eden or as an ape swinging from a tree, all of us are the product of thousands of years of breeding that results in the unique human qualities and unique DNA characteristics that each of us possess.

We have spoken repeatedly about the fact that there is a mind-body connection, that the mind affects the body, that the body affects the mind, and that the two interact together to create the whole person that we are. The interaction between mind and body is so precise, scientists can now rather amazingly and horrifyingly take a single piece of hair, a scrape of skin, or a bit of fingernail and clone a duplicate of me. That clone, that second *me,* would be physically and emotionally exactly like me and while its history of interaction with society would give it a different persona and view of life than me, at conception it would share with me exactly those traits, including the ancestral inheritance that I had at conception.

Like our DNA aspects, those ancestral aspects of self get passed on genetically to us, a little different combination for each of us because each of us is a unique blend and mixture of our mother and father, who in turn were themselves a unique blend of the mixture of their parents, and so on, back an eon. Thus our genetic inheritance is a treasure of qualities that have been passed on from generation to generation.

When you have personally taken thousands of people through eidetic imaging sessions, you find a common thread; people frequently experience images that have their source not in their own lifetime but in a genetic essence that has its source in their primordial roots.

When people are specifically taken back into their ancestral time zone, accessing their genetic roots, they often come up with amazing information and detail about their ethnic roots. These roots are accessible by people of all ethnic backgrounds, but the images are frequently striking when the person is a product of a culture where there has been a sustained inner cohesion for a great length of time (Africans, Jews, Celts, Japanese, Scandinavians, etc.).

As I say, you see this in all ethnic groups. From Italians, we frequently get images that have a kind of sensual connection to the earth, from Germans images with a more methodical feel to them. I worked with a woman whose mother was a Scot and the father a Native American. She had been raised by her mother and had little physical connection to her father, because he died when she was a toddler, so her Native American side was more alien to her. When she made the journey to her Native American ancestral zone, powerful images, inherited from the genetics of her father's ethnicity, came forth, which surprised and delighted her. In her images she experienced ecstatic feelings of a fundamental connection to nature. She saw herself part of a tribe, sitting on the earth on a hill, delighting in watching birds soar in blue skies. For the first time in her life she felt whole, as if she had reconciled a side of her own personality that had lain undiscovered.

Images of people with African ancestry often have a sense of a rising spirit that comes from the very roots of the soil of Africa and is connected to the sound and rhythm of drums and a heartbeat. The ancestral strength that is found in their roots is not found in other races or in any other people. Each ethnicity and culture has its unique genetic gift that can be shared with the rest of mankind. The African images seem to personify the vast richness of the land and its people, people closely connected to earth and nature.

These are not my perceptions but those of people of African heritage with whom I have worked in imaging sessions. That power that comes out in imaging, power linked to the very soil itself, typifies not only their spiritual images but also their whole history. When you think about the history of black-skinned people, visions of men and women and children shackled and tortured on slave ships can come to mind. Yet as a people they survived slavery with an incredible strength of spirit, which became a religious spirit, seen in prayer, music, and dance.

African descendants spontaneously connect to ancestral images containing the rhythm of a heartbeat and the soil, such as images of mothers dancing with their children on their backs, with their babies sensing the heartbeat through the rhythm of the dance, connecting it to the music. This sort of image is common to all women, but I hear it expressed more often and more powerfully by women of African ancestry. However, when both men and women do imaging, they access a powerful depth of spirit from their ancestors that can't be broken. That strength of spirit is a gift of great value from Africa to share with all humanity.

This beautiful image is what one African American woman saw when she accessed her ancestral time zone: "I see drums, I see dancing, I see people celebrating. I see that in the dance there is a wholeness; it's almost as if something moves out of the rhythm, the rhythm of the universe. The drumbeat brings out the spirit, it brings the spirit up."

Eastern European Jews have ancestral images that reflect the complexity of their heritage. Arthur Koestler's book *The Thirteenth Tribe* has discussed the origins of the European Jews, and Dr. Ahsen has discussed the issue of European Jewish identity in his imagery research. Most Eastern European Jews' personal images do not take them back to Israel, as one might think, but to bands of nomadic people moving across steppes and plains in horse troops. This is not an unexpected result since most Eastern Europeans, Slavs and Jews alike, are products of the great migration of barbarian tribes from the East, Huns and Goths and the like, who filled the vacuum created by the crumbling Roman Empire.

Jews are also people who have been tightly woven genetically through intermarriage over the centuries, and people who have suffered persecutions for so long that its memory is passed on from generation to generation. As a people, European Jews feel connected to the Covenant and part of that is the notion that God never abandons you; nor that you abandon His purpose for you on earth—to bring light and illumination to humanity.

With this spiritual vision, that God will never abandon the Covenant Jew, many Jews ask how could God have let the Holocaust happen. I'm sure that people of African descent, Native Americans, Bosnian Muslims, Cambodians, Armenians, and a host of other people who have suffered genocide have wondered the same thing.

Madeline, a Jewish woman and child of Holocaust survivors, did an image that answered the question by touching on the teachings of her ancestral roots.

She saw her father in the home in which she grew up, holding a glass filled with tea. All of a sudden she saw her father, still holding the glass, but in a different setting. The scene had shifted. "I saw my father hold the water glass while sitting in a city of rubble, death, and destruction, a concentration camp. His hands were bloodied as if he had crushed the glass with his bare hands. In the image he raised his bloodied hands toward the heavens and cried out, 'Why hast thou forsaken me?' This was exactly how I felt. I wondered how God could have abandoned humanity and left it in so much pain," she said.

Madeline was asked to see herself in the image with her father in order to understand his experience. However, in the imaging she took it a step further, and her question was answered.

"I see myself there. I walk past him in this city of death, to a pile of bodies. I climb the mound of bodies to the very top. The heavens part and a hand descends from the clouds and gives me a torch of light (this all happens spontaneously in the image). I carry the torch back down the mound and continue walking, and words come to me: 'Even though you walk through cities of death and destruction, I AM always with you.' " Seeing the image and hearing the words, Madeline had a profound shift in her understanding. "I feel no fear and know that I can walk through anything as long as I know that I have the light within me. No one can destroy that light inside me. They may take everything from me, even my life, but the light within is eternal. This gives me immense strength."

Madeline's image was a revelation to her and important in her life because it made her realize that when she could not change the external events that befell her, she could profoundly alter the way in which she carried herself through life's circumstances. She said, "It is we who abandon the connection to divine sources, to the powers within us, to our inner light. We can be an example to others of what is possible for the human spirit to contain because the divine connection never abandons us, it continues to reside within the deepest core of our being and it is us who fail to keep the connection active."

Madeline had brought forth the religious teachings of her ancestors—from the Old Testament—through her images.

I don't want to leave you with the impression that our spiritual connection to the ancestral zone brings forth nothing but incidents of death and destruction, slave ships and concentration camps. I have related those images because war, slavery, and genocide are historically dramatic memories and continue to affect us through the legacy of our heritage. Even though these images are sometimes of unimaginable horrors, victory over them carries powerful messages to us about how to deal with our own lives.

Most ancestral images are not of war and destruction, but are connections to the sources of strength our ancestors drew from the earth and the elements, the flora and the fauna around them. I have spoken to people of Slavic and Germanic heritage, who experience invigorating ancestral images of thunder and wind; to people of Latin heritage, who find themselves relaxed and peaceful by ancestral images of the sun and warm brown earth; to a British man, who saw images of Druids and circles of stones.

At times ancestral images bring forth memories of the painful history of a people. But going more deeply into the image, peeling back the layers of history, great genetic strength may be found. Madeline described how she found strength in the images of her mother. "The year before my mother died of cancer, I was already married and she came for a visit. She told me stories of her experience during the war that she had never told before.

"One story she told me really stayed with me and haunted me. I couldn't get it out of my mind. Just as I had to work on the image of my father to understand in a deeper way the question of God forsaking us when evil things happen, I had to understand things from another level from my mother. Images bring out deep knowledge. Until I did the image about my father, I had no idea that no matter where you go that the spiritual light is inside you.

"The story my mother told me was that toward the end of the war she and my father and little sister were moving toward the Russian front while the fighting was still going on. My parents tried to make their way toward the battle front to avoid the Nazi troops because they believed that they would be free the minute they reached the Russian lines. Moving across the countryside, they were captured by German soldiers, who thought they were Polish peasants because they had false identity papers and pretended they were Christian. My little sister had been raised as a Christian and didn't know anything about her Jewish heritage because to teach her any Jewish rites would have meant certain death for her and my parents.

"The German soldiers took them to an infirmary, a makeshift field hospital for wounded soldiers on the front lines. They put my parents to work helping in the infirmary and kitchen. This was standard practice among the Nazis and German soldiers—they would take whoever they could find and put them to work; if they were Jews, they would probably kill them or put them in concentration camps.

"My mother was made a nurse responsible for the care of a German general with a wounded arm, and my sister hung around my mother while she took care of him. My father was sent to the kitchen to peel potatoes and help with the meals. Mother said it was really hard to take care of this general and pretend because she knew that the Nazis had killed her whole family. She said trucks would come in from the front lines every day, open trucks with wooden slats, exposing young German soldiers who had been wounded. Some were missing limbs; others looking very gory with their stomachs torn open. It was the rainy season in Poland and the rain created a lot of mud. When the trucks came to the infirmary with the wounded and bleeding soldiers, their blood dripped from the trucks and mixed with the mud.

"My mother said that her feeling of revenge was so intense that when she saw the Nazi blood mixing with the mud, she could barely contain herself from ripping off all her clothes and bathing in the mud and blood.

"That startling image of my mother throwing herself into the mud and blood really affected me. Shortly after she died, I became obsessed with my mother's memory of the mud and blood and her feelings of revenge. I couldn't put it out of my mind. I don't know if it was stimulated by the trauma of her death, but I felt that she had passed away and left behind unfinished business, as if she had passed the emotion to me, that feeling of revenge that had haunted her.

"As I was led through an image, I was instructed to see my mother rip off her clothes and jump into the mud and blood. I did that in the image because that was her unfinished business, where the energy in the image was, something she could barely contain herself from doing during her own life. I saw her rip her clothes off and jump into the mud and blood. After she jumped in, I saw her rise up. When she rose up, I saw a feeling of utter peace, with all of the strain and worry and sorrow and rage completely washed away, as if the bath in mud and blood brought peace and completion to her.

"Then I was instructed to see myself rip off my clothes and jump into the mud and blood. I knew this was asked of me because I was still trying to understand my mother's experience. So I saw myself ripping off my clothes and jumping into the mud and blood, and something happened. As I came up out of it I saw myself rising taller and taller, becoming this huge figure of a woman, like a giant mythic figure, very tall and wide and high. I felt almost holy, like the Virgin Mary, and as I looked around from this very tall, large perspective, it was as if I was looking through stained-glass windows. There was a holy feeling to the image.

"As I looked out over the countryside I saw German soldiers coming back injured, young boys, seventeen, eighteen, and I saw that they were innocent victims of a big propaganda machine. They were brainwashed and didn't know what they were doing. And I was filled with this incredible compassion for them. I was raised to think that the Nazis were the most horrible people on the earth and even to be wary of anything German; certainly not to have compassion for them. But here I was in this amazing state of utter compassion for the German soldiers.

"Then I looked over and saw the American soldiers and Russians, and they were all just young boys, innocent participants in this incredible war. The image made me enter into a state of compassion, deep and profound, for all of the mass of suffering humanity. As I stood there in this state of forgiveness and compassion and love, I saw all these men as part of tiny armies. I was in a state of utter bliss. I saw them crawling up my hands and arms, like the tiny men in *Gulliver's Travels*, the whole mass of broken humanity moving up my body.

"It brought me into a deep transformed awareness about the whole nature of humanity, and I had a feeling of peace and relief and love for all of them. Seeing their innocence and being filled with that compassion has never left me.

"The image taught me a transcendent type of love, even for people I was taught to hate. And that knowledge also comes from my ancestral roots, whose wisdom and teachings are part of Abraham, Isaac, and Jacob."

Madeline had touched the depth of her genetic roots and found compassion for *all* humanity. She moved beyond revenge to a greater awareness of love for all.

Madeline's images of the Holocaust lived on in her mind and haunted her, even though she had never been there. This is a phenomenon that Dr. Ahsen researched in depth. He found that Jewish people who had not directly experienced the Holocaust, but had heard stories about it from their parents or had seen it in the media, developed a storehouse of subliminal images in their minds that were so powerful that they suffered similar emotional consequences as those who had lived directly through the trauma. Their images were of a dramatic and astonishing intensity and authenticity. They reported feeling exactly like someone who had experienced it by physically being there firsthand. Although a product of their imagination they carried an undeniably deep empathic capacity that they shared with actual Holocaust sufferers.

Following this discovery, Jews and non-Jews, who were not victims of the Holocaust, were asked to see Holocaust images and they too experienced the same level of intensity. Everyone reported feeling like they had been there. Non-Jewish people tended to hold the experience at a distance and did not automatically empathize with it. However, when they were encouraged to see the images with all their emotion, their empathy came into full bloom. For some, their capacity for natural empathy had been covered over by prejudiced ideas they had learned about Jewish people. Once they were encouraged to experience Holocaust imagery without fear or prejudice, they too experienced a personal horror without any emotional distance toward the event.

In researching this type imagery further, it was discovered that global images of social horrors, such as those of the enslavement of African peoples, the destruction of Native Americans, Hiroshima and Nagasaki, Bosnia, etc., perpetually exist in people's minds. When attention is *not* paid to the full experience of these images, by avoidance or by discounting them, emotional flight results in injury to that person and to their knowledge. When people avoid the pain that others have suffered, a vacuum is created in their minds and a special vulnerability weakens them because they become incapable of dealing with the realities of the world. One who becomes defensive, racist, or fearful of facing the themes of traumatic social situations cannot transform the pain into greater wisdom, compassion, and resolution toward a better world.

From this perspective, one can understand that images of the Black social experience are not so distinct from images of the Holocaust and

Bosnia, and the two have a definite resonance with one another. As the groups experience empathy toward each other, through witnessing the traumatic images of one another, they manifest a profound bond between them as victims of all social holocausts. That people carry the pain of others, therefore a unified empathy into each other's experiences, is important for the sake of all humanity. If one can see it and bear witness to it, then one can be a bearer of the other's sins, pains, and agonies. Like Madeline, one can discover solutions and find resources of strength that are illuminating and can move us to a greater love for one another, rather than perpetuating fear and separation.

A gentile man seeing the images of the Holocaust in his mind said, "The Jewish suffering is very Christ-like. It evokes total compassion in me. As I lived the images of what actually happened in my mind, I could not take it anymore. I switched my mind off and on. This is enlightening at a deep level. I dare not be him. I am afraid of being him. It is like watching and sliding into a horror movie."

A Muslim, looking into the experience of Christians said, "At this moment they are bewildered and confused about what is going on in the world and they do not have a clear idea of their own participation. It is a difficult situation to be a Christian in the world as things have ultimately developed. I feel disoriented and I have lost my identity when I think of myself as a Christian." Rather than animosity, the Muslim had compassion for the Christian position in current world affairs.

A Jew looking at the Muslim experience said, "I see that they suffer like we do. They are in pain and feel that they have not been honored and have been seen in a demeaning light by the rest of the world. Seeing their pain, passion, and anger, I feel at one with them. We are brothers and sisters, descendants from Abraham's seed. I do not feel separate from them and welcome them into my heart."

Whether we are Jews, Christians, or Muslims, we are not alone. Through imagination, all of humanity can be united. By being willing to break down the barriers in our own minds and empathize into what other religions, races, and cultures experience, we have the possibility of truly knowing and loving one another and healing the divisive splits of ignorance that divide us. Through imagination humanity can heal and come together as ONE.

"One going to take a pointed stick to pinch a baby bird should first try it on himself to feel how it hurts."

African Traditional Religions. Yoruba Proverb

The Earth we left behind a few generations ago, or a few thousand years back, is still there, and so are the people who inhabited it. We can go to this ancestral time zone and meet all of them again, and they will tell us what we lost because they still have it.

Dr. Akhter Ahsen

Below I have set forth the Ancestral Zone Image. When you explore with it, keep in mind that it may take more than one session to access layers of our genetic history.

ANCESTRAL ZONE IMAGE

This image takes you back in time to your ancestors. If you have mixed ancestry, first choose one to explore and then you can choose to explore the other.

1. See an image of yourself in the present time.
2. Where are you? What do you see?
3. Now go back in time, back to your ancestors, and see an image of your ancestors.
4. What country do you go to? What kind of geography are you in? (If the Image is not clear, go further back in time until you make a connection.)
5. See that they come and greet you. How do they receive you?
6. How do you feel as they receive you? What are the feelings that come over you?
7. Explore the area and feel at home.
8. Are you discovering another part of yourself?
9. Allow yourself to explore the image fully.

35

Eidetic Imaging
The Science of Our Emotions

The modern science of imaging and the name Dr. Akhter Ahsen are synonymous. For most of the second half of the twentieth century, Dr. Ahsen's research and seminal reports about eidetic imaging have resulted in the birth of a science.*

> *An approach which enables the patient to cut through the mind/body problem and deal with the essential unity, which is himself as a human being.*
> The International Journal of Clinical and Experimental Hypnosis

Today Dr. Ahsen is the world's leading theoretician of mental imaging and has authored thirty books and hundreds of articles on the subject. He is editor and founder of the *Journal of Mental Imagery*. The *Journal's* editorial staff is international with participants from major United States universities such as Harvard, Stanford, Yale, plus universities in Britain, France, Japan, India, Sweden, Australia, Canada, and others.

> *"Unmatched in the clinical literature . . . a methodological advance."*
> The American Journal of Psychiatry

Dr. Ahsen did not "invent" eidetic imaging. On the contrary, the concept goes back thousands of years to the ancient Greeks. Dr. Ahsen's contribution, like Freud's with psychoanalysis and Skinner's with behaviorism, was to lay the scientific framework for what had been mere theory before.

> *"An exciting and ingenious way of getting to conflict areas."*
> Contemporary Psychology

*This discussion of eidetic imaging and Dr. Ahsen's contributions to the science also appeared in my book *Images of Desire*.

Dr. Ahsen is both a scientist and a philosopher. Joseph Campbell, the legendary, world-renowned mythologist, said of Dr. Ahsen's epic poem *Manhunt in the Desert* that it was "inspired" and proclaimed that Dr. Ahsen did not *write* the poem, he *received* it.

In his introduction to the book, Joseph Campbell wrote: "Akhter Ahsen's *Manhunt in the Desert* is a magnificent poem of powerful images, rendering its legend of spiritual quest and realization, as through a medium of prophetic vision. The work has a quality of revelation about it and should be read by all."

Dr. Ahsen is also the author of numerous technical books encompassing almost every major issue in the field of imaging.

"This exposure to treatment through images was transforming to my view of medicine and my later psychiatric practice. The effectiveness of this type of treatment by Dr. Ahsen was startling in both the extent of its cure and the rapidity and directness which it was obtained through a systematic, definite technique."

Anna T. Dolan, M.D., chief of psychiatry,
Yonkers General Hospital, Yonkers, New York

EIDETICS ARE NO LONGER THE EXCLUSIVE DOMAIN OF THE "GIFTED"

Eidetic imaging is not new to psychology—on the contrary, imaging concepts have been part of the general theory of psychology since giants like Freud and Jung began putting their discoveries on paper. In the 1920s, E. R. Jaensch of the Marburg school made an extensive study of eidetics, but rather than exploring the more practical and useful aspects of imaging, he was attracted to the esoteric aspects of it. Jaensch's theories left early practitioners of psychology the impression that only "gifted" persons—writers, artists, poets—and young children were capable of evoking true eidetic images.

Dr. Ahsen, whose research into the science of the mind began several decades ago, discovered that eidetic images were not the exclusive domain of the gifted few but could be applied in a practical way by most people once they learned the technique. It's true that "gifted" people, ranging from noted authors to world-class athletes, have made dynamic use of imaging to put themselves into the winning zone, but countless others have used imaging to deal with the common problems of relationships and work that so many of us encounter on a daily basis.

"A unique and important contribution to the scientific study of healing with imagery."

New Age Magazine

We can see the external world with our two eyes, but there is an internal world and a mental eye, the *psyche eye*, which we can use to see into our own *self*. That third eye is the least used of our ocular abilities and for many of us it is almost unused. Imaging uses the psyche eye to peer into our own inner processes, initiating a deep probing, getting past shallow states of mind and peeling away our emotions to reveal new truths as one peels away the layers of an onion.

"When I began my research on the eidetic image in the early 1950's, it was being studied only in the experimental psychology field, as a vivid, lifelike image of astounding clarity, found among the gifted and in children. As my work unfolded, the image with these characteristics was consistently revealed in all normal people as an expression of positive life, and also connected with areas of emotional conflict, especially with parents. Following this finding, extensive evidence soon emerged showing eidetics to be a system of sensuous life in the psyche which makes the sensibilities of each individual readily available to him in consciousness. This indicated the presence of a vast and self-motivated therapeutic potential in the individual's own mind."

Dr. Ahsen, *Psycheye,* Brandon House, 1977, Preface

THE LANGUAGE OF THE MIND-BODY CONNECTION

A fundamental difference between eidetic imaging and other forms of psychotherapy is that with imaging the person is able to see a situation clearly, experience the emotions connected to it, and have an immediate understanding of themselves by evoking and seeing images of the situation. In traditional therapy, the person explains things verbally to a therapist, who listens and then tries to help the person find the meaning.

Many people using eidetics are not doing so in a psychotherapy context, but are merely interested in increasing creativity, productivity, and so on.

For example, a woman named Marge is suffering from stress due to an inability to communicate with her male boss. With traditional therapy, the clinician asks the client a series of questions concerning the situation. Marge uses words to explain her physical and emotional condition, telling the clinician that when her boss raises his voice, she feels tension in her throat and chest and so her fears keep her from replying back in an effective manner. During the course of the treatment, the clinician asks Marge to probe back in time for possible historical antecedents for the behavior.

Marge relates that her father frequently yelled at her during her childhood, and the clinician concludes that her core inadequacies stem from these early episodes. The clinician then discusses this interpretation with her and attempts to get her to come to an understanding about her problems with dealing with authority figures by relating the situation with the boss to the tyrannical parent.

Thus, in classical psychoanalysis, the clinician asks questions, and the person seeking help verbally responds to the questions, using words to describe feelings and emotions. The clinician then tries to explain to the person the meaning of the responses.

With eidetic imaging, the person is asked to evoke an image of the boss and to examine the image. Because of the link between current fears and the shaping of our personalities, the person may also be asked to evoke an image of home life and parents.

An eidetic image is composed of three aspects: the *image* itself, the *somatic*, or bodily, response to the image, and the *meaning* (insight or new perspective) revealed to the patient as he or she examines the image. Dr. Ahsen referred to an eidetic image as ISM because of its structure of Image, Somatic, and Meaning. Most eidetic practitioners use this nomenclature.

"Somatic" refers to the body's reaction to the image. (I frequently use the word emotional as a shorthand term for the bodily reaction the person seeing an eidetic image experiences.) When I asked one person to see an image of his father, he experienced cold chills. Another felt the radiation of warmth. Others feel physical tightening in their chest and stomach, or a welling up of love. Fear, anger, hate, love, and even ambivalence manifest themselves to us with our bodily responses. We "experience" and "feel" our emotions in a unity of mind and body.

When prime images—eidetic images—are evoked, the person will internally experience the sensations, good or bad, that they stimulated from examining the image and experiencing the emotional responses to it. One experiences a revelation of the situation rather than have the meaning of one's internal experiences suggested by a third person. A somatic response to the image by the person is an automatic response from the sensations created while examining the image: the image is created, the body reacts emotionally to it, and from the image and the reaction the person gains instant and automatic understanding about the situation.

This is not to imply that one throws down all of one's emotional crutches and walks after a single eidetic imaging experience. What the person ordinarily gains is greater understanding of the situation, fresh perceptions, and deeper abilities and strengths for dealing with it. Eidetic images bring not just insight to the fore, but also the wholeness that is stored biologically in the person. That is a critical distinction between eidetic imaging and therapies that only provide insight.

In the example we are using, Marge, unable to stand up to her boss, gains insight into the current problem by imaging her father. She gains this insight herself. It is not suggested to her by a clinician but arises spontaneously within her. Also, inside of Marge is the knowledge, in the form of images, of her true power, and this is revealed and made available to her through further images. Eidetics brings forth one's most potent genetic abilities.

> "The central need in psychotherapy has been the development of a true language of emotions which breaks through artificial barriers, a language which is deep, authentic, and everyone can understand and share. The eidetic is this pictorial language of the mind which as been, in the literature, rightly called a new means of communication more subtle than verbalization of facts and associative thinking. This pictorial language is highly effective in presenting and elucidating mental issues."
>
> Dr. Ahsen, *Psycheye,* Brandon House, 1977, Preface

An eidetic image is a clear, lucid, visual sensation. It is a language of the mind that carries with it bodily excitement in terms of tension, love, or other emotional states. Seeing the image stimulates the physical response and imparts meaning to the observer. It is not simply a memory image, such as a memory of what an apple tastes like, but a composite of visual and emotional states within us. Commonly, the image that is evoked has been repressed by us and needs to be exposed to our examination in order to deal with current problems. Marge, who was emotionally battered by her father, repressed the image of his haranguing and gained insight into her current problems when she accessed the image and examined it. She also found her true strength to deal effectively with her boss.

Eidetic imaging lends itself well to use in a self-help context. The person using it not only *experiences* the situation but is the *analyzer* of the data as well; the person projects the image and learns from the perceptions. That is one of the fundamental differences between eidetic imaging and classical psychotherapy. With imaging, the patient journeys into self to explore his or her own experiences and discover unique strengths and powers as he or she works with the clinician or with themselves. The image has the power for transformation.

As Dr. Ahsen put it, it's an "exciting invitation to individuals who would like to know more about themselves."

Are images more powerful, more insightful, than words? We've all heard the expression, "A picture is worth a thousand words." An eidetic image is not just a picture, but is a composite of many pictures and situations.

> "My words cannot constitute my experience. At best they can describe experiences to me . . . Words in this sense are not idols but tools—words are secondary to experience. . . . In the stream of experience there are little whirlpools which follow a different law of continuous repetition—a particular brand of images—eidetics—represent these parts. In a sense they are like words, static and repeatable—but, unlike words, available to experience. . . . It [an Eidetic] is a life-like visual image which, if attended to, completely absorbs the individual to the exclusion of everything else. Because of this absorption, it concretizes a part of the psyche in lucid detail . . . it is an independent self-motivated image that responds to a special kind of handling."
>
> (Dr. Ahsen, *Basic Concepts in Eidetic Psychotherapy*, Brandon House, 1968, page 24)

Words are secondary to experience, and the eidetic image is experience itself, not as verbalized to someone else, but as lived and relived, bringing with it revelations about ourselves and solutions to our goals.

Almost as ancient as the pyramids, yet on the cutting edge of modern psychology, eidetic imaging is an exciting and profound way to rediscover our gifts from the gods.

Appendix of Images

As you have already discovered, imaging is very easy. The process is the same for all images. The fact that one image may have three instructions and another a dozen is irrelevant—you don't have to memorize the instructions. Once you see an image, it will still be there when you go back to it after reading the next instruction.

It is best that you read all of the instructions prior to beginning so that they will be familiar to you. The instructions are not complicated, and if you need to look at them again while you are imaging, feel free to do so. This should not affect the quality of the image.

Once you are in a good place mentally and physically to see an eidetic image, you are ready to begin. Remember, an eidetic is neither mere memory nor a figment of your imagination. An eidetic is an image recalled from the storage of visions in your mental bank. It may be of the lover you met last month or the parent who died thirty years ago. How long it has been in storage is not relevant.

Keep in mind that the eidetic contains three individual parts to it: the *image* itself, which can be vague or vivid; the *somatic*/emotional response or feeling that accompanies it, and the *meaning* revealed by it.

The emotional response may be very subtle or it may be earth-shattering. Sometimes people experience very profound emotional responses—they will laugh, cry, feel great joy or intense anger. Other times, the response may be much more subtle, such as a slight tension in the stomach or chest, a vague feeling of coolness or warmth, feeling ill at ease, or just feeling good.

Meaning refers to the insight you gain from the image. It is an automatic function of the image and you do not have to dig for it. If the eidetic is there, the meaning will also be there. Often times it is an *Aha!* revelation, a sudden insight and understanding that shouts out to you—"So that's what Jack or Jane is all about! So that's why I can't do this or that, so that's what he means, so that's why she's so distant. . . ."

Other times, it does not strike like lightning or flash like a neon sign but is a generalized sense of knowledge in which you gain information about the situation or person you are imaging. The image may be vague or vivid. The important thing is that you understand and leave yourself open to *see* the image, *feel* the image, and gain *insight* from it.

You begin the exercise by finding a quiet place where you can completely relax and can sit or lay comfortably. You may keep your eyes open or closed, whichever you prefer.

Index of Images

1. ANCESTRAL ZONE IMAGE

1. See an image of yourself in the present time.

2. Where are you? What do you see?

3. Now go back in time, back to your ancestors, and see an image of your ancestors.

4. What country do you go to? What kind of geography are you in? (If the image is not clear, go back in time until you make a connection.)

5. See that they come and greet you. How do they receive you?

6. How do you feel as they receive you? What are the feelings that come over you?

7. Explore the area and feel at home.

8. Are you discovering another part of yourself?

9. Allow yourself to explore the image fully.

2. APHRODITE

1. See an image of Aphrodite in your mind's eye. Aphrodite is full of love, warmth, sensuality, wisdom, and power.

2. Now see Aphrodite is seeing herself naked in front of a mirror. Her breasts appear sensuous and proportional in the mirror.

3. See that she is admiring her sensuous breasts. Her breasts are reflective of beauty, power, nourishment, of giving love.

4. There is a sensuous aroma of perfume flowing out of the mirror . . . experience the perfume flowing in the image.

5. See that the perfume expands your awareness of your feminine nature.

6. See that the reflection in the mirror reveals your true feminine essence.

7. See that you have the essence of feminine sensuality emanating from within you.

3. APPLAUSE

1. See that you are on a stage and people are clapping their hands in applause for you.

2. Keep your mother in mind and see the image of people applauding you.
   What do you see? How do you feel as you see the image?

3. Keep you father in mind and see the image of people applauding you.
   What do you see? How do you feel as you see the image?

4. Is there a difference when you keep mother in mind and when you keep father in mind during the applause?

4. CO-CONSCIOUSNESS

This technique is used to see yourself through the eyes of someone you are having a problem with or that you just want to know better. You can gain insight and understanding about yourself and how others feel about you.

1. Relax, close your eyes if you like, and see an image of yourself in a situation with the person.

2. Where are you? See yourself in the environment where you normally spend time with the person (home, school, workplace, etc.).
   What are you doing?

3. See the person. What are they doing? How do you feel as you see them? Let the information unfold. The information will come forward. Don't worry if the image is vague or vivid.

4. Now see that the person is seeing you.
   Now see through their eyes—they are seeing you. (In the image you can literally do this. Simply look through their eyes.)

   Allow the image to unfold.
   Don't second-guess the information coming to you. Just look at yourself through their eyes. You may see a full vivid image or just get a sense impression.

5. What do they see?

6. Now go back to your eyes. See that you are seeing them.
   What do you see?
   How do you feel as you see this image?

You can keep doing this, going back and forth seeing them through your eyes and then seeing you through their eyes. As you do, more and more information will unfold.

The images are holographic, which means that there are stored pieces of information connected in the mind to other stored pieces of information. Keep reversing the process, looking at the other person and at yourself, until you come to an understanding that is valuable to you.

5. CROSSING THE ROAD

1. Think of the front of a shop that you often go to. Consider the picture that comes to your mind's eye. See the overall appearance of the shop from the opposite side of the road.

2. Picture in your mind that you are crossing the road in order to go over to the shop on the other side. Describe how you cross the road, what images you see, and what happens until you reach the shop on the other side of the road.

3. Think of your mother. Keeping mother in mind, see the image of yourself crossing the road again. Describe how you cross the road, and what happens until you reach the shop on the other side.

4. Think of your father. Keeping father in mind, see the image of yourself crossing the road again. Again, describe how you cross the road, and what happens until you reach the shop on the other side.

6. EIDOLA IMAGE: THE FUTURE TODAY

1. There is a past, a present, and the future.

2. The past is way back, and appears remote and covered over.

3. The present has a lack, a void.

4. This void is painful.

5. Something from the future is needed to fill the void.

6. See an image in this void of lights or of a Being who is a visitor from the future.

7. It is beautiful, awesome, with an omen and a special power.

8. This is a visitation that is futuristic. It a visit taking you to the future.

9. This is called *Eidola*. This is a futuristic visitor.

10. See this image, this Eidola from the future.

11. Now feel its awesomeness.

12. There is a feeling of a message in the image. What is the message?
    Experience your feeling and vibrations from the Eidola.

13. How does it change you when you look at the Eidola?

14. Let the futuristic message from the Eidola pass through your mind and transform you.

15. Do not resist; become like the Eidola. Experience feelings and vibrations.

16. Become vibrant like the Eidola.

17. Now experience these special feelings within you.

18. There are messages of the future in your body.

19. Experience the energy in your body.

20. Let the energy move you into the future.

7. EMANATION

1. Relax and clear your mind. Close your eyes and go inward.

2. See an image of a person in a situation in which you feel stuck, powerless, or that you are unable to deal with effectively.

3. How does the person appear to you?

4. How do you feel as you see the image? Allow your feelings and body sensations to come into awareness.

5. If you could say or do anything to this person, what would that be? Let that desire come into your awareness.

6. Now see a big wind come from the high heavens into the room and surround you. This wind is a gift from the gods.

7. Feel the sensation of the wind swirling and swirling all around you.

8. See another "you" jump out of your image. (For some, it pops right out of their head.) The old you disappears and you become the "new you" in the image.

9. What is this "new you" like?

10. See that this new you does or says whatever it wants.

11. What does it do or say?

12. How do you feel as you see the image? Become aware of your shift to the new you.

13. How is the other person reacting to your new self? In the image when you see the new you—with your new

strengths, powers, or abilities—interacting with the other person, notice how the other person reacts.

14. How does the other person now react to you? If the new you that came out does not have enough strength, ability, or power, repeat the process.

15. Now see a wind come from the heavens and surround this new you. Feel the wind, this gift from the gods, swirling around.

16. Now see another you jump out of the "new" you.

17. See how this one interacts with the person.

8. HEART AND DESIRE

1. Think of all the desires you have.

2. Let all of these desires come into your mind and let your heart beat with these desires.

3. Let the world know your desires and let your heartbeat know the world. Go with your desires into the world.

9. HEART DRUMMING IMAGE

1. Your heartbeat becomes stronger during physical performance.

2. Feel your heartbeat and see that it pumps stronger.

3. See that you can hear the drumming of your heart.

There is imagination in this heartbeat. As your heart beats, it goes in rhythm with your imagination.

4. See you performing and let the heart beat.

5. You become stronger, your performance is more pleasurable and easier to release.

6. How does your performance change when you add the image of your heart?

This image can be used when engaging in any sport or physical activity (running, dance, soccer, etc).

10. "HIGH" IN YOUR WORK

1. See an image of the work you do.

2. See yourself doing it.

3. See what you enjoy about it. Focus on the aspect that gives you the most energy or pleasure.

4. See that what you enjoy gives you a "high" feeling.

5. Feel the high feeling and let it get stronger.

6. This is the high or passion in what you do.

7. See yourself at work in a high state.

8. Let the pleasure, the high state, get stronger.

9. See yourself at work expressing this passion, this high.

10. How is your work now?

11. High Executive Performance

1. See an image of performing in an executive activity you enjoy.

2. See what you love about it, what makes you high as you do it.

3. Let this high feeling envelop you. Feel it in your body.

4. Let it get you high.

5. This is the passion in your performance.

6. See that you perform your executive duties with this high feeling. This is the power in you.

12. High Sports Image

1. See an image of performing in an athletic activity you enjoy.

2. See what you love about it, what makes you high as you do it.

3. Let this high feeling envelop you. Feel it in your body.

4. Let it get you high.

5. This is the passion in your performance.

6. See that you perform with this high feeling. This is the power in you.

13. HOME IMAGE

Picture your parents in the house (or apartment) where you lived most of the time with them, the place that gives the feeling of a home.

1. Picture your parents in the house. Where do you see them? What are they doing?

2. How do you feel as you see the house?

3. See your father. Where is he? What is he doing in the picture?

4. Do you experience pleasant or unpleasant feelings when you see him?

5. Relax and recall memories about the place where your father appears.

6. Now see your mother. What is she doing?

7. Do you experience pleasant or unpleasant feelings when you see her?

8. Relax and recall memories about the place where your mother appears.

9. Where are your siblings? What are they doing? How do you feel as you see them?

10. Now see yourself in the picture. What are you doing?

11. Does the place give you the feeling of a home?

14. IDOL OF LOVE

1. Remember yourself in love, and the person you touched, or who touched you, the first time you realized you were in love with them.

2. Remember the touch and see the person before you again.

   This is an early image of love. All other images are late images of love, even of this person. There is Cupid in this early image. The god is present here. The more you look at this image, the more it becomes like an icon.

3. See the image. You have bodily feelings and sensations of the god of love being near you. Keep this image at this early stage. Do not bring to your mind later images of this person.

4. Feel your body relaxing, your bones and muscles relaxing. This is Cupid, the god of love, in the image. All other human images of love are late images, which only contain the problems between you.

15. IMAGES OF DARKNESS

1. See yourself in total darkness, descending into a very dark space in which there is no light—a rich darkness, pitch black.

2. Feel yourself enveloped in the darkness and let a nourishing feeling of calm pass through you. Relax your body and your mind.

3. See that darkness is the source of all creation, that everything starts in darkness; it's rich and full, not empty.

4. Walk in the darkness, feeling the darkness, getting comfortable with it.

5. You can't see in the dark, so as you walk use your instincts to guide you. Your senses can't help you, so let your feelings and intuitions guide you.

6. Walk in the darkness, guided by your intuition, with a feeling that you know things intuitively.

7. Let your feelings flow as you walk . . .

8. Now reach out and open a window.

9. Explore what is beyond the window.

10. Breathe freely and explore that place in an active way.

11. How do you feel about what you are seeing?

Imagination begins in darkness. This image allows us to connect to the primordial source of creativity within us by freeing up the mind and letting the information flow.

16. IMAGES OF YOUR HEART

1. See your heart which is beating inside your chest on the left side of your body.

2. Now, imagine that you are doing things with your whole heart in it.

3. Become aware that your heart is made of essence (feeling of the heart) and it is made of flesh also (the physical side). When you put the essence of the heart and the flesh together, you have the feeling of the "whole" heart. Pay

attention to this whole-heart feeling, with the essence and the flesh both in the feeling.

4. Now see that you are doing things with your "whole" heart in it.

5. See yourself doing other things with the "whole" heart in it.

6. Now see that you are putting your "whole" heart into being with a person with whom you want to relate better. How are you with them? Allow the revelations of your heart to unfold.

17. Imaging a Child

1. See your child somewhere in the home.

2. Where is he/she?

3. What is your child doing?

4. Notice his/her moods, actions. What do you see?

5. How do you feel as you see your child?

6. Look in the child's eye. There is a feeling or story there. What story do you see?

18. Imaging with Filters

1. See a person or difficult situation in your mind's eye.

2. What do you see? How do you feel as you see it?

3. Keep mother in mind and see the problem or situation. This means to think of her as if you can sense her presence.

4. What happens in the image, keeping mother in mind? Let the images unfold without interference.

5. Now keep father in mind and see the problem or situation. This means to think of him as if you sense his presence.

6. What happens in the image, keeping father in mind?

19. LIGHT OF THE RUNNING STREAM

When we do the Images of Darkness to connect to our inner spirit, we can add the Light of the Running Stream to probe further into our creative resources. This image is similar to the ordinary Running Stream image but has points directed solely toward creativity.

1. See that you are a running stream.

2. See that running stream which you are.

3. See something in front of you as you experience yourself as the running stream. What do you see?

4. Now see an obstacle in front of you. When you see yourself as the running stream, see how you run through this obstacle or the problem it involves.

5. Now see your parents in front of you, as you see yourself as a running stream.

6. See your father in front of you, and you are the running stream.

7. Now see your mother in front of you, and you are the running stream.

8. Now see the world in front of you, and you are the running stream.

9. See the whole world and feel "what will be will be" and be the running stream.

10. See history in front of you, and that you are the stream, the running stream. People make the history of the world. Do not fear history.

11. See history and you as the running stream battling each other. Who has the more authentic power?

12. Are you afraid of anything now?

13. See that you are working on a creative project and you are the running stream.

14. See you are a running stream and that there is an obstacle to your project.

15. See how the stream deals with the obstacle.

20. PARENTS' ACCEPTANCE OF YOU

1. Picture your parents standing in front of you.

2. Look at your parents' skin and concentrate on it for a while.

3. Does it seem to accept you or reject you?

4. How do you feel as you look at their skin?

5. Whose skin gives you the feeling of acceptance? To what degree?

6. Whose skin gives the feeling of rejection? To what degree?

7. Concentrate on your feelings concerning your father's skin.

8. How do you feel as you experience father's skin?

9. Concentrate on your feelings concerning your mother's skin.

10. How do you feel as you experience mother's skin?

11. Which parent usually touches you more?

12. Which parent do you usually touch more?

21. Parents' Brains

1. Picture your parents' brains.

2. Touch each parent's brain and feel the temperature there. Is it cold, warm, or hot?

3. Now touch your father's brain. What is the temperature?

4. Is touching your father's brain pleasant or unpleasant?

5. Now touch your mother's brain. What is the temperature?

6. Is touching your mother's brain pleasant or unpleasant?

7. What does hot temperature of a brain mean to you?

8. What does cold temperature of a brain mean to you?

9. What does neutral temperature of a brain mean to you?

10. Which parent's brain do you tend to avoid touching?

22. Parents' Heartbeat

1. Picture your parents' complete images standing in front of you.

2. Image a window opening in each parent's chest so you can see his or her heart beating there.

3. See your father's heart beating. Describe its beat and its appearance.

4. Is there any sign of anxiety in father's heartbeat?

5. Imagine a picture in your father's heart. Who do you see?

6. See your mother's heart beating. Describe its beat and its appearance.

7. Is there any sign of anxiety in mother's heartbeat?

8. Imagine a picture in your mother's heart. Who do you see?

9. In what way do you wish your father's heart to appear different?

10. In what way do you wish your mother's heart to appear different?

23. PARENTS' LEFT/RIGHT POSITION

1. Picture your parents standing directly in front of you.

2. As you look at them, who is standing on your left and who is standing on your right?

3. Now try to switch their positions. Are you able to switch them?

4. Notice any difficulty or discomfort when you switch them.

5. See your parents standing in front of you again.

6. Who is standing on the left and who is standing on the right now?

7. Switch your parents' position again.

8. Do you again experience a problem when you switch them?

9. Notice the two different feelings: spontaneous and forced.

10. Notice that you have no control over your parents' spontaneous images.

24. PARENTS' LISTENING TO YOU

1. Picture yourself talking to both your parents.

2. Who seems to hear you better?

3. How does the other parent hear you by comparison?

4. Concentrate on how your father hears you in the image.

5. When he hears you, do you feel secure or insecure?

6. Concentrate on how your mother hears you in the image.

7. When she hears you, do you feel secure or insecure?

8. Concentrate on the parent whose hearing creates security for you.

9. Concentrate on the parent whose hearing creates insecurity for you.

10. Which parent do you approach more for listening to you?

25. PARENTS' UNDERSTANDING YOU

1. See yourself talking to both of your parents again.

2. Who seems to understand you better, mother or father?

3. Concentrate on how your father understands you in the image.

4. Do you feel understood?

5. Concentrate on how your mother understands you in the picture.

6. Do you feel understood?

7. See father. What kind of ideas would you like to exchange with him?

8. See mother. What kind of ideas would you like to exchange with her?

9. Which parent exchanges ideas with you more?

10. Which parent do you feel should exchange ideas with you more?

26. PARENTS' VOICES

1. Picture your parents and hear their voices.

2. Whose voice sounds louder to you? Describe the voice.

3. How is the voice of the other parent in comparison?

4. Concentrate on your father's voice. Is the sound pleasant or unpleasant?

5. Relax and recall memories as you continue to hear his voice.

6. Concentrate on your mother's voice. Is the sound pleasant or unpleasant?

7. Relax and recall memories as you continue to hear her voice.

8. Whose voice do you pay attention to less, mother's or father's?

9. What is this voice you attend less saying to you?

10. Why do you pay less attention to this voice?

27. PARENTS' WARMTH AND CONNECTION

1. Picture your parents standing directly in front of you.

2. Which parent's body has more personal warmth?

3. How is the other parent's body in comparison?

4. Concentrate on your feelings concerning father's body.

5. How do you feel as you see his body?

6. Relax and recall memories as you concentrate on your father's body.

7. Concentrate on your feelings concerning mother's body.

8. How do you feel when you see her body?

9. Relax and recall memories as you concentrate on your mother's body.

10. Which parent's body do you wish to know more? Why?

28. PERIPHERY

1. See an image in which you feel hopeless or despairing.

2. Go to the edge, to the periphery of the image. What do you see? How do you feel?

3. Now go to the edge of the new image. What do you see? Do you feel any different?

4. If needed, go to the edge, the periphery of this image. What do you see? How do you feel?

5. Repeat going to the edge of each new image until you get a shift in your original stuck feeling. Allow the relief and illumination to come over you.

29. Physical Preparation

1. See that you come into an empty place. This empty place is where your energies come together.

2. See that you are preparing to launch out.

3. Concentrate on this feeling of coming together in this empty place and getting ready for the activity.

4. See that your energies are coming together.

5. See that you are getting ready.

6. See that you are going to launch out.

7. See that you will do the impossible.

30. Poseidon

1. See Poseidon coming out of the sea. He is coming ashore. He's holding a trident in his hand, the symbol of his power.

2. See his chest. It is strong and broad.

3. See that you become Poseidon. As you move towards the shore, the waves crash against your chest but the force of your power surging forward pushes against them as you move through them.

4. See that you have come onto the shore dripping water.

5. See that your body is hot and the cool air dries your body as you move. Feel the coolness against your warm body.

6. See that there's a temple on a hill. It is the temple of the virgin priestesses.

7. See a priestess in the temple. Feel the heat in your body as you walk towards the temple.

8. See that as you move towards the temple there's a warm fire in it and an intoxicating essence of perfume. Smell the perfume.

9. See that you're drawn to the nectar in the temple, to the priestess.

10. Experience the sexual energy flowing through your body.

31. RUNNING STREAM

1. See that you are a running stream.

2. See that running stream which you are.

3. See something in front of you as you experience yourself as the running stream. What do you see?

4. Now see an obstacle in front of you. When you see yourself as the running stream, see how you run through this obstacle or the problem it involves.

5. Now see your parents in front of you, as you see yourself as a running stream.

6. See your father in front of you, and you are the running stream.

7. Now see your mother in front of you, and you are the running stream.

8. Now see the world in front of you, and you are the running stream.

9. See the whole world and feel "what will be, will be" and be the running stream.

10. See history in front of you, and you are the stream, the running stream. People make the history of the world. Do not fear history.

11. See history and you as the running stream battling each other. Who has the more authentic power?

12. Are you afraid of anything now?

13. See a negative situation, and run through it as the stream.

14. See a negative person, and be this running stream.

15. See constraints, prohibition, and other fears, and run through them one by one, as the running stream.

32. RUNNING STREAM FOR BUSINESS

1. See that you are a running stream.

2. See that running stream that you are.

3. See something in front of you as you experience yourself as the running stream. What do you see?

4. Now see an obstacle in front of you. When you see yourself as the running stream, see how you run through this obstacle, or the problem it involves.

5. Now see your bosses, your workers in front of you, as you see yourself as a running stream. What happens to the stream?

6. See your colleagues in front of you when you see yourself as the running stream.

7. Now see your competitors in front of you, and be the running stream.

8. Now see the world in front of you, and you are the running stream.

9. See the whole world and feel "what will be, will be" and the running stream.

10. Now see past history in front of you, and you are the stream, the running stream.

11. See the present in front of you, and you are the running stream.

12. See the future in front of you, and you are the running stream.

13. See a negative situation or a negative person and run through it as the stream, and be this running stream.

14. See constraints, prohibition, and other fears, and run through them one by one, as the running stream. Who has more power?

15. Do not fear anything and be this running stream.

33. SMELL IMAGE

1. See that you are playing at a sport where there is a target or goal (basketball, pitching, soccer, golf, hockey, archery, etc).

2. See an image that you are ready to aim or shoot at the target/goal.

3. See that you are aiming/shooting at the target/goal while you are only visually looking at it.

4. What happens as you see this image?

5. Now see that you aim at the target while you are visually looking at it and also while smelling the target at the same time. Imagine an olfactory connection with the visual target/goal.

6. What happens as you see this image? As a result the target/goal comes closer.

7. Notice that you become closer to the target/goal when you add the smell.

34. SPORTS ACTION WITH FILTERS

1. See yourself involved in a physical activity (tennis, golf, basketball, jogging, bicycling, etc.).

2. Perform an action in regard to that activity (hit the ball, jog, pedal the bike, lift weights, etc.).

3. As you perform the action, keep your father in mind. What do you see? How does it affect your performance?

4. As you perform the action, keep your mother in mind. What do you see? How does it affect your performance?

35. SPORTS ASSESSMENT: VOSI TEST

SUCCESS ASSESSMENT IMAGES WITH FILTERS

The following is an image similar to the sixteen-element Success Assessment we used in the careers section, only this one is geared toward sports and other physical activities. In assessing our performance, we use parental filters.

1. See yourself thinking of the event.
    Keep mother in mind while you are thinking of the event.
    Keep father in mind white you are thinking of the event.
    Is there a difference in your feelings when you keep a
    different parent in mind?

2. See yourself preparing for an activity or physical event.
    Keep mother in mind while you are thinking of the event.
    Keep father in mind while you are thinking of the event.
    Is there a difference in your feelings when you keep a
    different parent in mind?

3. See yourself during the activity, experiencing the event.
    Keep mother in mind while you are thinking of yourself
    having success.
    Keep father in mind while you are thinking of yourself
    having success.
    Is there a difference in your feelings when you keep a
    different parent in mind?

4. See yourself improving in an area in which you need work.
    Keep mother in mind while you are thinking of the task.
    Keep father in mind while you are thinking of the task.
    Is there a difference in your feelings when you keep a
    different parent in mind?

5. See yourself being applauded for your achievement.
    Keep mother in mind while you are being applauded for
    your achievement.
    Keep father in mind while you are being applauded for your
    achievement.
    Is there a difference in your feelings when you keep a
    different parent in mind?

36. STORY IN THE EYES

1. See a person you desire to know more about, standing in front of you.

2. Look into the person's eyes.

3. Concentrate on the eyes.

4. Do their eyes give you any feeling or tell you any story?

5. Concentrate on the story or feeling in the person's eyes. What do you see?

37. SUCCESS ASSESSING

This is a detailed image taking a look at a person's success assessment from the time of high school to the present. The purpose is to permit us to gain insight into where we have been blocked in our goals.

EDUCATION

1. See yourself at high school.
    Keep mother in mind while you are at school.
    Keep father in mind while you are at school.
    Is there a difference in your feelings when you keep a different parent in mind?

2. See yourself dealing with a difficulty at high school.
    Keep mother in mind while you deal with the difficulty.
    Keep father in mind while you deal with the difficulty.
    Is there a difference in your feelings when you keep a different parent in mind?

3. See yourself at college.
   Keep mother in mind while you are at college.
   Keep father in mind while you are at college.
   Is there a difference in your feelings when you keep a
   different parent in mind?

4. See yourself dealing with a difficulty at college.
   Keep mother in mind white you deal with the difficulty.
   Keep father in mind while you deal with the difficulty.
   Is there a difference in your feelings when you keep a different
   parent in mind?

INTERVIEW

5. See yourself thinking of a job.
   Keep mother in mind while you think of a job.
   Keep father in mind while you think of a job.
   Is there a difference in your feelings when you keep a
   different parent in mind?

6. See yourself thinking of an interview.
   Keep mother in mind while you think about the interview.
   Keep father in mind while you think about the interview.
   Is there a difference in your feelings when you keep a
   different parent in mind?

7. See yourself preparing for an interview.
   Keep mother in mind while you prepare for the interview.
   Keep father in mind while you prepare for the interview.
   Is there a difference in your feelings when you keep a
   different parent in mind?

8. See yourself having an interview.
   Keep mother in mind while you deal with the interview.
   Keep father in mind while you deal with the interview.
   Is there a difference in your feelings when you keep a different
   parent in mind?

PROBLEM SOLVING

9. See yourself dealing with a problem at work.
   Keep mother in mind while you deal with the difficulty.
   Keep father in mind while you deal with the difficulty.
   Is there a difference in your feelings when you keep a
   different parent in mind?

10. See yourself dealing with an obstruction.
    Keep mother in mind while you deal with the obstruction.
    Keep father in mind while you deal with the obstruction.
    Is there a difference in your feelings when you keep a
    different parent in mind?

11. See yourself working out details.
    Keep mother in mind while you work out the details.
    Keep father in mind while you work out the details.
    Is there a difference in your feelings when you keep a
    different parent in mind?

12. See yourself implementing a solution.
    Keep mother in mind while you implement the solution.
    Keep father in mind while you implement the solution.
    Is there a difference in your feelings when you keep a
    different parent in mind?

SUCCESS

13. See yourself successful at work.
    Keep mother in mind while you are successful at work.
    Keep father in mind while you are successful at work.
    Is there a difference in your feelings when you keep a
    different parent in mind?

14. See yourself wanting a promotion at work.
    Keep mother in mind while you want a promotion at work.
    Keep father in mind while you want a promotion at work.

Is there a difference in your feelings when you keep a different parent in mind?

15. See yourself being promoted at work.
Keep mother in mind while you are being promoted at work.
Keep father in mind while you are being promoted at work.
Is there a difference in your feelings when you keep a different parent in mind?

16. See yourself being applauded for your achievement.
Keep mother in mind while you are being applauded for your achievement.
Keep father in mind while you are being applauded for your achievement.
Is there a difference in your feelings when you keep a different parent in mind?

38. Swimming Image

1. See yourself as a running stream. See that running stream that you are.

2. See your competitor (coworker, boss, employees, etc.) swimming in the running stream.

3. Watch how they swim.

4. How are they swimming (fast, slow, easily, or with difficulty, aggressive, just flowing with the current, etc.)?

5. How do you feel as you see the image?

6. What meaning or insight do you gain about them as you see the image?

39. Vague and Vivid

1. See an image of a person you want to know better.

2. See that the person is *vivid* and you are *vague*.

3. What do you see?

4. How do you feel as you see the image?

5. Now see that the person is *vague* and you are *vivid*.

6. What do you see?

7. How do you feel as you see the image?

8. Switch again and see that the other person is *vivid* and you are *vague*.

9. What do you see?

10. How do you feel as you see the image?

You can keep going back and forth, *vague* and *vivid*, until you have gained all you need from the images.

40. Walk-Around

1. Relax, close your eyes if you like, and see an image of a person that you want insight into.
   If the image is vague just keep looking. The information will come in sense impressions or feelings.

2. Look at the person from the front. What do you see?
    Notice their body language, the emotions that you can read
    on their face, and anything that strikes you. Let the
    information about the other person simply come to you.

3. How do you feel as you see the image?

4. Now move to the right side of the person and look at the
    person from that side. As you look at them, be aware of
    how they look, their body posture, the emotions you sense
    on that side. What do you see about them?
    Let all of the impressions come forward.
    How do you feel now that you see them from this side?
    Pleasant? Unpleasant? Neutral?

5. Now move to the back of their head and observe them from
    that angle.
    What do you see?
    Again, just let the information come, whatever it is.
    How do you feel as you see them from the back?
    Pleasant? Unpleasant? Neutral?

6. Now go to the left side of them.
    What do you see? How do you feel?

7. Go back to the front.
    What do you see? How do you feel?

8. Do you have a different understanding of this person than
    when you started?

41. WORK SITUATION USING A FILTER

1. See a situation (or person) at work that you are having
    difficulty with.

2. What do you see?

3. How do you feel as you see the image?

4. Think of your mother. Keep your mother in mind and see the same image in your mind. Let the image unfold like a movie.

5. What do you see?

6. How do you feel as you see the image?

7. Think of your father. Keep your father in mind and see the same image in your mind. Let the image unfold like a movie.

8. What do you see?

9. How do you feel as you see the image?

Note: You can use other people as filters to gain more perspectives in a situation, such as a mentor, friend, spiritual figure, etc.

42. THE "IT" IMAGE FOR WOMEN

1. Close your eyes, picture your womb.

2. It is soft, dark, and mysterious. Allow yourself to experience the feelings and sensations as you see this image.

3. See its beauty.

4. See how you have both the male and female shapes within you.

5. Experience the sensation of having both and be with this feeling for a while.

6. Be aware of the subtle shift of feelings and sensations that come over your whole being. How do you feel?

7. You have it all. You are complete, a microcosm of life.

8. Concentrate on this image.

9. Let this whole feminine feeling go with you wherever you go.

Bibliography

Ahsen, Akhter. (1987). *ABC of Imagery*. Bronx, NY: Brandon House, Inc.

Ahsen, Akhter. (1988). *Aphrodite: The Psychology of Consciousness*. Bronx, NY: Brandon House, Inc.

Ahsen, Akhter. (1968). *Basic Concepts in Eidetic Psychotherapy*. Bronx, NY: Brandon House, Inc.

Ahsen, Akhter. (1972). *Eidetic Parents Test and Analysis: A Practical Guide to Systematic & Comprehensive Analysis*. Bronx, NY: Brandon House, Inc.

Ahsen, Akhter. (1990). *Hyponoia: The Underneath Sense of Being*. Bronx, NY: Brandon House, Inc.

Ahsen, Akhter (2001). "Imagery in Sports, General Performance and Executive Excellence." *Journal of Mental Imagery*. Volume 25, No. 3–4.

Ahsen, Akhter. (1993). *Imagery Paradigm*. Bronx, NY: Brandon House, Inc.

Ahsen, Akhter. (1993). *Learning Ability & Disability: An Image Approach*. Bronx, NY: Brandon House, Inc.

Ahsen, Akhter. (1996). *Menstruation and Menopause: Imagery Therapeutics In Social Context*. Bronx, NY: Brandon House, Inc.

Ahsen, Akhter. (1992). *New Surrealism: The Liberation of Images in Consciousness*. Bronx, NY: Brandon House, Inc.

Ahsen, Akhter. (1977). *Psycheye: Self-Analytic Consciousness*. Bronx, NY: Brandon House, Inc.

Bent, Nancy A. (1995). *Beyond MS: It's All in the Image,* Bronx, NY: Brandon House, Inc.

Dolan, Anna T. (1997). *Imagery Treatment of Phobias, Anxiety States and Other Symptom Complexes in Akhter Ahsen's Image Psychology*. Bronx, NY: Brandon House, Inc.

Hochman, Judith. (1994). *Ahsen's Image Psychology*. Bronx, NY: Brandon House, Inc.

Hochman, Judith. (2000). *Image and Word in Ahsen's Image Psychology*. Bronx, NY: Brandon House, Inc.

Koestler, Arthur. (1978). *The Thirteenth Tribe*. New York: Random House.

Nixon, Toni. (1997). *New Treatment of Alcohol and Drug Abuse in Akhter Ahsen's Eidetic Image Therapy*. Bronx, NY: Brandon House, Inc.

Sussman, Jaqueline. (2001). *Images of Desire*. New York: Tom Doherty Associates, LLC, Forge Books.